CIVIL PROCEDURE 2017

FIRST SUPPLEMENT TO THE 2017 EDITION

Up-to-date generally to 9 June 2017.

TO ACCESS THE WHITE BOOK UPDATING SERVICE VIA
HTTP://WWW.SWEETANDMAXWELL.CO.UK/WHITEBOOK YOU NEED TO ENTER THE
FOLLOWING PASSWORD:
WB2017

SWEET & MAXWELL

 THOMSON REUTERS

Published in 2017 by Thomson Reuters (Professional) UK Limited (Registered in England &
Wales, Company No 1679046.
Registered Office and address for service: 5 Canada Square, Canary Wharf, London E14 5AQ)
trading as Sweet & Maxwell.
Typesetting by Sweet & Maxwell electronic publishing system.
Printed and bound in the UK by CPI Group (UK) Ltd, Croydon, CR0 4YY.
For further information on our products and services, visit
http://www.sweetandmaxwell.co.uk.

No natural forests were destroyed to make this product; only farmed timber was used and
replanted.

British Library Cataloguing in Publication Data
A catalogue record for this book is available from the British Library

ISBN–978-0414-06227-6

Civil Procedure First Supplement to the 2017 Edition

Civil Procedure 2017 published on 23 March 2017. The First Supplement contains updating material for both Volumes of *Civil Procedure 2017* and brings the work up-to-date to 9 June 2017.

This Supplement covers the following updates:

- A new Pre-Action Protocol for Debt Claims, which comes into force on 1 October 2017
- Amendments to Court Guides: Admiralty & Commercial, Chancery and Queen's Bench
- A Queen's Bench Practice Note listing changes to the procedure for obtaining trial listing appointments with the QB Judges' Listing Office
- Updated and new commentary on case law including:
  - *Merrix v Heart of England NHS Foundation Trust* (Part 3—The Court's Case & Costs Management Powers)
  - *Libyan Investment Authority v Société Générale* (Part 6—Service of Documents)
  - *Redbourn Group Ltd v Fairgate Development Ltd* (Part 13—Setting Aside or Varying Default Judgment)
  - *Football Association Premier League Ltd v O'Donovan* (Part 15—Defence & Reply & Part 17—Amendments to Statements of Case)
  - *Cameron v Hussain, Armes v Godfrey Morgan Solicitors* (Part 19—Parties & Group Litigation)
  - *Harb v Aziz* (Part 23—Applications for Court Orders)
  - *Holyoake v Candy* (Part 25—Interim Remedies & Security for Costs)
  - *Re RBS Rights Issue Litigation* (Part 31—Disclosure)
  - *Tchenguiz v Grant Thornton UK LLP* (Part 32—Evidence)
  - *Brown v Mujibal* (Part 33—Miscellaneous Rules about Evidence)
  - *OMV Petrom SA v Glencore International AG* (Part 36—Offers to Settle)
  - *Bath v Escott* (Part 39—Miscellaneous Provisions Relating to Hearings)
  - *NGPOD Global Limited v Aspirate N Go Limited* (Part 63—IP Claims)
  - *Hourani v Thomson* (Contempt of Court)
  - *Agarwal v Cardiff University, Weatherilt v Cathay Pacific Airways Ltd* (Employment)
  - *Briggs v First Choice Holidays and Flights Ltd, Thakkar v Patel* (ADR)
- A host of further commentary and case law updates to other Parts and Sections.

The Second Cumulative Supplement is due to publish in the Autumn. *Civil Procedure News* will continue to keep you abreast of developments for the remainder of the subscription year.

We welcome feedback from subscribers—please email *whitebook@sweetand maxwell.co.uk* with any comments or suggestions.

The White Book Team
June 2017

EDITOR-IN-CHIEF

THE RIGHT HONOURABLE LORD JUSTICE JACKSON
Lord Justice of Appeal; Honorary Fellow of Jesus College, Cambridge

GENERAL EDITORS

SENIOR MASTER B. FONTAINE
Senior Master of the Senior Courts in the Queen's Bench Division and Queen's Remembrancer; Central Authority for the Hague Conventions on Service and Taking of Evidence; Central Body under the EC Service and Evidence Regulations; Former Member of the Civil Procedure Rule Committee
PROFESSOR I. R. SCOTT Q.C. (Hon)
Emeritus Professor, University of Birmingham; Honorary Bencher of Gray's Inn

EDITOR OF CIVIL PROCEDURE NEWS

DR J. SORABJI
Barrister; Principal Legal Adviser to the Lord Chief Justice and the Master of the Rolls; UCL Judicial Institute

SENIOR EDITORIAL BOARD

SENIOR COSTS JUDGE A. GORDON-SAKER
Senior Courts Costs Office
THE RIGHT HONOURABLE LORD JUSTICE HAMBLEN
Lord Justice of Appeal
ROBERT N. HILL
Recorder, Deputy District Judge and Regional Costs Judge, North Eastern Circuit; Former District Judge and Former Member of the Civil Procedure Rule Committee
HIS HONOUR JUDGE NIC MADGE
Inner London Crown Court and Central London Civil Justice Centre
THE RIGHT HONOURABLE SIR GEOFFREY VOS
Chancellor of the High Court

EDITORS

JONATHAN AUBURN
Barrister, 11 King's Bench Walk
DR SIMON AUERBACH
Recorder and Employment Judge, Central London Employment Tribunal
DR STUART BARAN
Barrister, Three New Square
REGISTRAR BARBER
Registrar in Bankruptcy of the High Court
V. C. BELL
Barrister, High Court Chancery Chambers
HIS HONOUR JUDGE NIGEL BIRD
Manchester Civil Justice Centre
DEPUTY DISTRICT JUDGE SUZANNE BURN
A Deputy District Judge on the South Eastern Circuit; Former Member of the Civil Procedure Rule Committee
MARTIN CHAMBERLAIN Q.C.
One of Her Majesty's Counsel
SARA COCKERILL Q.C.
One of Her Majesty's Counsel
MASTER DAVID COOK
A Master of the Senior Courts, Queen's Bench Division
THE HONOURABLE MR JUSTICE COULSON
Judge of the Queen's Bench Division of the High Court; Presiding Judge of the North Eastern Circuit; Member of the Civil Procedure Rule Committee

MASTER R. EASTMAN
A Master of the Senior Courts, Queen's Bench Division
LAURA FELDMAN
Senior Associate (Barrister), Eversheds
M. GIBBON Q.C.
One of Her Majesty's Counsel, Maitland Chambers
JOAN GOULBOURN
Of the Public Guardianship Office
DISTRICT JUDGE MICHAEL HOVINGTON
Manchester County Court; Member of the Civil Procedure Rule Committee
R. JAY
Solicitor
E. JEARY
Of the Court Funds Office
MASTER JERVIS KAY Q.C.
Admiralty Registrar and a Master of the Senior Courts, Queen's Bench Division; One of Her Majesty's Counsel
CHRISTOPHER KNIGHT
Barrister, 11 King's Bench Walk
DISTRICT JUDGE M. LANGLEY
A District Judge of the Central London County Court
THE HONOURABLE MR JUSTICE LEWIS
Judge of the Queen's Bench Division of the High Court; Presiding Judge, Wales
SARA MASTERS Q.C.
One of Her Majesty's Counsel
MASTER VICTORIA MCCLOUD
A Master of the Senior Courts, Queen's Bench Division
DISTRICT JUDGE SIMON MIDDLETON
Truro Courts of Justice and Bodmin County Court
KARON MONAGHAN Q.C.
One of Her Majesty's Counsel
HELEN MOUNTFIELD Q.C.
One of Her Majesty's Counsel
JOHN O'HARE
Deputy Costs Judge; formerly a Master of the Senior Courts Costs Office
HIS HONOUR JUDGE RICHARD PARKES Q.C.
A Circuit Judge on the South Eastern Circuit
EDWARD PEPPERALL Q.C.
One of Her Majesty's Counsel, St Philips Chambers; Deputy High Court Judge; Former Member of the Civil Procedure Rule Committee
MASTER N. PRICE
A Master of the Senior Courts, Chancery Division
MASTER ROBERTS
A Master of the Senior Courts, Queen's Bench Division; Member of the Civil Procedure Rule Committee
DISTRICT JUDGE RICHARD ROBINSON
Principal Registry of the Family Division
DEPUTY DISTRICT JUDGE PHILIP ROGERS
A Deputy District Judge on the South Eastern Circuit
C. SANDERS
Solicitor
IAN SEWELL
Costs Clerk, Supreme Court of the United Kingdom
DR J. SORABJI
Barrister; Principal Legal Adviser to the Lord Chief Justice and the Master of the Rolls; UCL Judicial Institute

CONTENTS

TABLE OF CASES

TABLE OF STATUTES

TABLE OF INTERNATIONAL AND EUROPEAN LEGISLATION, TREATIES AND CONVENTIONS

VOLUME 1

SECTION A   CIVIL PROCEDURE RULES 1998

PART 2

APPLICATION AND INTERPRETATION OF THE RULES

Proceedings to which CPR do not apply

Replace the last paragraph with:

Although (as r.2.1 states) the CPR apply to "all proceedings" in the High Court, as a result of **2.1.3**
amendments made by s.174 of the Anti-social Behaviour, Crime and Policing Act 2014, to the Civil
Procedure Act 1997 s.1 and to the Courts Act 2003 s.68, with effect from 1 October 2014, Civil
Procedure Rules do not govern the practice and procedure to be followed in the High Court "in
relation to its jurisdiction under the Extradition Act 2003". From that date such practice and
procedure is governed by the Criminal Procedure Rules: see Criminal Procedure Rules 2015 Pt 50
(SI 2015/1490).

Effect of rule

In the first paragraph, after "Courts Act 2013", add:
see Vol.2, para.9A-419+) **2.4.1**

Replace the sixth paragraph (beginning with "By virtue of") with:

There is nothing to prevent a High Court judge with Administrative Court experience from sitting in the County Court for the purpose of trying a claim in which the claimant claimed (1) a
declaration that a public body had acted incompatibly with their Convention rights, and (2) damages for false imprisonment (*D. v Home Office* [2005] EWCA Civ 38; [2006] 1 W.L.R. 1003, CA
(where held that the bringing of such an action in a county court, rather than by way of proceedings under Pt 54, is not an abuse of process)).

Documents filed under Electronic Working Scheme

At the end of the paragraph, replace "a twelve month period." with:
two years. **2.8.6**

PRACTICE DIRECTION 2B—ALLOCATION OF CASES TO LEVELS OF JUDICIARY

Section III—The County Court

Injunctions, Anti-social Behaviour Orders, Committal and Freezing Orders

Add new paragraph at end: **2BPD.8**
Paragraphs 8.1, 8.1A and 8.3 contain references to ss.153A, 153B and 153D
of the Housing Act 1996 and to ss.1B and 1D of the Crime and Disorder Act
1998, all of which provisions were repealed and replaced by the Anti-social
Behaviour, Crime and Policing Act 2014.

Human Rights

After the first paragraph, add new paragraph:
15 The Race Relations Act 1976 was repealed and replaced by the Equality **2BPD.14**
Act 2010.

PART 3

THE COURT'S CASE AND COSTS MANAGEMENT POWERS

I. Case Management

Making orders subject to conditions

To the end of the fifth paragraph (beginning with "In Deutsche Bank AG"), add:

3.1.4   *Huscroft* was cited with approval in *IPCO (Nigeria) Ltd v Nigerian National Petroleum Corp* [2017] UKSC 16; [2017] 1 W.L.R 970, at para [44].

Ordering security

After the sixth paragraph (beginning with "In Societe Generale SA"), add new paragraph:

3.1.5   *Societe Generale v Saad Trading* was followed in *BCS Corporate ACC Ltd v Terry* 23rd February 2017, Green J, unrep., in which a defendant who was the subject of a default judgment which he contended had been obtained through fraud and abuse of process was ordered to pay outstanding costs orders before he could pursue any application to have that judgment set aside or struck out. He had previously flouted court orders, had access to funds and his case would not be stifled by the imposition of such a condition.

Stay of proceedings

After the first paragraph, add new paragraph:

3.1.7   The broad discretion to stay proceedings or judgments given to the court by r.3.1(2)(f) is limited by the opening words of r.3.1(2): "Except where these Rules provide otherwise". Rule r.3.1(2)(f) does not apply to applications to stay a money judgment since they are governed by r.83.7; The court's discretion under that rule is exercisable only where the court is satisfied that "(a) there are special circumstances which render it inexpedient to enforce the judgment or order; or (b) the applicant is unable from any reason to pay the money ..." (r.83.7(4); *Michael Wilson & Partners Ltd v Sinclair* [2017] EWCA Civ 55).

Varying or revoking orders subject to a liberty to apply

In the first paragraph, replace "Russell-Cooke Trust Co v Prentis [2002] EWHC 1435 (Ch), January 21, 2003, unrep.)." with:

3.1.13   *Russell-Cooke Trust Co v Prentis* [2003] EWHC 1435 (Ch), 21 January 2003, unrep.).

Attempts to re-litigate decided issues

Replace the fifth paragraph (beginning with "The making of such an application") with:

3.4.3.2   The making of such an application in the first proceedings commenced has come to be known as the *Aldi* requirement, non-compliance with which involves the claimant running a risk that the pursuit of a second claim would constitute an abuse (*Stuart v Goldberg Linde* [2008] 1 W.L.R. 823, noted below; *Gladman Commercial Properties v Fisher Hargreaves Proctor* [2013] EWCA Civ 1466; [2014] P.N.L.R. 11 (CA) at [65]–[67], [82], [83]). In *Clutterbuck v Cleghorn* [2017] EWCA Civ 137, the Court of Appeal examined the guidelines in *Aldi Stores* and concluded that a judge had been entitled to strike out two claims as an abuse of process for the claimants' failure to bring them before the court in earlier proceedings involving the same defendant. The *Aldi* guidelines were mandatory and they applied to the instant proceedings. However, their third claim against a party who was not part of the earlier proceedings should not have been struck out. The court stated that an inexcusable failure to comply with the *Aldi* guidelines was a relevant factor in assessing whether a party was abusing the process of the court. In assessing whether there was an abuse, the court had to carry out a broad merits-based judgment which took account of the public and private interests involved and also of the facts of the case.

After the fifth paragraph, add new paragraph:

In *Otkritie International Investment Management Ltd v Threadneedle Management Services Ltd* [2017] EWCA Civ 274, the claimant commenced a second action having, in the first action, wrongly failed to comply with the *Aldi* guidelines. Knowles J refused to strike out the second action but did impose a costs penalty on the claimants and this decision, and the order for costs, were both upheld by the Court of Appeal. Knowles J found that it was likely that, if the *Aldi* guidelines had been followed, the court would not have required the defendant in the second action to be joined as a party to the first action. The claims in *Otkritie* concerned losses on an investment scheme. In the first action the claimants had brought proceedings against their own employees for making false representations with regard to investments. A tenth defendant, a member of an asset management company, was later added when the claimants accused him of fraudulently assisting the employees. After a trial lasting more than nine weeks, judgment for the US$150 million was given against the tenth defendant and others. In the second action, the claimants brought proceedings for vicarious liability against the asset management company. Knowles J dismissed that company's application to strike out the claim but nevertheless awarded it 75% of its costs of the application. These decisions were upheld by the Court of Appeal.

Collateral attacks upon earlier decisions

In the last paragraph, replace "Shalabayev v JSC BTA Bank [2016] EWCA Civ 987," with:
  Shalabayev v JSC BTA Bank [2017] 1 W.L.R. 603,   **3.4.3.3**

Add new paragraphs at end:
  In *Barnett Waddington Trustees (1980) Ltd v Royal Bank of Scotland Plc* [2017] EWHC 834 (Ch); Mann J, the point was made that the doctrine of abuse of process was as capable of applying to defendants and defences as to claimants and claims. In previous related proceedings between the parties, the defendant did not put forward the costs of unwinding an interest rate swap as a funding transaction. It was held that the claimants would be entitled to resist such a claim as an abuse of process; *Johnson v Gore Wood* applied.
  In *Michael Wilson & Partners Ltd v Sinclair* [2017] EWCA Civ 3; the appellant consultancy company appealed against a decision striking out its proceedings against the respondents as an abuse of process on the basis that an arbitration tribunal had already rejected its claim. It was held that the court was not precluded from finding that a court claim which had already been determined in a prior arbitration was an abuse of process, but should be cautious about doing so. The instant case had been wrongly characterised as such because the parties were not the same in both sets of proceedings; the defendant to the court proceedings had declined to be a party to the arbitration. He could not therefore claim that he was being vexed twice and could not seek to take the benefit of the arbitration award; *Secretary of State for Trade and Industry v Bairstow* [2003] EWCA Civ 321 applied.

Failure to comply with a rule, practice direction or court order (r.3.4(2)(c))

Replace the first paragraph with:
  Rule 3.4(2)(c) gives the court an unqualified discretion to strike out a claim or defence where a   **3.4.4**
party has failed to comply with a rule, practice direction or court order. In *Nomura International Plc v Granada Group Ltd* [2007] EWHC 642 (Comm) (noted in para.3.4.3, above and para.16.2.1, below) a failure to comply with r.16.2 led to the striking out of the claim form; this was held to be the only appropriate sanction because, on the facts, the very commencement of proceedings amounted to an abuse of process. In *Walsham Chalet Park Ltd v Tallington Lakes Ltd* [2014] EWCA Civ 1607, the Court of Appeal held that, in exercising its discretion under r.3.4(2)(c), the court is entitled to have regard to the *Mitchell/Denton* principles (which apply to applications under r.3.9; and see further, paras 3.9.3 and 3.9.4, below). However, in that case, the Court of Appeal stressed that the ultimate question for the court in deciding whether to impose the sanction of strike-out is materially different from that in deciding whether to grant relief from a sanction that has already been imposed. In a strike-out application under r.3.4 the proportionality of the sanction itself is in issue, whereas an application under r.3.9 for relief from sanction has to proceed on the basis that the sanction was properly imposed (and see further, para.3.4.1, above). In many cases there may be alternatives to a strike out which may be more appropriate: awarding costs on the indemnity basis payable forthwith, ordering a party to pay money into to court and awarding interest at a higher or lower rate (*Biguzzi v Rank Leisure Plc* [1999] 1 W.L.R. 1926, CA; and see also *Summers v Fairclough Homes Ltd* [2012] UKSC 26; [2012] 1 W.L.R. 2004, noted in para.3.4.3.6, above). In *Candy v Holyoake* [2017] EWHC 373 (QB), Warby J held that, although the defendants had been in serious breach of their obligations under a consent order made for disclosure, and there was no good reason for the failures, it was not a just and proportionate response to strike out their defences. The admitted faults and the gravity of their failures could be reflected in costs orders. It was not suggested that the admitted defaults had prevented the possibility of a fair trial.

Striking out sanction effective without need for further order ("unless" orders)

Add new paragraph at end:
  In *Workman v Forrester* [2017] EWCA Civ 73, the claimants had obtained a default judgment for   **3.4.4.1**
damages to be assessed and also an order for disclosure of documents. Because the defendant persistently failed to comply with the disclosure order, the district judge made a further order that, unless the previous order was complied with, there would be judgment for the sum of £1,503,579.50, plus interest and costs. The defendant's appeal against that order was upheld by the circuit judge and by the Court of Appeal. Although such an order was more onerous than the usual order (an unless order under which the defendant might be debarred from defending the assessment of damages) it was justified given that the defendant's failure to comply with the disclosure order had been calculated to frustrate proceedings to his own advantage.

Consequences of non-payment

Add new paragraph at end:

3.7.2   As to applications for relief from the sanctions imposed by r.3.7 see *R. (on the application of DPP) v Stratford Magistrates' Court* [2017] DC 22nd March 2017, unrep. noted in para.3.9.6.9, below.

Effect of rule

In the first paragraph, replace "3.9.5.14" with:

3.8.1   3.9.10

Formulation of rule since April 2013

Add new paragraph at end:

3.9.3   In *Patterson v Spencer* [2017] EWCA Civ 140, the refusal of relief from sanctions was overturned where the judge (before the guidance in *Denton* had been given) had erred in his approach by relying extensively on *Mitchell*. The judge had erred, albeit understandably and the matter was considered afresh with the benefit of the guidance given in *Denton*.

No good reason for breach

Replace the first paragraph with:

3.9.6.9   Case examples of reasons held not to be good reasons explaining a failure to comply with a rule, practice direction or order include the following: "...overlooking a deadline will rarely be a good reason" ([41]); "...well-intentioned incompetence, for which there is no good reason, should not usually attract relief from a sanction unless the default is trivial" ([48]). See also *Newland Shipping & Forwarding Ltd v Toba Trading FZC* [2014] EWHC 210 (Comm); [2014] 2 Costs L.R 279; Hamblen J (the loss of legal representation as a result of a dispute over fees payable in respect of it); *British Gas Trading Ltd v Oak Cash & Carry* [2014] EWHC 4058 (QB) (upheld on appeal; [2016] EWCA Civ 153; [2016] 1 W.L.R. 4530; [2016] All E.R. 129; (noted in para.3.9.4.1, above and 3.9.6.10, below), McGowan J (personal difficulties suffered by the applicant's solicitor whose wife was subject to ongoing medical problems, where the solicitor was a member of a firm large enough to enable work to be delegated to other fee earners with sufficient experience and skill to ensure that tasks were properly completed; and see also, *Intellimedia Systems Ltd v Richards (Ch)* Warren J, 1 February 2017, unrep. noted in para.3.14.1, below).

Relevance of "all the circumstances"

To the end of the paragraph, add:

3.9.6.11   In *R. (on the application of DPP) v Stratford Magistrates' Court* [2017] DC 22nd March 2017, unreported, the DPP was granted relief from sanctions in judicial review proceedings after its claim was struck out for the inadvertent failure to pay a court fee. Relief from that sanction was granted. The case fell towards the bottom of the scale of seriousness. The underlying issue was not frivolous and was potentially of general public importance. The judicial review was on a question of law and there would be no forensic disadvantage to the interested parties and relatively little time would be lost (and see also, *R. (on the application of Muir) v Wandsworth LBC* [2017] QBD (Admin) Ousley J., 23rd March 2017, unrep.).

In *Michael v Phillips* [2017] EWHC 142 (QB) Green J, the defendants who had seriously breached an unless order requiring them to disclose documents by a certain date had their defence and counterclaim struck out and were debarred from defending the claim. Their application for relief from sanctions under r.3.9 was refused as the way in which they had lost and/or suppressed data was profoundly unsatisfactory, and significantly and unfairly prejudiced the claimants' ability to prepare for trial in a case turning on the forensic analysis of that data.

Meaning of "procedural error"

After the eighth paragraph (beginning with "In Cardiff County Council"), add new paragraph:

3.10.3   In *Thompson v Reeve* [2017] QBD, Master Yoxall, 20th March 2017, unrep., it was held that r.3.10 could be used to remedy a defect in the method of service of a Part 36 withdrawal notice (service by email where the opponent had not indicated a willingness to accept service by email). The court accepted that Part 36 was a self-contained code. However, it was not completely freestanding as shown by the fact that the respondents themselves had relied on an outside rule, r.6.20, to submit that service was irregular.

Civil restraint orders

Replace the twelfth paragraph (beginning with "The Court of Appeal also"), with:

3.11.1   The Court of Appeal also said that if the facts are clear and simple enough it might be appropriate for the court to proceed to make a civil restraint order immediately rather than adjourn the application. However, if the history of the previous litigation is complicated an adjournment might be appropriate. (In that case the previous history was complicated by the failure to record on previous orders that the applications or statements of case had been totally without merit; see r.3.3(7) and r.3.4(6) and see 3.4.10 above.

II. Costs Management

Effect of Section II and Practice Direction 3E

Add new paragraph at end:
    In *Various Claimants v MGN Ltd* [2016] EWHC 1894 (Ch); [2016] 4 Costs L.R. 695, Mann J held **3.12.1** that a budget approved by the court should not include any sum for any success fees or after-the-event ("ATE") insurance premiums which may be recoverable from the opponent if an order for costs is obtained. The Precedent H form did not provide for consideration of these additional liabilities or for the assumptions upon which they were based. Furthermore, under the CFA regime the relevant party did not have to disclose the terms of the CFA or the ATE premiums. By the same token, the litigant should not have to disclose any "assumptions" about them.

Costs management to be prospective not retrospective

Delete the last paragraph.   **3.12.2**

Filing "an agreed budget discussion report"

In the first paragraph replace "April 2013" with:
    April 2016;   **3.13.3**

Add new paragraph at end:
    As from 6 April 2017 a minor amendment was made to the opening words of Precedent R; the first line should now state the name of the party to whose budget the report relates.

Effect of rule

Add new paragraph at end:
    In *Intellimedia Systems Ltd v Richards* [2017] ChD 1st February 2017, Warren J, unrep., because of **3.14.1** staff illness, the claimant's solicitors failed to file or serve a budget or a budget discussion report on the defendants' budget before a CMC. This was a significant breach for which there had been no good reason. However, in all the circumstances, the sanction imposed by r.3.14 was not a proportionate one in the instant case. As the claimant had been inefficient, it was ordered to pay the costs of the instant hearing on an indemnity basis.

Minimising the adverse consequences of r.3.14 if relief from its sanction is not given

To the end of the third paragraph, add:
    In *Asghar v Bhatti* (QBD) 24 May 2017, unrep., Lewis J dismissed an appeal against a master's **3.14.3** order which approved a revision to a budget limited to court fees, the significant development being an increase in the likely duration of trial from 6 days to 12 days.
    The adverse consequences will be reduced by half if the party whose costs are limited to court fees makes a Pt 36 offer which his opponent does not accept within the relevant period for acceptance (usually 21 days from service of the offer) or which his opponent does not accept and later fails to achieve a more advantageous result at trial (see r.36.23 and the commentary thereto; para.36.23.1, below).

Add new paragraph 3.18.3:

Interplay between costs budgeting and detailed assessment
    In *Merrix v Heart of England NHS Foundation Trust* [2017] EWHC 346 (QB), (Carr J); [2017] 1 **3.18.3** Costs L.R.91., on appeal, the court considered the interplay between costs budgeting and detailed assessment under CPR Pt 47. The appellant, the successful party in a clinical negligence claim against the respondent, appealed against a decision that a costs judge's discretion at a detailed assessment of costs was not fettered by the costs budgeting regime. The costs judge (District Judge Lumb sitting as a Regional Costs Judge) held that costs budgeting did not replace detailed assessment, but was supposed to be a "strong guide" on "likely costs", thereby reducing the scope of any disagreement. Carr J held that the costs judge was wrong and that where a costs management order had been made, a costs judge assessing costs on the standard basis would not depart from the receiving party's last approved or agreed budget unless satisfied that there was good reason to do so. That applied equally whether the receiving party claimed less, the same as, or more than the sums budgeted. The central message was that set out in r.3.18, namely that an approved budget would bind the parties at detailed assessment unless there was a good reason to find otherwise. That was clear, mandatory, language, the purpose of the provision being to reduce the scope of,

and need for, detailed assessment. Costs budgeting was not an exercise in identifying the maximum amount of future costs; it was to identify what future costs were reasonable and proportionate. The proportionality test would be applied when fixing the budget. That was why a costs budget could not be departed from without good reason, *MacInnes v Gross* [2017] EWHC 127 (QB) applied, *Sarpd Oil International Ltd v Addax Energy SA* [2016] EWCA Civ 120 considered. Nothing in CPR PD3E para.7.3 impinged on that approach. There was no need to examine what constituted a "good reason" for the purposes of r.3.18, but clearly if the receiving party had spent less than was approved in the budget, the need to comply with the indemnity principle would require departure from the budget; there was no question of a party receiving more by way of costs than had actually been spent, *Henry v News Group Newspapers Ltd* [2013] EWCA Civ 19 considered.

Merrix is not now proceeding to a second appeal. However, a leapfrog appeal from Master Whalan in a somewhat similar case (*Harrison v Coventry NHS Trust (SCCO)* 16 August 2016 (unrep.)) was heard by the Court of Appeal on 10 May 2017 (judgment reserved).

PRACTICE DIRECTION 3E—COSTS MANAGEMENT

Precedent H—Costs budget

3EPD.5

In the first paragraph, replace "Precedent h", with:
"Precedent H"

Replace Precedent H with:

page 1

Work done / to be done	Incurred		Estimated		Total (£)
	Disbs (£)	Time costs (£)	Disbs (£)	Time costs (£)	
In the: xxx					
Parties: yyy					
Claim number: zzz					
Pre-action costs	£0.00	£0.00			£0.00
Issue / statements of case	£0.00	£0.00	£0.00	£0.00	£0.00
CMC	£0.00	£0.00	£0.00	£0.00	£0.00
Disclosure	£0.00	£0.00	£0.00	£0.00	£0.00
Witness statements	£0.00	£0.00	£0.00	£0.00	£0.00
Expert reports	£0.00	£0.00	£0.00	£0.00	£0.00
PTR			£0.00	£0.00	£0.00
Trial preparation			£0.00	£0.00	£0.00
Trial	£0.00		£0.00	£0.00	£0.00
ADR / Settlement discussions	£0.00		£0.00	£0.00	£0.00
Contingent cost A:			£0.00	£0.00	£0.00
Contingent cost B:			£0.00	£0.00	£0.00
GRAND TOTAL (including both incurred costs and estimated costs)	£0.00	£0.00	£0.00	£0.00	£0.00

This estimate *excludes* VAT (if applicable), success fees and ATE insurance premiums (if applicable), costs of detailed assessment, costs of any appeals, costs of enforcing any judgment and [complete as appropriate]

Approved budget	£
Budget drafting	1% of approved budget or £1,000	£
Budget process	2%	£

Statement of Truth

This budget is a fair and accurate statement of incurred and estimated costs which it would be reasonable and proportionate for my client to incur in this litigation.

Signed _____ Dated _____
Position _____

version 23/09/2016

In the:
Parties:
Claim number:

xxx
yyy
zzz

	RATE (per hour)	PRE-ACTION COSTS				ISSUE / STATEMENTS OF CASE				CMC			
		Incurred costs £	Estimated costs Hours	Estimated costs £	TOTAL £	Incurred costs £	Estimated costs Hours	Estimated costs £	TOTAL £	Incurred costs £	Estimated costs Hours	Estimated costs £	TOTAL £
Fee earner time													
1 grade		£0.00			£0.00	£0.00	0.00	£0.00	£0.00	£0.00	0.00		£0.00
2 grade		£0.00			£0.00	£0.00	0.00	£0.00	£0.00	£0.00	0.00		£0.00
3 grade		£0.00			£0.00	£0.00	0.00	£0.00	£0.00	£0.00	0.00		£0.00
4 grade		£0.00			£0.00	£0.00	0.00	£0.00	£0.00	£0.00	0.00		£0.00
5 Time value (1 to 4)		£0.00			£0.00	£0.00	0.00	£0.00	£0.00	£0.00	0.00	£0.00	£0.00
Expert's costs													
6 Fees		£0.00			£0.00	£0.00		£0.00	£0.00	£0.00			£0.00
7 Disbursements		£0.00			£0.00	£0.00			£0.00	£0.00			£0.00
Counsel fees													
8 Leading counsel		£0.00			£0.00	£0.00		£0.00	£0.00	£0.00		£0.00	£0.00
9 Junior counsel		£0.00			£0.00	£0.00		£0.00	£0.00	£0.00		£0.00	£0.00
Other Disbursements													
11 Disbursements		£0.00			£0.00	£0.00			£0.00	£0.00			£0.00
13 (6 to 11)		£0.00			£0.00	£0.00		£0.00	£0.00	£0.00		£0.00	£0.00
14 Total		£0.00			£0.00	£0.00		£0.00	£0.00	£0.00		£0.00	£0.00

Assumptions: Pre-action costs.

Assumptions: Issue / statements of case.

Assumptions: CMC.

page 3

In the:
Parties: xxx
Claim number: yyy
zzz

	RATE (per hour)	DISCLOSURE				WITNESS STATEMENTS			
		Incurred costs £	Estimated costs Hours	Estimated costs £	TOTAL £	Incurred costs £	Estimated costs Hours	Estimated costs £	TOTAL £
Fee earner time									
1 grade	£0.00	£0.00	0.00	£0.00	£0.00	£0.00	0.00	£0.00	£0.00
2 grade	£0.00	£0.00	0.00	£0.00	£0.00	£0.00	0.00	£0.00	£0.00
3 grade	£0.00	£0.00	0.00	£0.00	£0.00	£0.00	0.00	£0.00	£0.00
4 grade	£0.00	£0.00	0.00	£0.00	£0.00	£0.00	0.00	£0.00	£0.00
5 Time value (1 to 4)		£0.00	0.00	£0.00	£0.00	£0.00	0.00	£0.00	£0.00
Expert's costs									
6 Fees		£0.00		£0.00	£0.00	£0.00		£0.00	£0.00
7 Disbursements		£0.00		£0.00	£0.00	£0.00		£0.00	£0.00
Counsel fees									
8 Leading counsel		£0.00		£0.00	£0.00	£0.00		£0.00	£0.00
9 Junior counsel		£0.00		£0.00	£0.00	£0.00		£0.00	£0.00
Other									
11 Disbursements		£0.00		£0.00	£0.00	£0.00		£0.00	£0.00
13 Total Disbursements (6 to 11)		£0.00		£0.00	£0.00	£0.00		£0.00	£0.00
14 Total (5 + 13)		£0.00		£0.00	£0.00	£0.00		£0.00	£0.00

Assumptions: disclosure.

Assumptions: witness evidence.

Page 4

In the:
Parties: xxx yyy zzz
Claim number:

EXPERT REPORTS (see separate breakdown for expert fees)

EXPERT FEE SUMMARY

Drafting note: Completing this summary will populate totals for fees in table on left.

	RATE (per hour)	Incurred costs £	Estimated costs Hours	Estimated costs £	TOTAL £	Type	incurred	estimated report	estimated conference	estimated joint stms	Total estimated
Fee earner time											
1 grade	£0.00	£0.00	0.00	£0.00	£0.00	xx	£	£	£	£	£
2 grade	£0.00	£0.00	0.00	£0.00	£0.00	xx	£	£	£	£	£
3 grade	£0.00	£0.00	0.00	£0.00	£0.00	xx	£	£	£	£	£
4 grade	£0.00	£0.00	0.00	£0.00	£0.00	xx	£	£	£	£	£
5 Time value (1 to 4)		£0.00	0.00	£0.00	£0.00	xx	£	£	£	£	£
Expert's costs											
6 Fees		£0.00		£0.00	£0.00	xx	£	£	£	£	£
7 Disbursements		£0.00		£0.00	£0.00	xx	£	£	£	£	£
Counsel fees											
8 Leading counsel		£0.00		£0.00	£0.00	xx	£	£	£	£	£
9 Junior counsel		£0.00		£0.00	£0.00	xx	£	£	£	£	£
11 Other Disbursements		£0.00		£0.00	£0.00	xx	£	£	£	£	£
Total Disbursements 13 (6 to 11)		£0.00		£0.00	£0.00	Sub total	£	£	£	£	£
14 Total (5 + 13)		£0.00		£0.00	£0.00	Total expert fees (incurred and estimated)	£				£0.00

Assumptions: expert evidence.

In the:
Parties:
Claim number:

xxx
yyy
zzz

Page 5

	RATE (per hour)	PTR			TRIAL PREPARATION		
		Estimated costs		TOTAL	Estimated costs		TOTAL
		Hours	£		Hours	£	
Fee earner time							
1 grade	£0.00	0.00	£0.00	£0.00	0.00	£0.00	£0.00
2 grade	£0.00	0.00	£0.00	£0.00	0.00	£0.00	£0.00
3 grade	£0.00	0.00	£0.00	£0.00	0.00	£0.00	£0.00
4 grade	£0.00	0.00	£0.00	£0.00	0.00	£0.00	£0.00
5 Time value (1 to 4)		0.00	£0.00	£0.00	0.00	£0.00	£0.00
Expert's costs							
6 Fees			£0.00	£0.00		£0.00	£0.00
7 Disbursements			£0.00	£0.00		£0.00	£0.00
Counsel fees							
8 Leading counsel			£0.00	£0.00		£0.00	£0.00
9 Junior counsel			£0.00	£0.00		£0.00	£0.00
11 Other Disbursements			£0.00	£0.00		£0.00	£0.00
13 Total Disbursements (6 to 11)			£0.00	£0.00		£0.00	£0.00
14 Total (5 + 13)			£0.00	£0.00		£0.00	£0.00

Assumptions: PTR.

Assumptions: Trial prep.

12

page 6

In the:
Parties: xxx yyy
Claim number: zzz

	RATE (per hour)	TRIAL				SETTLEMENT / ADR				
		Estimated costs		TOTAL		Incurred costs	Estimated costs		TOTAL	
		Hours	£			£	Hours	£		
Fee earner time										
1	£0.00	0.00	£0.00	£0.00		£0.00	0.00	£0.00	£0.00	
2	£0.00	0.00	£0.00	£0.00		£0.00	0.00	£0.00	£0.00	
3	£0.00	0.00	£0.00	£0.00		£0.00	0.00	£0.00	£0.00	
4	£0.00	0.00	£0.00	£0.00		£0.00	0.00	£0.00	£0.00	
5 Time value (1 to 4)		0.00	£0.00	£0.00		£0.00	0.00	£0.00	£0.00	
6 Fees	Expert's costs		£0.00	£0.00		£0.00		£0.00	£0.00	
7 Disbursements			£0.00	£0.00		£0.00		£0.00	£0.00	
Counsel fees										
8 Leading counsel			£0.00	£0.00				£0.00	£0.00	
9 Junior counsel			£0.00	£0.00				£0.00	£0.00	
11 Other Disbursements			£0.00	£0.00				£0.00	£0.00	
Total Disbursements						£0.00		£0.00		
13 (6 to 11)			£0.00	£0.00		£0.00		£0.00	£0.00	
14 Total (5 + 13)			£0.00	£0.00		£0.00		£0.00	£0.00	

Assumptions:Trial.

Assumptions:Settlement / ADR.

In the:
Parties: xxx
Claim number: yyy
zzz

	RATE (per hour)	CONTINGENT COST A: [explain in assumptions box below]			CONTINGENT COST B: [explain in assumptions box below]		
		Estimated costs		TOTAL	Estimated costs		TOTAL
		Hours	£		Hours	£	
Fee earner time							
1	£0.00	0.00	£0.00	£0.00	0.00	£0.00	£0.00
2	£0.00	0.00	£0.00	£0.00	0.00	£0.00	£0.00
3	£0.00	0.00	£0.00	£0.00	0.00	£0.00	£0.00
4	£0.00	0.00	£0.00	£0.00	0.00	£0.00	£0.00
5 Time value (1 to 4)		0.00	£0.00	£0.00	0.00	£0.00	£0.00
Expert's costs							
6 Fees			£0.00	£0.00		£0.00	£0.00
7 Disbursements			£0.00	£0.00		£0.00	£0.00
Counsel fees							
8 Leading counsel			£0.00	£0.00		£0.00	£0.00
9 Junior counsel			£0.00	£0.00		£0.00	£0.00
11 Other Disbursements			£0.00	£0.00		£0.00	£0.00
13 Total Disbursements (6 to 11)			£0.00	£0.00		£0.00	£0.00
14 Total (5 + 13)			£0.00	£0.00		£0.00	£0.00

Assumptions: CONTINGENT COST A

Assumptions: CONTINGENT COST B

GUIDANCE NOTES ON PRECEDENT H

1. Where the monetary value of the case is less than £50,000 [or the costs claimed are less than £25,000] the parties must only use the first page of Precedent H.

2. Save in exceptional circumstances, the parties are not expected to lodge any documents other than Precedent H and the budget discussion report. Both are available in Excel format on the MOJ website with PD 3E. If the Excel format precedent on the MOJ website is used , the calculation on page one will calculate the totals automatically and the phase totals are linked to this page also.

3. This is the form on which you should set out your budget of anticipated costs in accordance with CPR Part 3 and Practice Direction 3E. In deciding the reasonable and proportionate costs of each phase of the budget the court will have regard to the factors set out at Civil Procedure Rules 44.3(5) and 44.4(3) including a consideration of where and the circumstances in which the work was done as opposed to where the case is heard.

4. This table identifies where within the budget form the various items of work, **in so far as they are required by the circumstances of your case**, should be included.

5. Allowance must be made in each phase for advising the client, taking instructions and corresponding with the other party/parties and the court in respect of matters falling within that phase.

6. The 'contingent cost' sections of this form should be used for **anticipated costs** which do not fall within the main categories set out in this form. Examples might be the trial of preliminary issues, a mediation, applications to amend, applications for disclosure against third parties or (in libel cases) applications re meaning. Only include costs which are more likely than not to be incurred. **Costs which are not anticipated** but which become necessary later are dealt with in paragraph 7.6 of PD3E.

7. Any party may apply to the court if it considers that another party is behaving oppressively in seeking to cause the applicant to spend money disproportionately on costs and the court will grant such relief as may be appropriate.

8. Assumptions:

    a. The assumptions that are reflected in this guidance document are **not** to be repeated. Include only those assumptions that **significantly** impact on the level of costs claimed such as the duration of the proceedings, the number of experts and witnesses or the number of interlocutory applications envisaged. Brief details only are required in the box beneath each phase. Additional documents are not encouraged and, where they are disregarded by the court, the cost of preparation may be disallowed, and additional documents should be included only where necessary.

    b. Written assumptions are not normally required by the Court in cases where the parties are only required to lodge the first page.

9. Budget preparation: the time spent in preparing the budget and associated material must **not** be claimed in the draft budget under any phase. The permitted figure will be inserted once the final budget figure has been approved by the court.

Phase	Includes	Does NOT include
Pre-action	• Pre-Action Protocol correspondence • Investigating the merits of the claim and advising client • Settlement discussions, advising on settlement and Part 36 offers • All other steps taken and advice given pre action	• Any work already incurred in relation to any other phase of the budget
Issue/statements of case	• Preparation of Claim Form • Issue and service of proceedings • Preparation of Particulars of Claim, Defence, Reply, including taking instructions, instructing counsel and any necessary investigation • Considering opposing statements of case and advising client • Part 18 requests (request and answer) • Any conferences with counsel primarily relating to statements of case • Updating schedules and counter-schedules of loss	• Amendments to statements of case
CMC	• Completion of DQs • Arranging a CMC • Reviewing opponent's budget • Correspondence with opponent to agree directions and budgets, where possible • Preparation for, and attendance at, the CMC • Finalising the order	• Subsequent CMCs • Preparation of costs budget for first CMC (this will be inserted in the approved budget)
Disclosure	• Obtaining documents from client and advising on disclosure obligations • Reviewing documents for disclosure, preparing disclosure report or questionnaire response and list • Inspection • Reviewing opponent's list and documents, undertaking any appropriate investigations • Correspondence between parties about the scope of disclosure and	• Applications for specific disclosure • Applications and requests for third party disclosure

	queries arising • Consulting counsel, so far as appropriate, in relation to disclosure	
Witness Statements	• Identifying witnesses • Obtaining statements • Preparing witness summaries • Consulting counsel, so far as appropriate, about witness statements • Reviewing opponent's statements and undertaking any appropriate investigations • Applications for witness summaries	• Arranging for witnesses to attend trial (include in trial preparation)
Expert Reports	• Identifying and engaging suitable expert(s) • Reviewing draft and approving report(s) • Dealing with follow-up questions of experts • Considering opposing experts' reports • Any conferences with counsel primarily relating to expert evidence • Meetings of experts (preparing agenda etc.)	• Obtaining permission to adduce expert evidence (include in CMC or a separate application) • Arranging for experts to attend trial (include in trial preparation)
PTR	• Bundle • Preparation of updated costs budgets and reviewing opponent's budget • Preparing and agreeing chronology, case summary and dramatis personae (if ordered and not already prepared earlier in case) • Completing and filing pre-trial checklists • Correspondence with opponent to agree directions and costs budgets, if possible • Preparation for and attendance at the PTR	• Assembling and/or copying the bundle (this is not fee earners' work)
Trial Preparation	• Trial bundles • Witness summonses, and arranging for witnesses to attend trial • Any final factual investigations • Supplemental disclosure and statements(if required) • Agreeing brief fee	• Assembling and/or copying the trial bundle (this is not fee earners' work) • Counsel's brief fee and any refreshers

	• Any pre-trial conferences and advice from counsel • Pre-trial liaison with witnesses	
Trial	• Solicitors' attendance at trial • All conferences and other activity outside court hours during the trial • Attendance on witnesses during the trial • Counsel's brief fee and any refreshers • Dealing with draft judgment and related applications	• Preparation for trial • Agreeing brief fee
Settlement	• Any conferences and advice from counsel in relation to settlement • Settlement negotiations and meetings between the parties to include Part 36 and other offers and advising the client • Drafting settlement agreement or Tomlin order • Advice to the client on settlement (excluding advice included in the pre-action phase)	• Mediation (should be included as a contingency)

Precedent R—Budget Discussion Report

Replace Precedent R with: **3EPD.6**

Cost budget for the		
In the:	Party	
	Court	
Case Number	Case number	

Budget discussion report

Phase	Claimed	Offered	Budgeted costs	Note : include only budgeted costs
Pre action costs	£0.00	£0.00	£0.00	Agreed or summary of why not agreed
Issue / stm of case	£0.00	£0.00	£0.00	Agreed or summary of why not agreed
CMC	£0.00	£0.00	£0.00	Agreed or summary of why not agreed
Disclosure	£0.00	£0.00	£0.00	Agreed or summary of why not agreed
Witness stms	£0.00	£0.00	£0.00	Agreed or summary of why not agreed
Experts reports	£0.00	£0.00	£0.00	Agreed or summary of why not agreed
PTR	£0.00	£0.00	£0.00	Agreed or summary of why not agreed
Trial preparation	£0.00	£0.00	£0.00	Agreed or summary of why not agreed
Trial	£0.00	£0.00	£0.00	Agreed or summary of why not agreed
ADR	£0.00	£0.00	£0.00	Agreed or summary of why not agreed
Contingent cost A:	£0.00	£0.00	£0.00	Agreed or summary of why not agreed
Contingent cost B:	£0.00	£0.00	£0.00	Agreed or summary of why not agreed
Total budgeted costs	£0.00	£0.00	£0.00	

PART 5

COURT DOCUMENTS

Viewing the case record

Replace paragraph with:

5.4B.9   Other provisions, apart from r.5.4B, may provide for parties or their representatives to have access to court records. Particular examples are Practice Direction 7E (Money Claim Online) para.13 (see para.7EPD.13 below); Practice Direction 55B (Possession Claims Online), para.14.2 (see para.55BPD.14 below) which make provision for the viewing of case records on court-maintained websites in the proceedings to which they apply. Under the "electronic working" arrangements, as provided for by Practice Direction 51O–The Electronic Working Pilot Scheme (see para.51OPD.1 et seq below), parties are enabled in certain proceedings in certain courts to issue proceedings and file documents online. Directions in paras 14 and 16 therein provide that, subject to the provisions of r.5.4B, parties may obtain electronic copies of documents contained in the electronic working case file (see para.51OPD.14 below).

Effect of rule and practice direction

Replace the seventh paragraph (beginning with "A non-party wishing"), with:

5.4C.1   A non-party wishing to obtain a copy of a document under this rule must pay the prescribed fee and (a) if the court's permission is required, file an application notice in accordance with Pt 23, or (b) if permission is not required, file a written request for the document (r.5.4D(1)). Paragraphs 15 and 16 of Practice Direction 51O–The Electronic Working Pilot Scheme contain directions stating arrangements enabling non-parties to examine the electronic record of proceedings handled under that Pilot Scheme and to obtain copies of documents available in accordance with r.5.4C (see para.51OPD.15 below).

Application in opposition by party or person identified

Replace the fourth paragraph (beginning with "Paragraph (5) of"), with:

5.4C.6   Paragraph (5) of the rule, r.5.4D(2), and Practice Direction 5A (Court Documents), para.4.4 (see para.5APD.4 below) deal with matters of practice in relation to an application under r.5.4C(4). In *Bombardier Transportation Ltd v Mersey Travel* [2017] EWHC 575 (TCC), 24 March 2017, unrep. (Coulson J), the claimant in a public procurement action made an application for an order pursuant to r.5.4C(4) that neither the particulars of claim, nor the confidential annexes attached to it, should be provided to non-parties. The judge noted that in procurement disputes particular difficulties can arise in striking the balance between open justice and confidentiality, and explained that passages in the *Guidance Note on Procedures for Public Procurement Cases* set out a practice to be followed in the TCC so as to ensure that confidential information is protected where necessary by orders made under r.5.4C(4). The practice to be followed in variation of trust claims where initial applications are made to the court to preserve confidentiality, including applications for interim orders restricting access to claim forms and evidence on the court file, is stated in *Practice Note (Variation of Trusts: Confidentiality Orders Pending the Hearing of Application)*, 9 February 2017, unrep. (see para.64PN.1).

PART 6

SERVICE OF DOCUMENTS

II.   Service of the Claim Form in the Jurisdiction or in specified circumstances within the EEA

"first class post" or "other service" (r.6.3(1)(b))

After the first paragraph, add new paragraph:

6.3.3   As to service by post or by other service at address within the jurisdiction when resident defendant out of the jurisdiction temporarily or indefinitely, see para.6.9.7 below.

6.9.7 *Change title of paragraph:*

Resident out of jurisdiction at time of service

Replace paragraph with:
Rule 6.3 is concerned with "methods" of service and says nothing about "place" of service. Where service of a claim form is to be effected by first class post or by service by another comparable service, the appropriate place will be as provided by other rules, quite commonly by r.6.9 (Service of claim form where the defendant does not provide an address at which the defendant may be served). Under r.6.9 the appropriate place will turn on the nature of the defendant to be served; for example, where the defendant is an individual, his or her "usual or last known address", or where being sued in the name of a business, the "principal or last known place of business". Where the place to which the claim form is sent is an address within the jurisdiction then, obviously, the service is effected at a place within the jurisdiction. The question has arisen whether the service is valid if, at the time it is so effected at the address of a defendant resident within the jurisdiction, the defendant is absent from the jurisdiction because abroad on a business trip, or a holiday, or (by withdrawing temporarily or indefinitely) to avoid service. The relevant Court of Appeal authorities are *City & Country Properties Ltd v Kamali* [2006] EWCA Civ 1879; [2007] 1 W.L.R. 1219, CA; *SSL International plc v TTK LIG Ltd* [2011] EWCA Civ 1170; [2012] 1 W.L.R. 1842, CA; they were reviewed and applied in the context of service of documents other than claim forms (in particular, witness summonses) in *Clavis Liberty Fund 1 LP v Young* [2015] UKUT 72 (TCC); [2015] 1 W.L.R. 2949 (Warren J) at paras 26 to 32; and *Libyan Investment Authority v Société Générale* [2017] EWHC 781 (Comm), 6 April 2017, unrep. (Teare J) at paras 57 to 67. The principle that a defendant may be served with originating process within the jurisdiction only if he or she is "present in the jurisdiction" at the time is deeply embedded in English law (*Chellaram v Chellaram (No.2)* [2002] 3 All E.R. 17 (Lawrence Collins J) at para.47). The problem is that of reconciling that principle with the development of rules permitting service by post within the jurisdiction. The prevailing opinion seems to be that a defendant "resident" in the jurisdiction is "subject" to the jurisdiction and therefore "present" in the jurisdiction.
As to usual or last known address, see para.6.9.3.1 above.

"relevant step under rule 7.5(1)"

After the seventh paragraph (beginning with "Before October 1"), add new paragraph:
Note also the decision in *Brightside Group Ltd v RSM UK Audit LLP* [2017] EWHC 6 (Comm), **6.14.3** where Andrew Baker J held that compliance with the date for service of a claim form or notice of discontinuance under a r.7.7 notice was to be determined by reference to r.6.14 not r.7.5. He noted that there was no prior authority on the relationship between r.6.14 and r.7.7. He held that the decisions in *Godwin v Swindon Borough Council* and *Anderton v Clwyd County Council (No.2)* (above) remain binding, and make it clear that the deemed date of service is set out in r.6.14, which is a fixed and irrebuttable date. He distinguished previous authorities, *Ageas (UK) Ltd v Kwik-Fit (GB) Ltd* [2013] EWHC 3261 (QB) and *T & L Sugars Ltd v Tate & Lyle Industries Ltd* [2014] EWHC 1066 (Comm) on the ground that neither of those decisions were concerned with r.7.7.

Retrospective operation—"steps already taken"

Add new paragraph at end:
Popplewell J has given a helpful analysis of the principles applicable to CPR 6.15 and 6.16 in **6.15.5** *Societe Generale v Goldas Kuyumculuk Sanayi Ithalat Ihracat AS* [2017] EWHC 667 (Comm). He dismissed the claimant's retrospective application for permission for service by an alternative method in circumstances where there had been deliberate delay and abusive conduct by the claimant once it knew that its attempted service on defendants in Turkey was disputed and had no reason to believe that purported service in Dubai was valid.

III. Service of Documents other than the Claim Form in the United Kingdom or in specified circumstances within the EEA

"first class post, document exchange or other service" (r.6.20(1)(b))

After the first paragraph, add new paragraphs:
Rule 6.20 applies to the service of documents other than a claim form. Paragraph (1)(a) of that **6.20.2** rule states that a document may be served by first class post. Rule 6.9 provides for the service of claim forms and in that rule it is expressly provided that, where a claim is served by post on an individual defendant, the place of service will be that individual's "usual or last known residence". There is no such express provision in r.6.20, but it has become accepted that it is right to apply it to service of other documents (e.g. a witness summons) by analogy (*Clavis Liberty Fund 1 LP v Young* [2015] UKUT 72 (TCC); [2015] 1 W.L.R. 2949 (Warren J.) at para.21; *Libyan Investment Authority v Société Générale* [2017] EWHC 781 (Comm), 6 April 2017, unrep. (Teare J) at para.58). See further para.6.9.7 above.

In *Libyan Investment Authority v Societe Generale*, op cit, on 3 January 2017, some of several defendants (D) issued a witness summons for purpose of securing attendance of an individual (X) at a trial, and on 15 February 2017, sent it by first class post to the address of a London flat of which X was leaseholder since January 2014 and which X vacated on 18 February 2017, mid-way through the period of two-month's notice which his landlord had been required by statute to grant him for the termination of the lease. Earlier, on 24 December 2016, X had left London for Paris and subsequently travelled elsewhere abroad, returning to Paris on 3 March 2017. On 28 February 2017, in X's absence, the court declared that the witness summons had been validly served by post. Subsequently, a judge dismissed X's application to set aside service of the summons. In doing so the judge (1) found that X was resident within the jurisdiction until 18 February 2017, and (2) rejected X's submission that, as he was not physically within the jurisdiction when the summons was issued (on 15 February) and when it was deemed to be served (17 February), there could not be any valid service.

IV.   Service of the Claim Form and other Documents out of the Jurisdiction

Replace with:

Service out of jurisdiction with court's permission

6.36.1   A claimant does not require the permission of the court to serve a claim form on a defendant out of the jurisdiction in the circumstances provided for by r.6.32 (service on a defendant in Scotland or Northern Ireland) or by r.6.33 (where court has jurisdiction under Judgments Regulation etc). Rule 6.36 applies to proceedings to which those rules do not apply.

A claimant does not require the permission of the court to serve a counterclaim on a foreign claimant because, by bringing proceedings in the English court, the foreign claimant submits to the court's jurisdiction in regard to any counterclaim (*Derby & Co v Larsson* [1976] 1 W.L.R. 202, H.L.).

The expression "jurisdiction" in this context denotes the area of the territorial jurisdiction of the High Court and the County Court as the case may be.

The claimant may serve a claim form out of the jurisdiction with the permission of the court if any of the "grounds" set out in para.3.1 of Practice Direction 6B apply.

For text of para.3.1, see para.6BPD.3 below. For commentary on the scope of the several grounds, see para.6HJ.1 et seq below.

When the CPR came into effect, these grounds, or "heads of jurisdiction" (as they were traditionally named), or "gateways", as they are nowadays colloquially called, were enacted in CPR Sch.1 RSC Ord.11 r.1(1), and from 2 May 2000, until 1 October 2008, they were contained in r.6.20. From the latter date they were relegated from rule form to practice direction form, specifically as listed in para.3.1 of PD6B. (That arrangement caused some surprise, given that the grounds in effect extend the jurisdiction of the court, something that requires legislation.)

A claimant seeks the court's permission by application. See further r.6.37 and commentary thereon.

CPR r.7.2(1) states that proceedings are started when the court "issues a claim form at the request of the claimant". It may be noted that, before the CPR came into effect, RSC Ord.6, r.7(1) provided that no writ which is to be served on a defendant out of the jurisdiction "shall be issued for such service without the leave of the court" unless the action was one to which other rules applied, being rules that permitted service of the writ out of the jurisdiction without the permission of the court. There is no comparable provision in the CPR. An application under r.6.36 is for permission to serve, not for permission to issue.

In terms, r.6.36 is concerned with the service out of the jurisdiction of "a claim form". CPR r.81.10(2) states that, where a committal application is made against a person who is not an existing party to the proceedings, it is made against that person by an application notice under Pt 23. It has been held that in appropriate circumstances such notice could be "a claim form" within the meaning of r.6.36 (*Dar Al Arkan Real Estate Development Co v Al Refai* [2014] EWCA Civ 715; [2015] 1 W.L.R. 135, CA, where permission granted to serve a committal application on an individual out of the jurisdiction under para.3.1(3)(b) of Practice Direction 6B on ground that he was a necessary and proper party to contempt proceedings brought against a defendant).

Replace paragraphs 6.37.1-6.37.13 with:

The application for permission (r.6.37(1))

6.37.1   The provisions in r.6.37 deal sequentially with three topics (but not exhaustively). First, with the content of the application for permission (paras (1) and (2)), secondly, with the decision of the court whether or not to grant permission (paras (3) and (4)), and thirdly, with practical issues arising where permission is granted (para.(5)).

For interpretation in Pt 6 of "claim", and construing of "claim form", "claimant" and "defendant", see r.6.2(c).

In addition to the matters explained immediately below, note also the information contained in the Court Guides as follows: Chancery Guide Ch.7 paras 7-12 to 7-14 (Permission to serve out of the jurisdiction), and Ch.11 paras 11-7 and 11-8 (Service out) (Vol.2 paras 1A-56 and 1A-77);

Queen's Bench Guide (Service of the claim form—out of the jurisdiction—with permission) paras 4.4.27 to 4.4.30, in particular para.4.4.28 (Vol.2 para.1B-27); Admiralty and Commercial Courts Guide Appendix 15 paras 2 to 5 (Application for permission), and paras 7 to 9 (Practice under rule 6.36) (Vol.2 paras 2A-176 and 2A-180.1); Mercantile Court Guide paras 3.10 to 3.12 (Service of the claim form out of the jurisdiction) (Vol.2 para.2B-20).

Normally, for obvious reasons, an application to serve a claim form out of the jurisdiction under r.6.36 will be made ex parte and without notice. In the High Court an application in the Chancery Division or Queen's Bench Division will be dealt with by a Master or a District Judge (CPR r.2.4) (who may refer the matter to a Judge), and in the Commercial Court or a Mercantile Court by a Judge. In para.7B.1 of Practice Direction 2A (Chancery Proceedings) it is expressly provided that a Master may make a service out order in proceedings in the Patents Court. Usually an application will be dealt with on paper, without an oral hearing.

Where the claim form is to be served out of the jurisdiction, it must be served in accordance with Section IV of Pt 6 within six months of the date of issue (r.7.5(2)). It should be noted that that time limit runs from the date of issue; not from the date on which permission to serve out is given. That is an important point to be kept in mind where the claimant does not, before the claim form is issued, make an application for permission to serve out. As to the period for service where the claim form (though naming a foreign defendant) is, at issue, marked by the court "not for service out of the jurisdiction", see para.6.37.10 below. The claimant may apply for an order extending the period for service of a claim form (r.7.6(1)). Where the period of initial validity of a claim form (whatever that might be and however determined) has expired the court retains power to extend it retrospectively, and to entertain an application to serve the claim form out of the jurisdiction made within the extended time. See commentary following r.7.6 (Extension of time for service a claim form).

Content of application for permission (r.6.37(1))

6.37.2

Applications for permission to serve a claim form out of the jurisdiction under r.6.36 are made in accordance with CPR Pt 23. Rule 23.6 states that an application notice must state (a) what order the applicant is seeking and (b) briefly, why the applicant is seeking the order. If an applicant wishes to rely on matters set out in his application notice as written evidence, the notice must be verified by a statement of truth (r.22.1(3)). Where convenient, the written evidence should be included in the form of an application notice, rather than in a separate witness statement, and the notice may extended for this purpose. The applicant for permission under r.6.36 should use **Form N244** (Application notice) and include in it the additional information referred to in **Form PF 6A** (Application for permission to serve claim form out of the jurisdiction (rules 6.36 and 6.37)).

The information relied on in the notice in support of the application should be verified by a statement of truth in the normal way. **Form PF 6A** reflects the requirements imposed on applicants by r.6.37. That Form states that the claimant must be set out either in the application notice itself or within a witness statement to be filed with the application notice, the matters referred to in r.6.37(1), the facts relied on under r.6.37(3), and the grounds, facts etc relied on for satisfying r.6.37(2) and (4) (where those sub-rules are relevant). The written evidence may be given by any person with knowledge of the facts but it is more usually made by the claimant's solicitor upon knowledge, information and belief. The evidence should be sufficiently full to establish the matters referred to in r.6.37 and reflected in **Form PF 6A**. The burden of establishing that the claimant's claim falls within one of the grounds stated in para 3.1 of Practice Direction 6B (r.6.37(1)(a)) and that the claimant's claim has a reasonable prospect of success (r.6.37(1)(b)) falls on the claimant; see further, as to burden and standard of proof, para.6.37.15 et seq below.

Paragraph (2) of r.62.5 (Service out of jurisdiction of arbitration claims) states that an application under that rule must be supported by written evidence (a) stating the grounds on which the application is made and (b) showing in what place or country the person to be served is, or probably may be found (Vol.2 para.2E-12).

Application in respect of claim in para.3.1(3) of PD6B (r.6.37(2))

6.37.3

In terms, the effect of para.(2) of r.6.37 is confined to applications to the court for permission to serve a claim form out of the jurisdiction where the claim is made under para.3.1(3) of Practice Direction 6B, that is to say, where the claimant, having brought a claim against a defendant, applies for permission to serve the claim form on "another person" out of the jurisdiction on the ground that that other person is a necessary or proper party to the claim against the defendant. The width of that head of jurisdiction and its potential for abuse by claimants bringing against a defendant a specious or weak claim (or perhaps one in which the defendant connived) as a pretext for bringing proceedings against "another person" attracted judicial concern. In response to that concern, in 1987 the formulation for the head of jurisdiction was significantly amended and at the same time what is now r.6.37(2) was first introduced into the rules (and has remained largely in the same terms since). The phrase "a real issue which it is reasonable for the court to try" replicates the terms of para.3.1(3) of Practice Direction 6B. See further para.6HJ.4 below.

Application under r.6.36 to serve out—duty of disclosure

6.37.4

On an ex parte application (particularly where it is made on paper) the applicant is under an obligation to make full and fair (or "frank") disclosure. The duty arises on any ex parte application, and certainly so on one made under r.6.36, where what is being sought is the exercise of an exorbitant jurisdiction, bringing a foreign defendant within the jurisdiction even if only to incur the cost and inconvenience of fighting a jurisdiction application successfully.

For an explanation of variations in the extent of the duty to disclose more generally, and of the gravity of any lack of frankness, depending on the character of the application, contrasting applications under r.6.36 with ex parte applications made in other contexts (especially for interim injunctions), see *Payabi v Amstel Shipping Corporation* [1992] Q.B. 907 (Hobhouse J), at p.918; *MRG (Japan) Ltd v Engelhard Metals Japan Ltd* [2003] EWHC 3418 (Comm); [2004] 1 Lloyd's Rep. 731 (Toulson J), at paras 25 & 26.

In the context of ex parte applications under r.6.36, the disclosure duty has been summarised in various ways. In para.6 of **Form PF 6A** (Application for permission to serve claim form out of the jurisdiction (rules 6.36 and 6.37) it is stated that the application "should also bring to the attention of the court any matter which, if the other party were represented, that party would wish the court to be aware of" (adopted from *ABCI v Banque Franco-Tunisienne* [1996] 1 Lloyd's Rep. 485 (Waller J) at p.489). In para.2(c) of Appendix 15 of the Admiralty and Commercial Courts Guide it is said (in a formulation that has stood since that Guide was first published in 1986) that the applicant should "draw attention to any features which might reasonably be thought to weigh against the making of the order sought" (Vol.2 para.2A-176). See also *Masri v Consolidated Contractors International Company SAL* [2011] EWHC 1780 (Comm), 13 July 2011, unrep. (Burton J) at para.59 ("any material facts, and in particular any which may constitute a defence or some ground for not granting the order sought").

Such features, matters, material facts, etc., must be clearly drawn to the judge's attention. Those preparing statements in support of applications under r.6.36 should not proceed on the assumption that it is sufficient if, somewhere in the exhibits or in the statement, a point of materiality can be discerned (*ABCI v Banque Franco-Tunisienne* op cit at p.491).

A failure to refer to arguments on the merits which the defendant may seek to raise in answer to the claimant's claim at the trial should not generally be characterised as a failure to make a full and fair disclosure, unless they are of such weight that their omission may mislead the court in dealing with the application (*BP Exploration Co. (Libya) Ltd. v Hunt* [1976] 1 W.L.R. 788 (Kerr J), at p.798; approved *The Electric Furnace Company v Selas Corporation of America* [1987] R.P.C. 23, CA, at p.29 per Slade LJ). In *MRG (Japan) Ltd v Engelhard Metals Japan Ltd* [2003] EWHC 3418 (Comm); [2004] 1 Lloyd's Rep. 731 (Toulson J), a judge, in dismissing the defendant's application to set aside an order for service out, rejected the submission that if an applicant knew matters which would not on any reasonable view make any difference to whether there was a serious issue to be tried, or to any of the other questions which the judge had to consider, but which were relevant to the ultimate merits of the action, they must be disclosed.

Where an order is made on an ex parte application under r.6.36 (or on any other ex parte application), and it is subsequently established that the applicant deliberately misled the court or deliberately withheld information which he or she knew would, or might, be material, the order should be set aside (e.g. *Gunn v Diaz* [2017] EWHC 157 (QB); [2017] 1 Lloyd's Rep. 165 (Andrews J)). The mere fact that the non-disclosure may have been innocent does not deprive the court of its discretion to set aside an order for service out of the jurisdiction if the applicant has failed to make sufficient disclosure of material facts in the course of his application for permission (*Lazard Bros. & Co v Midland Bank* [1933] A.C. 289, HL, at p.307 per Lord Wright). In *The Hagen* [1908] P. 189, CA, Farwell LJ said (at p.201) that a failure to make full and fair disclosure would justify the court in discharging an order for service out "even although the party might afterward be in a position to make another application" (a dictum subsequently much-quoted).

It is not uncommon for applications to set aside orders for service out to be dismissed on the ground that, although there was material non-disclosure, if the full facts had been before the judge, permission would still have been given (e.g. *Kuwait Oil Co (KSC) v Idemitsu Tankers KK (The "Hida Maru")* [1981] 2 Lloyd's Rep. 510, CA). Failure to disclose to the court a limitation defence available to the defendant has been regarded as a serious omission (*ABCI v Banque Franco-Tunisienne* op cit), especially where the application is accompanied by an application to extend the period of validity of the claim form which would, if granted, deprive the defendant of an accrued right of limitation (*BUA International v Hai Hing Shipping Co Ltd (The "Hai Hing")* [2000] 1 Lloyd's Rep. 300 (Rix J)).

One of the matters which may well be material on an ex parte r.6.36 application is the existence of foreign proceedings between the same or related parties (whether pending or prospective), as not only may that go to the issue as to whether it is an appropriate case to be tried in England, but also to the possible applicability of any provisions in a civil procedure convention or the Judgments Regulation (recast) affecting priority of jurisdiction (*Masri v Consolidated Contractors International Company SAL* op cit at para.59). In normal circumstances that matter must be disclosed, and the non-disclosure of it may well of itself lead to the order for permission being set aside (*Ophthalmic Innovations International (UK) Ltd v Ophthalmic Innovations International Inc* [2004] EWHC 2948 (Ch); [2005] I.L.Pr.10 (Lawrence Collins J) at para.45).

In *NML Capital Limited v Republic of Argentina* [2011] UKSC 31, 273; [2011] 2 A.C. 495, SC, Lord Collins explained (at para.136) that in cases of non-disclosure, the court has a discretion (a) to set aside the order for service and require a fresh application, or (b) to treat the claim form as validly served, and deal with the non-disclosure if necessary by a costs order. For further information on the court's powers and procedural consequences where, on a defendant's application to set aside an order made under r.6.36, material non-disclosure is established (leading to the order for permission being set aside), see commentary following CPR r.11 (Procedure for disputing the court's jurisdiction).

"the court will not give permission unless satisfied" (r.6.37(3))

6.37.5

Rule 6.36 and para.3.1 of Practice Direction 6B state the grounds upon which the court may grant a claimant permission to serve a claim form out of the jurisdiction. In a given case, assuming that the court concludes that it has such power, that does not conclude the matter. As para.(3) of r.6.37 states, the court will not give permission unless satisfied that England and Wales is "the proper place in which to bring the claim". It is an over-simplification to say that this provision gives the court a discretion. In effect it flags up sophisticated conflict of law rules, particularly as regards the doctrine of forum non conveniens, which would come into play, whether or not their existence was noted and acknowledged in r.6.37. See paras 6.37.15.3 and 6.37.15.4 below.

Where proceedings are started in an English court, on application the court has power to stay the proceedings in favour of foreign proceedings where the court determines that England is not the proper place in which to bring the claim. That power also is exercisable in accordance with conflict of law rules. It is quite separate from the power exercisable by the court in accordance with r.6.37(3), but similar considerations may arise; see para.6.37.16 et seq below.

Permission to serve a claim form elsewhere in the United Kingdom (r.6.37(4))

6.37.6

Since the coming into effect of the Civil Jurisdiction and Judgments Act 1982, generally service of a claim form in Scotland or Northern Ireland may be made without permission under r.6.32. In the rare circumstances where permission is required r.6.37(4) applies. The rule was initially enacted in the late nineteenth century to placate Scottish concerns that English courts then too readily granted claimants permission to serve writs on defendants in Scotland. The effect of r.6.37(4) is confined to its context. Thus, where service is effected on a defendant in Scotland or Northern Ireland in circumstances where it was not necessary for the claimant to obtain the court's permission, and the defendant applies to set aside the service on forum non conveniens grounds, r.6.37(4) does not add anything to the defendant's submissions.

The effect of the rule may be misunderstood. In *Williams v Cartwright* [1895] 1 Q.B. 142, CA, it was explained (at p.146 per Lord Esher M.R.) that it is not an additional ground for giving permission to serve out of the jurisdiction; it is an additional obstacle that the applicant has to surmount. The cost and convenience of all parties to the action, not of the claimant alone, is relevant (ibid, at pp.147 and 149). There is no comparable reciprocal rule in the Rules of the Court of Session. For other early authorities on the rule, see *White Book* 2008 Vol.1 para.6.21.8. The early cases show that the chief considerations of convenience are the obvious ones of the residence of the parties and witnesses, the inconvenience of double litigation and the fact of one of the courts having already acquired seisin of the case, the location of documents for convenience of disclosure, the probability of despatch or delay, and the enforcement of the remedy sought in the action. Those cases were decided at a time when the differences between the considerations that the court had to take into account in this context, and where defendants were resident in other countries, were more marked than they subsequently became.

Directions as to service etc where court gives permission (r.6.37(5))

6.37.7

The appropriate form where an order for permission is granted is **Form PF 6B** (Order for permission to serve claim form out of jurisdiction (r.6.37(5)), formerly Queen's Bench Masters' Practice Form No. PF6.

Various rules in the CPR impose time limits within which a defendant served with a claim form should take certain procedural steps, if minded to do so. Paragraph (5) of r.6.37 acknowledges that the periods specified in such time limits should not apply where the defendant is served out of the jurisdiction, because it would be unrealistic to expect compliance. Those time limits are not disapplied, but instead the court is required to specify alternative periods for the procedural steps referred to in sub-paras (i) to (iv) of r.6.37(5).

As the parenthesis at the end of r.6.37(5) indicates, the periods referred to in sub-paras (i), (ii) and (iii) of r.6.37(5) are as specified in para.6.1 of Practice Direction 6B (see para.6BPD.5 below). The period specified by the court should be inserted in para.2 of **Form PF 6B**.

Where the claim form is to be served out of the jurisdiction it must be served in accordance with Section IV of Part 6 within six months of the date of issue (r.7.5). The court may give directions about "the method of service" and give permission for other documents in the proceedings to be served out of the jurisdiction (para.(b) of r.6.37(5)) and normally such directions will be sought by the claimant. For general provisions as to methods of service of claim forms out of the jurisdiction, see r.6.40 below. For commentary on the question whether the court may permit service out of the jurisdiction by "an alternative method", and for relevance of r.6.37 to that issue, see para.6.40.5 below.

Where an application notice is to be served out of the jurisdiction on a person who is not a party to the proceedings, paras (i), (ii) and (iii) of r.6.37(5)(a) do not apply (r.6.39(1)).

For procedure where service is to be through foreign government judicial authorities and British Consular authorities, see r.6.42 and r.6.43, and commentary thereon.

Amendment of claim form before service

6.37.8   A claimant's application for permission to serve out of the jurisdiction under r.6.36 must set out which of the grounds in para.3.1 of Practice Direction 6B relied (r.6.37(1)(a)). In practice this means demonstrating to the court in the application how the claimant's claim comes within one or more of those grounds. Rule 17.1(1) provides that a party may amend his statement of case at any time before it is served on any other party. (Subject to what is said immediately below, this rule and other rules relating to amendment apply to claim forms served out of the jurisdiction in the same way as they apply to other actions.) It is conceivable that a claimant, having been granted permission to serve out of the jurisdiction on one ground may, before serving it, resolve to amend the claim adding a new cause of action. Where the new cause of action is not one falling within any of the grounds stated in para.3.1 such amendment is not permissible (*Waterhouse v Reid* [1938] 1 K.B. 743, CA). Where the claimant's position is that the amended claim does fall within one of the grounds he or she cannot proceed on the assumption that the court's order granting permission covers the amended claim; the claimant must make a fresh application under r.6.36 for permission to serve the claim form out of the jurisdiction relating the claim in its amended form to a ground in para.3.1 (*Trafalgar Tours Ltd v Henry* [1990] 2 Lloyd's Rep. 298, CA).

Amendment of claim form after service

6.37.9   An applicant for permission under r.6.36 must show that each claim made by them has the attributes set out in at least one of the sub-paragaphs listed under para.3.1 of 6BPD; each such sub-paragraph being read, generally speaking, disjunctively (*Matthews v Kuwait Bechtel Corp* [1959] 2 Q.B. 57, CA). This may be a straight-forward matter. On the other hand it may involve a detailed analysis of issues of fact and law (perhaps quite complicated), creating scope for well-founded rival submissions in the event of an order for service out being challenged by the defendant. Where the order is so challenged the claimants may seek to support it on a different analysis of their pleaded case to that upon which they relied at the ex parte hearing. A question which has arisen is whether the claimants, anticipating at an inter partes hearing a formidable challenge to the order granting service out may seek the court's permission to amend their pleaded case, putting the claim on a different basis to that for which permission to serve out was granted ex parte and relating the amended claim to one or other of the grounds set out in para. 3.1 of Practice Direction 6B.

In the case of *In re Jogia* [1988] 1 W.L.R. 484 (Sir Nicolas Browne-Wilkinson V.-C.), at the hearing of the defendant's application to set aside the service of a writ on them outside the jurisdiction, for which the court had granted permission, the claimants applied for leave to amend their claim by abandoning a particular claim and raising others based on an alternative hypothesis and for which permission to serve out could be given. The judge accepted the defendant's submission that permission to amend had to be refused because the court was bound, by the Court of Appeal decision in *Parker v Schuller* (1901) 17 T.L.R. 299, CA, to hold that, in deciding whether service should be set aside, it had to confine itself to considering only those matters relied on as bringing the case within, what is now, para.3.1 of Practice Direction 6B when the original permission was given. Subsequently, that Court of Appeal decision was referred to or applied in numerous decisions at first instance or in the Court of Appeal (well summarised in *Al-Sadi v Al-Sadi* [2011] EWHC 976 (Comm), 4 April 2011, unrep. (Beatson J) at paras 18 & 19 and para.34 et seq) in support of the proposition that a claimant who has been given permission to serve out cannot resist an application challenging the jurisdiction by pleading a new cause of action. An effect of the decision was that the court was required to decide an application for permission to serve out of the jurisdiction on the basis of the cause or causes of action expressly mentioned in the pleadings, and the claimant would not be allowed to rely on an alternative cause of action which he or she sought to spell out of the facts pleaded if it had not been mentioned (*NML Capital Limited v Republic of Argentina* [2011] UKSC 31; [2011] 2 A.C. 495, SC, at para.132 per Lord Collins). If the claimants wished to rely on the amended claim (perhaps because forced to in order to keep the action alive), they had to make a fresh application for permission to serve out (which almost invariably would involve applying for an extension of time for service).

In the Supreme Court case of *NML Capital Limited v Republic of Argentina*, op cit, Lord Phillips (with whom the other Justices agreed on this point) stated that he was prepared to hold, should it be necessary to do so, that the so-called rule in *Parker v Schuller* should no longer be applied. His lordship explained (at paras 76 & 77) that there are a number of authorities, starting with *Holland v Leslie* [1894] 2 Q.B. 450, CA, which suggest that there is, in principle, no objection to amending a pleading which has been served out of the jurisdiction (whether by amending to add a cause of action or to substitute one), unless the effect will be to add a claim in respect of which leave could not, or would not, have been given to serve out. There was no obvious reason why it should be mandatory for the claimant to be required to start all over again rather than that the court should have a discretion as to the order that would best serve the overriding objective. Where a claimants' application to amend involves a defendant outside the jurisdiction who is already before the court, the court should not adopt any different approach to that adopted in a domestic case, provided that the new cause of action is one for which permission to serve out could be obtained if necessary (*JSC VTB Bank v Skurikhin* [2013] EWHC 3863 (Comm), 28 June 2013, unrep. (Flaux J), at para.9).

See further commentary on r.11 (Disputing the court's jurisdiction)

Claim form marked "not for service out of the jurisdiction"

In para.4.4.23 of the Queen's Bench Guide it is explained that a claimant may issue a claim **6.37.10** form against a defendant who appears to be out of the jurisdiction, without first having obtained permission for service, provided that, if the case is not one where service may be effected without permission, the claim form is endorsed by the court "not for service out of the jurisdiction" (Vol.2 para.1B-25). See also, to similar effect, para.11.7 of the Chancery Guide (Vol.2 para.1A-77). That practice is of very long-standing. Before the enactment of the CPR it was dealt with in practice directions (including *Practice Note (Writ: Service Abroad)* [1987] 1 W.L.R. 86).

The explanation usually given for the purpose of the practice has been (1) that it ensures that the claim form issued by the court is not valid for service in a country for which permission to serve is required, and (2) that it is convenient where the defendant with a foreign address has a solicitor within the jurisdiction willing to accept service and/or where there are other defendants who could be served out of the jurisdiction without permission.

The introduction (in 1990) of different and short periods of initial validity for service of a claim form (four months or six months) depending on whether it is to be served (respectively) within or without the jurisdiction, created problems not incidental to the practice previously (illustrated by *Vitol Energy (Bermuda) Ltd v Pisco Shipping Co Ltd* [1998] 1 Lloyd's Rep 509, CA). After the CPR came into effect the problems were resolved in principle by the Court of Appeal in *Anderton v Clwyd County Council (No.2)* [2002] EWCA Civ 933; [2002] 1 W.L.R. 3174, CA, at paras 97 and 98 (where the Court disposed of one of the joint appeals in those proceedings; i.e. the appeal in *Cummins v Shell International Manning Services Ltd*, 5 September 2001, unrep. (Gray J)). Since that authoritative decision, examples have routinely appeared of cases where the claim form was marked at issue "not for service out of the jurisdiction" (permission to serve out having not by then been obtained and not then sought) and the court subsequently granted the claimant (on an application under r.7.6 made during a period of extended validity for service) permission to serve the claim form out of the jurisdiction (see e.g. *Cecil v Bayat* [2011] EWCA Civ 135; [2011] 1 W.L.R. 3086, CA, where in the event the Court of Appeal held that the lower court erred, not in granting permission to serve out, but in extending the validity for service period). First instance cases dealing with disputes as to the fixing of the period of initial validity where the claim form was so marked (perhaps mistakenly) and as to whether, in that circumstance, the extension of the period should be permitted include: *S T Shipping & Transport Inc v Vyzantio Shipping Ltd (The "Byzantio")* [2004] EWHC 3067 (Comm); [2005] 1 Lloyd's Rep. 531 (Judge Havelock-Allan QC); *Nesheim v Kosa* [2006] EWHC 2710 (Ch), 4 October 2006, unrep. (Briggs J); *American Leisure Group Limited v Garrard* [2014] EWHC 2101 (Ch); [2014] 1 W.L.R. 4102 (David Richards J); *TMT Asia Limited v BHP Billiton Marketing AG* [2016] EWHC 287 (Ch), 14 January 2016, unrep. (Burton J).

Admiralty claims

In Part 61 (Admiralty claims) special rules as to the service out of the jurisdiction of claim forms **6.37.11** for collision claims and for limitation claims are stated in, respectively, r.61.4(7) and r.61.11(5). Claim forms may not be served out of the jurisdiction unless the conditions stated in those provisions are met, and "the court grants permission under Section IV of Part 6"; see Vol.2 paras 2D-29 & 2D-73. See further paras N5.3 and N6.2 of the Admiralty and Commercial Courts Guide (Vol.2 paras 2A-133 & 2A-134).

Application to set aside the order or service

See commentary in CPR Pt 11.   **6.37.12**

Appeal

An appeal from a refusal by a Master to give permission to serve the claim form out of the **6.37.13** jurisdiction lies to a judge of the High Court. Should a party wish to challenge a decision of a judge of the High Court which was itself an appeal from a decision of a Master, permission to appeal must be sought from the Court of Appeal to which any such appeal (a second appeal) lies (see CPR r.52.3 to 52.7, and Table 1 to CPR PD52A).

Delete paragraph 6.37.14 "Appeal".

Principles upon which permission to serve outside the jurisdiction is granted

Rule 6.36 and para.3.1 of 6BPD

Replace the fifth paragraph (beginning with "In CH Offshore Ltd") with:

In *CH Offshore Ltd v PDV Marina SA* [2015] EWHC 595 (Comm) the court rejected a defendant's **6.37.15.1** argument that a third party was a necessary and property party under CPR PD 6B para.3.1(4). There was no single investigation to be carried out in respect of the main claim and the third party claim, and they were not bound by a common thread. They arose under very different contracts which gave rise to different and separate issues and were not back-to-back. In *Brownlie v Four Seasons Holdings Inc* [2015] EWCA Civ 665; [2015] C.P. Rep. 40 the CA held that consequential loss suffered in England as a result of an accident abroad is insufficient to found English jurisdiction. Such loss does not constitute "damage ... sustained within the jurisdiction" for the purposes of the tort jurisdiction gateway in CPR PD 6B para.3.1(9)(a). This gateway has to be interpreted consistently with the European regime on jurisdiction and applicable law. The judgment also contains clarification on the standard of proof: see *Canada Trust Co v Stolzenberg* above. It follows *Erste Group Bank AG (London) v JSC (VMZ Red October)* [2015] EWCA Civ 379, where a differently constituted CA doubted whether it was correct to interpret "damage" for the purposes of the tort jurisdictional gateway as extending to consequential loss, and expressly stated that it had "serious reservations as to whether those first instance cases were right" in relation to the first instance decisions of *Booth v Phillips* [2004] EWHC 1437 (Comm); [2004] 1 W.L.R. 3292, *Cooley v Ramsey* [2008] EWHC 129 (QB) (see para.6.37.43 below). The effect of those decisions is to reverse the trend of those first instance decisions in widening the test for the jurisdictional gateway under CPR PD6B para.3.1(9)(a).

After the fifth paragraph (beginning with "In CH Offshore Ltd"), add new paragraphs:

Note also *Gunn v Diaz and others* [2017] EWHC 157 (QB) where following the decision in Brownlie Andrews J set aside the order giving permission for service outside the jurisdiction. Although she considered that the court had discretion to permit the claimants to rely on a different ground of jurisdiction to the original application (the necessary and proper party gateway (PD6B.3.1(3)), to fulfil the requirements for this gateway, service on the "anchor defendant" must have been legally permissible. As the court should never have granted permission to serve on any of the defendants at the original application (applying Brownlie), prior service on the fourth defendant and prospective service on the fifth defendant could not be relied upon.

Similarly in *Microsoft Mobile OY (Ltd) v Sony Europe Ltd* [2017] EWHC 374 (Ch), permission to serve out of the jurisdiction against two of four defendants was set aside, because the claims against the first two defendants were stayed because the claims against them fell within an arbitration clause, and as the first defendant was the 'anchor' defendant it was no longer possible to proceed with claims against the third and fourth defendants on the basis of the necessary and proper party gateway (PD 6B.3.1(3)).

In the last paragraph, replace "NML Capital Limited v Republic of Argentina [2011] UKSC 31, 273, [2011] 3 W.L.R. 273, S.C." with:

NML Capital Limited v Republic of Argentina [2011] UKSC 31, 273; [2011] 3 W.L.R. 273, S.C.

Service Regulation

After the sixth paragraph (beginning with "Under art.14"), add new paragraph:

6.41.2   In *Henderson v Novo Banco SA (Case C-354/15)* the ECJ held that postal service of a document instituting proceedings is valid even if the document was not delivered to the addressee in person, provided that it was served on an adult person who was inside the habitual residence of the addressee and is either a member of his family, or an employee in his service. The court also confirmed that (i) service is valid even if the acknowledgment of receipt has been replaced by another document, provided that it is equivalent with regard to information and evidence; and (ii) national legislation providing that the absence of the Annex II form (which advises the addressee of his right to refuse the document in certain circumstances) rendered service invalid, was precluded by the Service Regulation, which required such an omission to be corrected by sending the Annex II form to the addressee.

PRACTICE DIRECTION 6A—SERVICE WITHIN THE UNITED KINGDOM

Editorial note

6APD.10.1   *Replace table with:*

METHOD OF SERVICE CPR 6.3 and 6.26	DEEMED DATE OF SERVICE OF CLAIM FORM CPR 6.14 and 7.5(1); 6.5(3)	DEEMED DATE OF SERVICE OF PARTICULARS OF CLAIM CPR 6.26
First Class Post, document exchange or other service that provides delivery on the next business day	The second business day after completion of the step. e.g. posted, left with, delivered to or collected by the relevant document delivery service on Monday, deemed served on Wednesday; or posted, left with, delivered to or collected	The second day after it was posted, or left with, delivered to or collected by the relevant service provider, provided that day is a business day, if not the next business day after that day. e.g. posted, left with, delivered to or collected by the

	by the relevant document delivery service on Friday, deemed served on the following Tuesday (unless Monday is a Bank Holiday, then deemed service on Wednesday).	relevant document delivery service on Monday, deemed served on Wednesday posted, left with, delivered to or collected by the relevant document delivery service on Friday, deemed served on the followingMonday (unless Monday is a Bank Holiday, then deemed service on Tuesday).
Delivery of the document or leaving it at the relevant place	Second business day after delivering to or leaving at the relevant place. e.g. delivered /left on Monday, served on Wednesday; delivered/left on Friday, deemed served on Tuesday (unless Monday is a Bank Holiday, then deemed service on Wednesday).	If delivered/left at permitted address on a business day before 4.30pm, on that day, or in any other case, the next business day. e.g. delivered/left 4pm Monday, deemed served Monday (unless Monday is a Bank Holiday, then deemed service on Tuesday); delivered/left 5pm Monday, deemed served Tuesday delivered/left 4pm Friday, deemed served Friday; delivered/left 5pm Friday, deemed served the following Monday (unless Monday is a Bank Holiday, then deemed service on Tuesday).
Personal Service	Second business day after leaving claim form in accordance with r.6.5 (3). e.g. left on Monday, deemed served on Wednesday; left on Friday, deemed served on the following Tuesday (unless Monday is a Bank Holiday, then deemed service on Wednesday).	If served personally before 4.30pm, on a business day, on that day, or in any other case, the next business day. e.g. personally delivered 4pm Monday, deemed served Monday (unless Monday is a Bank Holiday, then deemed service on Tuesday); personally delivered 5pm Monday, deemed served Tuesday personally delivered 4pm Friday, deemed served Friday; personally delivered 5pm Friday, deemed served the following Monday (unless Monday is a Bank Holiday, then deemed service on Tuesday).
Fax	Second Business day after transmission of the fax is completed. e.g. transmission of fax completed on Monday, deemed served on Wednesday; transmission of fax completed on Friday, deemed served on the following Tuesday (unless Monday is a Bank Holiday, then deemed service on Wednesday).	If transmission of the fax is before 4.30pm on a business day, on that day, or in any other case, the next business day. e.g. transmitted 4pm Monday, deemed served Monday (unless Monday is a Bank Holiday, then deemed service on Tuesday); transmitted 5pm Monday, deemed served Tuesday; transmitted 4pm Friday, deemed served Friday; transmitted 5pm Friday, deemed served the following Monday (unless Monday is a Bank Holiday, then deemed service on Tuesday).
Email or other Electronic Method	Second Business day after sending the email or other electronic transmission. e.g. transmission on Monday, deemed served on Wednesday; transmission on Friday,	If electronic transmission is before 4.30pm on a business day, on that day, or in any other case, the next business day. e.g. transmitted 4pm Monday, deemed served

	deemed served on the following Tuesday (unless Monday is a Bank Holiday, then deemed service on Wednesday).	Monday (unless Monday is a Bank Holiday, then deemed service on Tuesday); transmitted 5pm Monday, deemed served Tuesday; transmitted 4pm Friday, deemed served Friday; transmitted 5pm Friday, deemed served the following Monday (unless Monday is a Bank Holiday, then deemed service on Tuesday).

NOTES ON HEADS OF JURISDICTION IN PARAGRAPH 3.1 OF PRACTICE DIRECTION 6B

General Grounds (para.3.1(1) to (4A))

Paragraph 3.1(2): Claim for injunction restraining act within the jurisdiction

In the last paragraph, replace "(Fujifilm Kyowa Kirin Biologics Company Ltd v Abbvie Biotechnology Ltd [2016] EWHC 2204 (Pat), 8 September 2016, unrep." with:

6HJ.4   (*Fujifilm Kyowa Kirin Biologics Company Ltd v Abbvie Biotechnology Ltd* [2017] EWCA Civ 1 (CA); [2017] C.P. Rep 16

Admiralty claims (para.3.1(19))

In the last paragraph, replace "6.37.9" with:

6HJ.36   6.37.11

NOTES ON RULES OF JURISDICTION IN JUDGMENTS REGULATION (RECAST)

C.   Special Jurisdiction: Person May be Sued in Another Member State

1.   Special jurisdiction—general (arts 7 and 8)

(a)   Special jurisdiction—particular matters (art.7)

(ii) Matters relating to tort, delict or quasi-delict (art.7(2))

In the ninth paragraph (beginning with "For a consideration"), after "proceedings were commenced.", add:

6JR.16   This decision was upheld by the Supreme Court, see [2017] UKSC 13; [2017] 2 W.L.R. 853, SC.

After the ninth paragraph (beginning with "For a consideration"), add new paragraph:

In *Il Yas Khrapunov v JSC BTA Bank* [2017] EWCA Civ 40 (CA); 2 February 2017, unrep., the Court of Appeal considered jurisdiction under Article 5(3) of the Lugano Convention in the context of a conspiracy claim. The defendants were alleged to have conspired in England in breach of a world-wide freezing order by wrongfully dealing with assets located abroad. The Court of Appeal held that the place where the damage occurred was the relevant jurisdiction where the initial damage occurred being the place where the bank's opportunity to execute its judgment was lost or hindered, whilst the place of the event giving rise to the damage was the initial hatching of the conspiracy in England.

2.   Special Jurisdiction—Insurance, Consumer and Individual Employee Contracts (arts 10 to 23)

(c)   Jurisdiction over individual contracts of employment (arts 20 to 23)

In the sixth paragraph (beginning with "However, in Peter Miles"), replace "Peter Miles Bosworth v Arcadia Petroleum Ltd [2016] EWCA Civ 818, CA" with:

6JR.28   *Peter Miles Bosworth v Arcadia Petroleum Ltd* [2016] EWCA Civ 818, CA; [2016] C.P. Rep 48

D. Exclusive Jurisdiction: Jurisdiction Regardless of the Domicile of the Parties (art. 24)

4. Proceedings concerned with the registration or validity of patents etc

Add new paragraph at end:
The insertion of the words "irrespective of whether the issue is raised by way of an action or as a **6JR.32** defence" gives legislative endorsement to the decision of the Court of Justice of the European Union in *Gesellschaft fur Antriebstechnik mbH & Co. KG v Lamellen und Kupplungsbau Beteiligungs KG (C-4/03) EU:C:2006:457;* [2006] ECR I-6509. The interpretation and application of art.24(4) has been considered in a number of decisions of the English courts and of the CJEU. The authorities were examined in *Anan Kasei Co Ltd v Molycorp Chemicals & Oxides (Europe) Ltd* [2016] EWHC 1722 (Pat); [2016] Bus. L.R. 945 (Arnold J) at paras 18 to 23. In that case it was held that, where a claim for infringement in relation to the German designation of a patent was countered by a defence challenging the validity of the patent, for the purposes of allocation of jurisdiction the issue of whether there had been an infringement of a valid claim of that patent had to be treated as a single issue and was not divisible into the sub issues of infringement and validity.

5. "Reflexive" application of art.24

In the last paragraph, after "in BVI companies)", add:
and *Deutsche Bank AG v Sebastian Holdings Inc.* [2017] EWHC 459 (Comm), 13 March 2017, **6JR.33** unrep. (Teare J) (dispute regarding enforcement of judgment against defendant domiciled in Monaco).

E. Prorogation of jurisdiction (arts 25 and 26)

2. Jurisdiction by agreement (choice of court agreement) (art.25.1)

After the third paragraph (beginning with "The agreement must"), add new paragraph:
An asymmetric is an exclusive jurisdiction clause for the purposes of arts 25 and 31(2) of the **6JR.35** Judgments Regulation (recast), see *Commerzbank Aktiengesellschaft v Liquimar Tankers Management Inc.* [2017] EWHC 161 (Comm), 3 February 2017, unrep. (Cranston J).

F. Priority of Jurisdiction—Lis Pendens and Related Actions

Degree to which proceedings must be "related"

In the fourth paragraph (beginning with "For a further consideration"), replace "Eden" with:
Eder   **6JR.46**

PART 8

ALTERNATIVE PROCEDURE FOR CLAIMS

Editorial introduction

Add new paragraph at end:
Whilst difficulties arise if the Pt 8 procedure is used inappropriately, the converse is also the **8.0.1** case and the Pt 7 procedure should not be used where the Pt 8 procedure is more suitable, where for example issues of construction arise: see *Amey Birmingham Highways Limited v Birmingham City Council* [2016] EWHC 2191 (TCC).

PART 13

SETTING ASIDE OR VARYING DEFAULT JUDGMENT

Effects of court's approach following implementation of Jackson

Replace the second paragraph with:
An application under r.13.3 to set aside a judgment entered in default of defence is an applica- **13.3.5**

tion "for relief from any sanction" within the meaning of r.3.9. The tests for the application of r.3.9 laid down in *Denton v TH White Ltd (Practice Note)* [2014] EWCA Civ 906; [2014] 1 W.L.R. 3926, CA, are therefore engaged; *Gentry v Miller (Practice Note)* [2016] EWCA Civ 141; [2016] 1 W.L.R. 2696, CA, at para.23 per Vos LJ; *Regione Piemonte v Dexia Crediop SpA*, [2014] EWCA Civ 1298, 9 October 2014, CA, unrep., at paras 39 and 40 per Christopher Clarke LJ; *Redbourn Group Ltd v Fairgate Development Ltd* [2017] EWHC 1223 (TCC), 26 May 2017, unrep. (Coulson J) at paras 17 and 18; *Hockley v North Lincolnshire and Goole NHS Foundation Trust*, 19 September 2014, unrep. (Judge Richardson QC). See further commentary on r.3.9 at para.3.9.5 above.

PART 14

ADMISSIONS

"amend or withdraw an admission"

After the sixth paragraph (beginning with "An attempt to"), add new paragraph:

14.1.8   In *Mack v Clarke* [2017] EWHC 113 (QB) Master Davidson considered an application for permission to amend the defence in a clinical negligence claim by striking out one paragraph which could, on one view, have been taken to be a partial admission. It was held that the amendment, properly analysed, did not seek to withdraw an admission and that CPR Pt 14, taken as a whole, is primarily directed towards admissions which would entitle a claimant to enter judgment against a defendant. The Master held that Pt 14.1(1) is drawn somewhat more widely in that it refers to "any part" of another party's case but in his view, that must still comprise a distinct element or ingredient of that case, for example breach of duty, causation or a head of loss.

PART 15

DEFENCE AND REPLY

Effect of rule

Replace paragraph with:

15.11.1   This rule imposes an automatic stay after six months if the defendant fails to file an admission, defence or counterclaim and the claimant has not sought default judgment or summary judgment. Any party can apply for the stay to be lifted. Although in most cases the claimant is the party most likely to make the application, defendants may apply if, for example, they wish to raise a counterclaim. Practice Direction 15, para.3.4, provides that the application should be made in accordance with Pt 23 and should state the reason for the applicant's delay in proceeding with the claim, or in responding to it, as the case may be. In *Football Association Premier League Ltd v O'Donovan* [2017] EWHC 152 (Ch), Master Marsh expressed the view that the rule does not place a heavy burden on the applicant to discharge before the court will agree to the stay being lifted. The applicant would have to give an adequate explanation of his delay and show that his case (be it claim, defence or counterclaim) has real, as opposed to only fanciful, prospects of success. If the application is opposed, the court would have to weigh the competing interests of the parties in the balance. If the court were to characterise a stay under this rule as a sanction for delay it would be appropriate to apply the *Mitchell/Denton* principles (as to which, see further, para.3.9.4.1). If the delay in question is neither serious nor significant, the court is likely to lift the stay regardless of the adequacy of the reasons given for delay.

PART 16

STATEMENTS OF CASE

Related sources

At the end of the paragraph, replace "(Scottish Power UK Plc v Talisman North Sea Ltd, QBD (Comm), 22 September 2016, unrep. Leggatt J)." with:

16.0.2   *Scottish Power UK Plc v Talisman North Sea Ltd* [2016] EWHC 3569 (Comm).

PART 17

AMENDMENTS TO STATEMENTS OF CASE

Editorial introduction

Replace paragraph with:

    The rules in this Part deal with amendments to "statements of case", a term which means "a **17.0.1** claim form, particulars of claim where these are not included in the claim form, defence, Pt 20 claim or a reply to a defence" (r.2.3(1)). Every developed system of civil court procedure must provide a means by which the text of documents prepared for use in proceedings can be amended. In respect of acknowledgments of service (documents falling outside the definition of statements of case and, therefore, outside Pt 17) the existence of such a means is assumed but not explained in Practice Direction 10, para.5.4 (see para.10PD.5, above). In one reported case Master Matthews held that, for documents other than statements of case, r.3.1(2)(m) provides a power of amendment which would otherwise fall within the court's inherent jurisdiction (*Agents Mutual Ltd v Moginnie James Ltd* [2016] EWHC 3384 (Ch), noted in para.3.1.19, above).

Amendments to statements of case with the permission of the court

Replace r.17.3(2) with: **17.3**

(2)   **The power of the court to give permission under this rule is subject to—**

    (a)   **rule 19.2 (change of parties—general);**

    (b)   **rule 19.5 (special provisions about adding or substituting parties after the end of a relevant limitation period(GL)); and**

    (c)   **rule 17.4 (amendments of statement of case after the end of a relevant limitation period).**

Change title of paragraph: **17.3.3**

The date from which amendments take effect

Replace paragraph with:

    Under the previous rules, an amendment duly made, with or without leave, took effect, not from the date when the amendment was made, but from the date of the original document which it amended. This rule applied to every successive amendment of whatever nature and at whatever stage the amendment was made. Thus, when an amendment was made to the writ, the amendment dated back to the date of the original issue of the writ and the action continued as if the amendment had been inserted from the beginning: "the writ as amended becomes the origin of the action, and the claim thereon endorsed is substituted for the claim originally endorsed" (per Collins M.R. in *Sneade v Wotherton, etc.* [1904] 1 K.B. 295 at 297). Similarly in the pleadings: "once pleadings are amended, what stood before amendment is no longer material before the court and no longer defines the issues to be tried" (per Hodson LJ in *Warner v Sampson* [1959] 1 Q.B. 297 at 321). This, the so-called "doctrine of relation back" applied also to amendments to add or substitute parties to proceedings. In that context the doctrine has been disapproved (*Liff v Peasley* [1980] 1 W.L.R. 781; and *Ketteman v Hansel Properties Ltd* [1987] A.C. 189). Under the CPR the addition of a new party now takes effect on the date the amended claim form is served upon him, unless the court otherwise orders (Practice Direction 19A, para.3.3; see para.19APD.3, below).

    An amendment which is sought after the expiry of a relevant limitation period should be refused as futile if its effect will not relate back to a time before the limitation period expired. Another aspect of the doctrine of relation back was that it made absurd the notion that parties could raise, by amendment, causes of action or titles to sue that they did not have at the commencement of the proceedings in question (see, for example, *Ingall v Moran* [1944] K.B. 160). Instead of raising such matters by amendment claimants were left to commence new proceedings, so exposing themselves to extra costs liabilities and, possibly to limitation problems. Section 35 of the Limitation Act gives statutory effect to the doctrine of relation back but only for the purposes of the Act. Rule 17.4 gives effect to the section and relaxes the doctrine of relation back in three circumstances (new claims arising out of the same facts, or substantially the same facts as an existing claim; correcting the name of a party; and altering the capacity in which a party claims if the new capacity is one which the party had when the proceedings started or has since acquired. These relaxations are available only in the context of amendments made after the expiry of a limitation period which is statutory, and thus are not available after the expiry of a contractual limitation period (see further the several pages of commentary to r.17.4, below).

There is controversy as to whether the doctrine of relation back still survives as a freestanding doctrine that applies inflexibly to all claims. The CPR case law on this subject is classified in the following sub-paragraphs.

Add new paragraph 17.3.3.1:

Amendments to add a new claim which had not arisen when the claim form was issued

17.3.3.1   The leading case here is *British Credit Trust Holdings v UK Insurance Ltd* [2003] EWHC 2404 (Comm); [2004] 1 E.R. (Comm) 444, where the claimant was permitted to amend the claim to add a claim for declaratory relief in order to seek declaratory relief in respect of insurance claims arising after the proceedings had started. Having referred to the decisions in *Ketterman v Hansel Properties* (see above) and to *Maridive* (see below) Morrison J gave the guidance summarised below.

(a)   Where a new defendant is added the normal position is that the claim against him will date from the time he is joined and not from the date the action was begun.

(b)   There is no reason in principle why a different rule should apply to an application to add a new cause of action.

(c)   The doctrine of relation back will only be a relevant consideration if the other party's position will be prejudiced if the new claim takes effect earlier than the date on which permission to amend was granted.

In that case the claimant was given permission to amend which was expressed to take effect from the date of issue of the claim thereby preventing the defendant from relying upon a contractual limitation defence; the defendant had known that the claimant had intended to raise this new claim in these proceedings and had not been misled by the error the claimant had made in its pleading.

See also *Football Association Premier League Ltd v O'Donovan* [2017] EWHC 152 (Ch) noted in para.17.3.3.4 below.

Add new paragraph 17.3.3.2:

Amendments to regularise an existing claim by pleading facts which occurred after the claim form was issued

17.3.3.2   The leading case here is *Maridive & Oil Services (SAE) v CNA Insurance Company (Europe) Ltd* [2002] EWCA Civ 369; [2002] 1 All E.R. (Comm) 653; [2002] 2 Lloyd's Rep 9; before the commencement of the proceedings, one of two claimants had made a demand upon the defendant under an instrument called a lease bond. In the proceedings, the defendant pleaded in its defence that the demand had been made by the wrong claimant. Promptly thereafter and within the contractual limitation period, the claimants made a second demand, this time in the name of both of them, and served a reply referring to both demands. After the contractual limitation period had expired the defendant applied to strike out the reply as a wrongful attempt to raise a new cause of action without first obtaining permission to amend. The lower court held (amongst other things) that the second demand, but not the first, had been validly made but the claimants could not rely upon it because it had been made only after the commencement of these proceedings. The ruling as to the invalidity of the first demand was upheld on appeal. As to the second demand, the Court of Appeal unanimously allowed the appeal: there is no absolute rule of law or practice which precludes an amendment to rely on a cause of action which accrued only after the date of the original claim in circumstances even if, at the time the amendment was sought, the proceedings raised no arguable cause of action. The court has a discretion whether or not to allow the amendment; a discretion which is to be exercised as justice requires. The claimants' error in making an amendment without leave was, at most, an error of procedure which the court had power to remedy under r.3.10 (General power of the court to rectify matters where there has been an error of procedure). The new claim raised by the amendment took effect from the date of the reply, if not earlier (see [37], [58] and [75]).

Other post-CPR cases falling within this sub-paragraph are often called the "title to sue" cases: cases in which, but for an assignment made to him after the issue of proceedings, the claimant had no title to sue upon the cause of action he purported to raise in the claim form. The earliest post CPR "title to sue" case is *Haq v Singh* [2001] EWCA Civ 957; [2001] 1 W.L.R. 1594. In 1993 a discharged bankrupt brought a claim for damages, alleging that the defendants had given her negligent advice in 1987 culminating in her bankruptcy in 1988. The original defence was served in 1993 but, in 2000, after expiry of the relevant limitation period, an amended defence asserted her lack of capacity to sue, because the relevant cause of action had, upon her bankruptcy, vested and remained in her trustee. The claimant then obtained an assignment from her trustee of the cause of action. The issue was whether the judge was right to permit her to amend to plead the assignment. He had so held on the basis that before the assignment she had no capacity to sue, whereas after the assignment she had the capacity to sue as the trustee's assignee and therefore the case was within Pt 17.4(4). The Court of Appeal allowed the defendants' appeal, holding that since, both before and after the assignment, the claimant was suing in a personal capacity, her capacity had not altered and so she was not entitled to amend. Arden LJ, however, expressed the obiter view, as did Pill LJ, that: "The effect of CPR r 17.4(4) is therefore to remove the effect of *Ingall v Moran* [1944] 1 KB 160 ..." (as to which, see para.17.3.3, above, and see further, below).

In *Haq*, neither the Court of Appeal nor the lower court made any ruling as to whether the amendment sought in that case could have been permitted under r.17.4(2) (a new claim arising out of the same facts, or substantially the same facts as an existing claim). This point was taken in *Smith v Henniker-Major & Co (a firm)* [2003] Ch 182; [2002] EWCA Civ 762. In the lower court Rimer J had held that the cause of action arising under an assignment dated 2001 was not the same or substantially the same as the cause of action arising under an ineffective assignment dated 1998 and the Court of Appeal decided not to disturb the lower court's decision on this point. However, Robert Walker LJ (as he then was) whose judgment on this point was accepted by the other Lords Justices, expressed real doubt about Rimer J's conclusion that the case did not come within r.17.4(2). The matter is fact-sensitive. Permission to amend has been granted under r.17.4(2) in the other "title to sue" cases. In *Finlan v Eyton Morris Winfield (a firm)* [2007] EWHC 914 (Ch); [2007] 4 All E.R. 143, a claimant was permitted to amend his particulars of claim after expiry of the limitation period so as to allege a deed of assignment to him of the causes of action he was suing upon, which deed had been made a few hours after the claim form had been issued. Finlan was followed in *Parker v SJ Berwin* [2008] EWHC 3017 (QB); [2009] P.N.L.R. 17; and in *Courtwood Holdings SA v Woodley Properties Ltd* [2016] EWHC 1168 (Ch), the facts of which are noted in para.17.3.3.4 below (and see also *Munday v Hilburn* [2014] EWHC 4496 (Ch); [2015] B.P.I.R. 684).

Some "title to sue" cases are still governed by the older principles. These cases, concerning the estates of deceased persons, are considered in the next sub-paragraph, para.17.3.3.3, below.

Add new paragraph 17.3.3.3:

In a claim commenced on behalf of a deceased person's estate, an amendment to plead a grant of representation obtained after the claim form was issued

The main group of cases to which this sub-paragraph applies are cases in which the claimant is described as the personal representative of a deceased person's estate but is not in fact an executor of the deceased's will and, at the time of commencement, had not already obtained a grant of representation (for example, letters of administration, or letters of administration with will annexed, or a grant under s.116 Senior Courts Act 1981, (Power of court to pass over prior claims to grant). Whilst an executor can sue in the capacity of executor before obtaining a grant of probate (because he derives his title to sue from the will itself) an administrator has no title to sue until he has obtained a grant of administration (*Chetty v Chetty* [1916] 1 A.C. 603, at 608, 609, per Lord Parker of Waddington). **17.3.3.3**

The leading case here is *Milburn-Snell v Evans* [2011] EWCA Civ 577; [2012] 1 W.L.R. 41, as to which see further, para.19.8.2, below. In that case the Court of Appeal held, following *Ingall v Moran* [1944] K.B. 160, that the commencement of proceedings as a personal representative without first obtaining a grant of representation is an incurable nullity; such a claim is born dead and so is incapable of being revived (unless, fortuitously, the case falls within the Limitation Act s.35; briefly described in para.17.3.3, above). The Court doubted, obiter, the views stated by the Court in *Haq v Singh* [2001] EWCA Civ 957; [2001] 1 W.L.R. 1594 (cited in para.17.3.3.2, above). However, about a year before the *Milburn-Snell* decision, views similar to those expressed in *Haq* were also expressed in the Supreme Court in *Roberts v Gill & Co* [2010] UKSC 22; [2011] 1 A.C. 240 (see the judgment of Lord Collins at [2], [34] and [38]; and the judgment of Lord Walker at [97] and [98]; the facts of *Roberts v Gill & Co* are noted in para.19.5.8, below).

Milburn-Snell was followed in a differently constituted Court of Appeal in *Hussain v Bank of Scotland plc* [2012] EWCA Civ 264 (noted in para.19.8.3, below) and by Stewart J in *Kimathi v Foreign & Commonwealth Office* [2016] EWHC 3005(QB); [2017] 1 W.L.R. 1081 (noted in para.19.8.2, below).

Add new paragraph 17.3.3.4:

Later cases in which Milburn-Snell was distinguished

In *Meerza v Al Baho* [2015] EWHC 3154 (Ch), proceedings were commenced in 2011 on behalf of a deceased's estate by a claimant who did not obtain letters of administration in England until March 2012. On an application to strike out the proceedings citing *Milburn-Snell* (see above) Peter Smith J distinguished that case on the basis that the Court of Appeal there had considered only the court's powers under r.19.8 and had not been referred to the wide powers of amendment as explained in *Maridive and Oil Services SAE v CNA Insurance Co (Europe) Ltd* [2002] EWCA Civ 369 (as to which, see para.17.3.3.2, above, and as to *Meerza*, see further, para.19.8.2, below). **17.3.3.4**

Courtwood Holdings SA v Woodley Properties Ltd [2016] EWHC 1168 (Ch), concerned a commercial dispute over the development of land. The claimant relied upon an assignment dated 2010, but that was held to relate only to the causes of action existing at that time and the causes of action in these proceedings arose after 2010. A second assignment had been made but only in 2016, after the commencement of these proceedings. The defendants opposed an application to amend to rely on the second assignment on the basis that, on *Milburn-Snell* principles, the current proceedings were an incurable nullity. However Asplin J granted permission to amend, relying upon earlier cases including Maridive (see para.17.3.3.2, above) and distinguished *Milburn-Snell* ("[73] ...This case is not concerned with capacity to sue on behalf of the estate of a deceased person ...").

In *Haastrup v Haastrup* [2016] EWHC 3311 (Ch) (Master Matthews) the claim concerned a deceased person's estate but, on the facts, the claimant was entitled to sue in her capacity as a beneficiary and therefore the decisions in both *Milburn-Snell* and *Meerza* were distinguished.

Nevertheless the learned Master explained how, had that not been the case, he would have decided which of these two conflicting cases to follow. On the facts, *Meerza* differs from both *Milburn-Snell* and *Haastrup* in that, only in *Meerza*, had the claimant obtained a grant of representation before her title to sue was challenged.

In *Football Association Premier League Ltd v O'Donovan* [2017] EWHC 152 (Ch) (Master Marsh) the claimant commenced proceedings in May 2016 claiming remedies for infringement of copyright. Later, the claimant sought permission to amend in respect of, amongst other things, allegations of infringement of copyrights created after May 2016. Whilst acknowledging the two strands of Court of Appeal authority (*Milburn-Snell* and *Maridive*) the learned Master adopted and applied the guidance given by Morrison J in *British Credit Trust Holdings v UK Insurance Ltd* [2003] EWHC 2404 Comm; [2004] 1 All ER (Comm) 444 (see para.17.3.3.1, above) and stated that "[19] ... the issue of 'incurable nullity' in relation to the estate of a deceased person is some considerable distance from the issue I am considering.". Permission to amend was given, the amendments to take effect, not from the date of issue of proceedings or from the date of amendment, but from 13 August 2016, that being the opening date of the 2016/17 football season.

17.3.4 *Change title of paragraph:*

Other effects of amendment

Replace with:

Amendments to a claim which specify additional remedies or an increase in the claim value may place the claimant under a liability to pay an additional court fee: the difference between the court fee actually paid and the court fee which would have been payable had the additional remedies or increased claim value been specified from the outset. The fact that claimants may apply to increase the value of their claims only after the defendant had offered them the maximum sums previously claimed, was not, by itself, evidence that the original claim values had been deliberately understated (*Various v MGN Ltd* (Ch) (Mann J), 18 May 2017, unrep.).

Deliberately understating the value of claims in order to defer paying higher court fees is an abuse of process for which the court has power to strike out the claim, if it is just to do so (*Lewis v Ward Hadaway (a firm)* [2015] EWHC 3503 (Ch)); [2016] 4 W.L.R. 6). In the circumstances of that case and having regard to the overriding objective, it was held that it would have been disproportionate to strike out the claims. However, in respect of some of the claims, the claim form had not been issued within the relevant limitation period even though it had been delivered in due time to the court office, accompanied by a request to issue. In those cases, because of the claimants' abusive procedural conduct concerning court fees, the court summarily dismissed the claims under Pt 24 as being statute-barred; as to this aspect of the case, see further, Practice Direction 7A, para.5.1 (see Vol.1 para.7APD.5); *Page v Hewetts* [2012] EWCA Civ 805; [2012] C.P. Rep. 40 and *Dixon v Radley House Partnership* [2016] EWHC 2511 (TCC); [2016] 5 Costs L.R. 979; [2017] C.P. Rep 4).

A claim allocated to the fast track may remain on that track even though the court has permitted the claimant to amend the claim so as to claim damages for an amount in excess of that fixed by para.(4) of r.26.6 (Scope of each track). It does not follow that such a case must inevitably be re-allocated to the multi-track (*Maguire v Molin* [2002] EWCA Civ 1083; [2003] 1 W.L.R. 644).

When permitting an amendment which substantially changes the case other parties have to meet the court should not normally make an order as to all costs prior to the amendment. A decision as to those costs is usually best left for consideration by the court post-trial; at the amendment stage it is often not possible to determine the viability of the unamended case (*Chadwick v Hollingsworth (No.2)* [2010] EWHC 2718 (QB)).

At the trial the fact that a pleading had been amended can sometimes affect the order as to the costs prior to amendment:

"As a general rule, where a plaintiff makes a late amendment, as here, which substantially alters the case the defendant has to meet and without which the action will fail, the defendant is entitled to the costs of the action down to the date of the amendment" (per Stuart-Smith LJ in *Beoco Ltd v Alfa Laval Co Ltd* [1995] Q.B. 137).

However, such an order should not always be made. In *Begum v Birmingham City Council* [2015] EWCA Civ 386; [2015] H.L.R. 33, the claim originally raised causes of action in negligence and misrepresentation only. Some twelve months before trial, the claim was amended to allege also a breach of statutory duty. At trial the claimant prevailed as to the amended claim only and the trial judge awarded the costs prior to amendment to the defendants. This part of the trial judge's order was reversed on appeal: the pleaded claims for negligence, misrepresentation and breach of statutory duty were merely different labels applied to the same underlying facts. The case the defendants had to meet was essentially the same before and after the claimant's amendment, unlike the position in *Beoco Ltd v Alfa Laval Co Ltd* [1995] Q.B. 137 where the claimant's late amendment had substantially altered the case the defendant had to meet and the defendant had been prejudiced by a lack of opportunity to make settlement offers (i.e. a payment into court). In Begum the costs prior to amendment were awarded to the claimant limited to 85 per cent to take account of the fact that pursuing the original, unsuccessful, claims had increased her costs overall.

In *Gold v Mincoff Science & Gold* [2004] EWHC 2036 (Ch), the claimant made an amendment at trial (in reply to a limitation defence, which reply the defendants had anticipated some months earlier when making offers to settle): had the amendment been made earlier, the claimant would have been awarded 85 per cent of his costs; because of the real possibility that the late amendment had prejudiced the defendants, Neuberger J awarded the claimant only 62.5 per cent of his costs up to the date of the amendment and 85 per cent thereafter.

The making of an amendment on the basis of which the amending party ultimately succeeds at trial may affect the costs consequences which flow from a Pt 36 offer made shortly before the amendment. It is one of the circumstances the court may take into account in determining whether it would be unjust to make the usual order on a failure to beat a Pt 36 offer (see r.36.17(5) and *Norwegian Cruise Line Ltd v Thompson Holidays Ltd*, 15 December 2000, unrep., Ch D; the claimant made a Pt 36 offer and, some five weeks later made an amendment which in fact improved its case at trial and, after another three weeks, made another Pt 36 offer. The defendant, who, because of the amendment, lost at trial and failed to beat the first Pt 36 offer, was allowed a notional period in which to reconsider its case following the amendment. The claimant's entitlement to enhanced costs and enhanced interest deferred until a date four weeks after the second Pt 36 offer.

General principles for grant of permission to amend

Replace with:

Except in cases to which r.17.4 applies (i.e. cases in which a limitation period has expired), the **17.3.5** provisions as to amendment of statements of case in Pt 17 give no indication as to the principles which the court should apply in determining whether an amendment may be made and whether, in the exercise of the court's discretion, it should be permitted (*Thurrock BC v Secretary of State for the Environment, Transport and the Regions (No.1)* [2001] C.P. Rep. 55, CA).

A dictum of Peter Gibson LJ (see below) in *Cobbold v Greenwich LBC*, 9 August 1999, unrep., CA, has been relied upon in many cases, both at first instance and on appeal. However, sometimes the dictum was not stated accurately and so was misunderstood. This had the unfortunate effect of lending weight to the erroneous argument that the court should take a relaxed attitude to late amendments and allow them where a refusal would prejudice the party seeking the amendment. The true position is that the existence and weight of such prejudice is just one the factors to be taken into account.

In *Swain-Mason v Mills & Reeve LLP (Practice Note)* [2011] EWCA Civ 14; [2011] 1 W.L.R. 2735, CA the Court of Appeal described such an attitude as wrong in principle and contrary to current case law. In that case the court reversed a ruling by a judge who, in purported reliance on Cobbold, had permitted amendments to be made at the start of a trial: it is incorrect to assume that late amendments should always be allowed if the opposing party can be compensated in costs without injustice; instead, the court should pay greater regard to all the circumstances which are now summed up in the overriding objective (as to which, see r.1.1 and the commentary thereto). For further details of the decision in *Swain-Mason*, see para.17.3.7 below.

Having regard to the overriding objective on an application for permission to amend requires the court to exercise its discretion so as to deal "with the case justly and at proportionate cost" which includes (amongst other things) saving expense, ensuring that the case is dealt with expeditiously and allocating to it no more than a fair share of the court's limited resources (see r.1.1). As to this, see further, *Hague Plant Ltd v Hague* [2014] EWCA Civ 1609; [2015] C.P. Rep. 14, which is noted in para.16.4.1, above.

In considering whether to permit amendments withdrawing an admission previously made in a statement of case the court must have regard to r.14.1 and the practice under that rule (as to which, see para.14.1.8, above, and see *White v Greensand Homes Ltd* [2007] EWCA Civ 643). *Lenton v Abrahams* [2003] EWHC 1104 (QB), concerned a Fatal Accidents Act claim brought by the second claimant arising out of a road accident in which both drivers were killed; D admitted duty and breach of duty but did not admit that the second claimant had been a dependent of the other deceased driver "G". After the claimants had disposed of the car in which G had been travelling, D applied to amend the defence to allege that G had negligently contributed to her own death by failing to wear a seatbelt; the Master's decision refusing permission to amend was upheld on appeal. *Cluley v R.L. Dix Heating (A Firm)* [2003] EWCA Civ 1595 concerned a contractual claim in respect of plumbing works carried out at a dwelling house built for the claimants; in their defence the defendants admitted the existence of a contract between them and the claimants; later they obtained permission to amend to deny any such contract; by that stage it was too late for the claimants to take proceedings against the main contractor or the architect; the Court of Appeal struck out the amendment.

Late amendments

After the seventh paragraph (beginning with "The principles relevant"), add new paragraph:

In *M v Kings College Hospital NHS Foundation Trust (QB)*, HH Judge Pearce, 11 April 2017, **17.3.7** unrep., the defendant served a defence which differed in important respects from what had been stated earlier on its behalf. The claimant delayed amending the particulars of claim to deal with the new matter until witness statements had been exchanged (the claimant having applied for early exchange). On the claimant's application to amend the particulars of claim, made about a year after service of the defence and about seven months before the trial, permission was granted: in the circumstances the claimant had been entitled to wait for witness statements to be exchanged before deciding how to amend his case and the delay did not imperil the trial date.

Effect of rule

In the third paragraph (beginning with "This rule extends"), replace "(Lokhova v Longmuir [2016] EWHC 2579 (QB)" with:

17.4.1   (*Lokhova v Longmuir* [2016] EWHC 2579 (QB); [2017] E.M.L.R. 7

Correcting name of party (r.17.4(3))

Add new paragraph at end:

17.4.5   In *Armes v Godfrey Morgan Solicitors (a firm)* [2017] EWCA Civ 323, the Court of Appeal has further considered the interrelationship between r.17.4(3) and r.19.5(3)(a): r.17.4(3) cannot be used by a claimant to substitute as defendants two persons sued in the alternative where one of those persons had originally been sued as a sole defendant (see further, para.19.5.6, below).

PART 19

PARTIES AND GROUP LITIGATION

Add new paragraph 19.1.3:

Proceedings may be brought against unnamed defendants

19.1.3   Practice Direction 7A, para.4.1(1) provides that a claim form "should state ... the full name of each party ..." and Practice Direction 16, para.2.6 defines what amounts to a party's full name. Nevertheless, there is no doubt that proceedings may be validly commenced even though the defendant is not named in the claim form. Express provision for such proceedings is made by r.55.6 in respect of possession claims against trespassers. There are also many case examples of claims for other remedies, particularly injunctions. In *South Cambridgeshire District Council v Persons Unknown* [2004] 4 P.L.R. 88 (concerning an injunction to restrain breach of planning controls) the Court of Appeal readily accepted the ruling which had earlier been made by Sir Andrew Morritt V-C, in *Bloomsbury Publishing Group plc v Newsgroup Newspapers Ltd* [2003] 1 W.L.R. 1633 (injunction to restrain breach of copyright by an unknown person who had obtained a copy of an unpublished Harry Potter novel) that the overriding objective and the obligations cast upon the court were inconsistent with an undue reliance upon form over substance. Instead the Court of Appeal dwelt upon the importance of describing the unnamed persons with sufficient precision so as to identify both those who are included and those who are not; and to give directions for service of the claim form, injunction and other papers. In *South Cambridgeshire District Council* the claimant was permitted to effect service "by leaving such documents in clear plastic envelopes nailed to a stake or gatepost or other prominent location on each of the plots 1-11 [at the address] pursuant to [what is now] CPR 6.15" (see also *Hampshire Waste Services Ltd v Persons Unknown* [2004] Env. L.R. 9; an injunction "restraining persons from entering or remaining without the claimant's consent" on land described in the order in connection with an environmental protest which had been threatened).

In *Gate Gourmet London Ltd v Transport and General Workers Union* [2005] I.R.L.R. 881, Fulford J (as he then was) granted an interim injunction against named defendants and also against unnamed defendants, the latter being defined in the order as persons "engaging in unlawful picketing and/or otherwise assaulting, threatening, intimidating, harassing, molesting or otherwise abusing the employees of Gate Gourmet or its associated companies ..." In other cases in which harassment by protesters has been alleged, proceedings have been taken against named persons joined as representatives of the members of named protest groups (and see further as to this, *Astellas Pharma Limited v Stop Huntingdon Animal Cruelty* [2011] EWCA Civ 752).

In *Brett Wilson v Person(s) Unknown* [2016] 4 W.L.R. 69 (a libel claim) the claimants obtained a default judgment, including damages and final injunctions both prohibitory and mandatory, against the defendants who were described as persons 'responsible for the operation and publication of [the website upon which the libel had been published]". Previously, an order had been made under r.6.15 for service of proceedings by email. In a similar case concerning a libel published on the internet, *Smith v Unknown Defendant Pseudonym "LikeICare"* [2016] EWHC 1775 (QB), Green J granted a final injunction and damages of £10,000 summarily assessed under r.53.2 (summary disposal under the Defamation Act 1996) giving the defendant liberty to apply to vary the quantification within 14 days if he considered it to be excessive or otherwise unjustified.

Several of the High Court cases summarised above were considered and approved by the Court of Appeal in *Cameron v Hussain* [2017] EWCA Civ 366. In that case the claimant in a road accident claim for damages successfully appealed against an order refusing her permission to amend her claim by substituting for the original defendant (the registered keeper of the car driven into collision with her car) a new defendant described as "The person unknown driving vehicle [registration number given] who collided with vehicle [registration number given] on [date of accident]".

The Court of Appeal held that the principle applied in *Bloomsbury Publishing Group plc* (see above) was not limited to claims for injunctive relief or to claims in which the applicant would otherwise have no remedy. Under the CPR, the court has a broad discretionary power to permit proceedings to continue against an unnamed defendant where to do so would further the overriding objective of dealing with cases justly and at proportionate cost. In *Cameron*, although the claimant was unable to identify the defendant driver, she could identify the insurer of the vehicle he had been driving and so would be able to enforce any judgment she obtained against that insurer under s.151 of the Road Traffic Act 1988. In those circumstances it was appropriate to permit service on the unnamed defendant by an alternative method, for example, service on the insurer. The claimant was not required to seek alternative remedies, such as under the MIB Untraced Drivers Agreement. Enabling the claimant to exercise her rights under s.151 would not be unfair to the insurer, such enforcement being the statutory obligation of all insurers who are authorised to provide motor insurance. Had the claimant been unable to identify the insurer, proceedings in the name of a person unknown would have been futile, as would an order for service by an alternative method. In such a case her only remedies would have been under the MIB Untraced Drivers Agreement, or proceedings against the registered keeper requiring him to divulge the identity of the driver (as to which, see further, para.31.18.1, below) or a claim for damages for causing or permitting a person to use an uninsured vehicle on the road (as to which, see *Monk v Warbey* [1935] 1 K.B. 75).

In some cases, proceedings are commenced against persons unknown where the claimants do not intend to serve them upon any defendant unless and until they can be identified. In the meantime however, an interim injunction is sought, perhaps with the intention of serving it upon media organisations who might be approached by the unnamed defendants (see for example *Middleton v Person or Persons Unknown* [2016] EWHC 2354 (QB); injunction to restrain infringement of privacy and possible breaches of copyright; and see also *Kerner v WX* [2015] EWHC 1247 (QB) noted in para.31.17.2.1, below). Claimants are not obliged to give prior notice of hearings of the application to all media organisations who may, theoretically, be affected by the injunction being sought; only upon those persons they reasonably believe might be involved and upon whom they intend to serve the court's order if an injunction is granted (*TUV v Person or Persons Unknown* [2010] EWHC 853).

I. Addition and Substitution of Parties

Effect of rule

In the last paragraph, replace "Milton Keynes BC v Viridor (Community Recycling MK) Ltd [2016] EWHC 2764 (TCC)," with:
    Milton Keynes BC v Viridor (Community Recycling MK) Ltd [2016] EWHC 2764 (TCC); [2017] **19.2.1** B.L.R. 47; [2016] 6 Costs L.R. 1041,

Joinder or substitution after judgment

To the end of the paragraph, add:
    However, in *Prescott*, the substitution of the original claimant (a partnership) by a company to **19.2.6** whom partnership assets had been assigned, led to a reduction in the remedies, injunctive and financial, for which the defendant was liable.

After the first paragraph, add new paragraphs:
    In *Billington v Davies* 10 April 2017, Norris J (Ch), unrep., the claimant obtained judgment with liberty to apply for declaratory relief in relation to the tracing of sums sought to be recovered under the order. The claimant obtained a charging order over the defendant's interest in land he owned jointly with his wife. The claimant sought permission to add the wife as a new defendant in order to trace, into her interest in the land, sums of money paid to her by the defendant. Norris J held that it was not appropriate to use the court's power under r.19.2 in order to enable the claimant to launch proceedings against a third party without involving the original defendant; it was open to the claimant to commence a Pt 8 application against the wife.
    In *Stone v WXY* [2012] EWHC 3184 (QB) Eady J held that it was not desirable to join a person as a defendant to dormant litigation in which the court had ordered an interim injunction against "persons unknown" in order to prevent harassment by paparazzi. The intended defendant denied harassment, there had been no recurrence, and his joinder could not be justified simply on the basis that he was the only person who could be identified.

Relationship between r.19.5(3)(a) and r.17.4(3) mistakes

Add new paragraph at end:
    In *Armes v Godfrey Morgan Solicitors (a firm)* [2017] EWCA Civ 323, the claimant, Mr Armes, **19.5.6**

brought a claim in respect of negligence alleged against a solicitor who had been employed by, or who had been a member of, a firm of solicitors which, before these proceedings had commenced had changed from a firm into a registered company. Until September 2013 the firm and the company both existed as separate entities (hereinafter called "the Firm" and "the Company" respectively). In separate proceedings the Company sued Mr Armes for unpaid fees, which action was, in March 2013, defeated on the basis that Mr Armes had no contractual relationship with the Company. However, in June 2012, the letter before claim in this action had been addressed to the Company and had been responded to by solicitors acting on its behalf. This action was commenced against the Company, as sole defendant, in October 2013, on the last day before expiry of the limitation period. A few days later, before it was served, the claimant made amendments to the claim form, without leave, naming the Company as first defendant and the Firm as second defendant, the cause of action being described as "negligence ... in representing the claimant in relation to a claim in personal injury". In particulars of claim subsequently served, the claim was pleaded against each defendant in the alternative, on the basis that "it is unclear to the Claimant when precisely [the Firm] transferred its business to [the Company] (if ever) ..." The Firm applied under r.17.2 for the amendment to be disallowed. That application was initially refused by the district judge and, on appeal, by the circuit judge, but was allowed on a second appeal to the Court of Appeal. Because it had been made after the relevant limitation period had expired, the amendment fell outside what can be permitted under r.19.5. As to r.19.5(3)(a) the Firm had not been substituted for the Company; joining two parties where one of them was originally the sole defendant does not amount to a substitution even if the joinder being made is a joinder "in the alternative". As to r.19.5(3)(b) the addition of the claim against the Firm was not necessary to enable the claim to be "carried on ... against the original party".

II.   Representative Parties

Binding character of judgment in representative proceedings

19.6.4   *In the last paragraph, replace "Chandra v Mayor [2016] EWHC 2636 (Ch), 19 July 2016, unrep." with:*
      Chandra v Mayor [2016] EWHC 2636 (Ch); [2017] 1 W.L.R. 729

The death of a potential claimant is not covered by r.19.8

19.8.2   *In the last paragraph, replace "Kimathi v Foreign & Commonwealth Office [2016] EWHC 3005 (QB)" with:*
      Kimathi v Foreign & Commonwealth Office [2016] EWHC 3005 (QB); [2017] 1 W.L.R. 1081

Add new paragraph at end:
      See further as to all of the cases noted in this paragraph, and other linked cases, paras 17.3.3 to 17.3.3.4, above.

Claim form and application for permission to continue

19.9A.1   *Replace the second paragraph with:*
      Section 261 of the 2006 Act provides that a member of a company who brings a derivative claim must apply to the court for permission to continue it. Section 262 of the 2006 Act provides that, in a claim brought by a company on a cause of action which could be pursued as a derivative claim, a member of a company may apply to the court for permission to continue that claim as a derivative claim. The matters which the court should take into account in determining whether to grant permission are stated in s.263. For texts of those statutory provisions, see Vol.2 para.2G-3 onwards.

III.   Group Litigation

Editorial note

19.11.1   *After the fifth paragraph (beginning with "The requirement"), add new paragraph:*
      See *McGlone v Chief Constable of South Yorkshire Police* [2016] EWHC 3359 (QB), 21 December 2016 unrep., where the court considered whether it would be appropriate to defer a decision to make a GLO because the GLO issues identified may not be final, or whether the GLO should be made and a stay imposed for a limited time to allow the outcome of independent investigations and time for drafting generic Particulars of Claim. The court concluded in that case that there was no advantage to deferring the making of a GLO where all parties, and the court, were of the view that the case was suitable for a GLO.

PART 21

Children and Protected Parties

Effect of rule

In the last paragraph, replace "OH v Craven [2016] EWHC 3146 (QB)," with:
  OH v Craven [2017] 4 W.L.R. 25,   **21.2.1**

Effect of rule

In the fifth paragraph (beginning with "Where compromise"), replace "OH v Craven [2016] EWHC 3146 (QB)," with:
  OH v Craven [2017] 4 W.L.R. 25,   **21.10.2**

Discretionary and bare trusts for children

In the fifth paragraph (beginning with "In OH v Craven"), replace "OH v Craven [2016] EWHC 3146 (QB)," with:
  OH v Craven [2017] 4 W.L.R. 25,   **21.11.3**

In the last paragraph, replace "Watt v ABC [2016] EWCOP 2532," with:
  Watt v ABC [2017] 4 W.L.R. 24; [2017] P & C.R. DG9,

PART 23

General Rules about Applications for Court Orders

When does Part 23 apply?

In the fourth paragraph, amend the last line to read:
  A person who seeks a remedy from the court before proceedings are started, or in relation to **23.0.2**
proceedings which are taking place, or will take place, in another jurisdiction must make an application under Pt 23 (r.7.2(2)).

Change title of paragraph: **23.0.17**

Applications and the overriding objective—unnecessary applications and communications with court

After the first paragraph, add new paragraph:
  In *Agarwala v Agarwala* [2016] EWCA Civ 1252, 8 December 2016, CA, unrep., where litigants
in person, in bitterly contested proceedings running almost continuously for seven years,
"bombarded the court with endless applications", the Court of Appeal said that judges are entitled,
as part of their general case management powers, to order in the course of particular proceedings,
where they feel it to be appropriate, that parties may not make an application without the leave of
the court (para.71). Further, judges are entitled to give strict directions regulating communications
with the court concerning applications, and litigants should understand that failure to comply with
such directions will mean that communications that they choose to send, notwithstanding those
directions, will be neither responded to nor acted upon (para.72).

Applications by parties in contempt

To the end of the first paragraph, add:
  In *Harb v Aziz* [2017] EWHC 258 (Ch), 21 February 2017, unrep. (Arnold J), after the Court of **23.0.18**
Appeal had (1) allowed the defendant's (D) appeal, (2) directed that the claimant's (C) claim be
retried, and (3) ordered C to pay £250,000 on account of D's costs of the appeal, C applied to the
High Court for directions for the retrial. D submitted that C should not be heard by the court since
she was in contempt of court as a result of her failure to comply with the Court of Appeal's costs
order. The judge rejected C's submission, finding (1) that C (a bankrupt) was unable to comply
with the costs order, (2) that her default (a) was "an involuntary one", and (b) if technically
amounting to a contempt, was not one which impeded the course of justice. The judge explained
that non-payment of interim costs orders by litigants is a very common occurrence, and commented
that if it amounted to a contempt of court which justified courts in not hearing the defaulting parties, many litigants would be shut out from pursuing or defending claims even in the absence of
any substantive order to that effect (para.30). In the circumstances C's submission was "a remark-
able one".

Add new paragraph 23.6.3:

Amendment of application notice

23.6.3   The power of the court to permit a party to amend a statement of case (r.17.1(2)(b)) does not extend to an application notice, as an application notice is not a statement of case as defined (r.2.3(1)). However, the court's power within r.3.1(2)(m), that is, "to take any other step or make any other order" for the purpose of managing the case and furthering the overriding objective, does include such power (*Agents Mutual Ltd v Moginnie James Ltd* [2016] EWHC 3384 (Ch), 30 December 2017, unrep. (Master Matthews), where claimants permitted to amend application for summary judgment to add additional grounds in circumstances where a fresh application including those grounds could not be made because by operation of an earlier court order the proceedings were then stayed).

PRACTICE DIRECTION 23B—APPLICATIONS UNDER PARTICULAR STATUTES

Scientific tests to determine parentage

To the end of the fourth paragraph (beginning with "Under the Family"), add:

23BPD.3   In *Spencer v Anderson (Paternity Testing: Jurisdiction)* [2016] EWHC 851 (Fam); [2017] 1 F.L.R. 1204, Peter Jackson J held that there was a legislative void in relation to post-mortem paternity testing and in relation to paternity testing using extracted DNA. He ordered paternity testing under the inherent jurisdiction of the High Court, after balancing the competing interests

PART 24

SUMMARY JUDGMENT

Minimum period of notice of hearing

In the first paragraph, replace "Serene Construction Ltd v Barclays Bank Plc, 3 November 2016, unrep., CA," with:

24.4.8   *Serene Construction Ltd v Barclays Bank Plc* [2016] EWCA Civ 1379,

PART 25

INTERIM REMEDIES AND SECURITY FOR COSTS

I.   Interim Remedies

Interim injunction (r.25.1(1)(a))

Notification injunctions

Replace paragraph with:

25.1.12.6.1   The High Court has power under the Senior Courts Act 1981 s.37(1) to make an order for what may be called, a "notification injunction", that is to say a free-standing order (not ancillary to another order) requiring the defendant to notify the claimant prior to, or shortly after, entering into a transaction by which property is disposed of. The purpose is that, if such a transaction may seriously damage the claimant's position, a freezing order can be applied for. Depending on the wording, this may be a less invasive interference with the defendant's rights than a conventional freezing order (presumably with a less onerous potential liability under the cross-undertaking in damages). The Court of Appeal in *Holyoake v Candy* [2017] EWCA Civ 92, 28 February 2017, CA, unrep., accepted that the terms of the notification injunction in that case (though not necessarily in all cases) were a modified version of a conventional freezing order, rather than a distinct type of injunction (para.35). The test for the grant of such an injunction is the same as for a conventional freezing order, namely that the applicant must show a "good arguable case" or, in other words, a real risk, supported by solid evidence, that a future judgment would not be met because of an unjustifiable disposition of assets" (paras 39 to 43).

Freezing injunction (formerly Mareva injunction) (r.25.1(1)(f))

Jurisdiction—generally

Replace the second paragraph with:

25.1.25.1
The court will in an appropriate case, grant relief ancillary to a freezing order against the primary defendant by joining a third party as a defendant (even though there is no cause of action against it) and granting a freezing injunction against it to support the claimant's claim against the primary defendant: this is the so-called Chabra jurisdiction (see *TSB Private Bank International S.A. v Chabra* [1992] 1 W.L.R. 231 (Mummery J)). See commentary in Vol.2, para.15-63. The Chabra jurisdiction is not, however, unlimited. The reformulation of the scope of this relief accepted by the Court of Appeal in *Lakatamia Shipping Co Ltd v Su* [2014] EWCA Civ 636; [2015] 1 W.L.R. 291, CA, is that it arises when: (1) there is good reason to suppose that assets held in the name of a defendant against whom the claimant asserts no cause of action would be amenable to some process, ultimately enforceable by the courts, by which the assets would be available to satisfy a judgment against a defendant against whom the claimant asserts a cause of action; (2) the test of "reason to suppose" is equated with a "good arguable case" i.e. more than barely arguable but not necessarily one the Judge believes has better than a 50% chance of success; and (3) it is just and convenient to exercise the jurisdiction, which is exceptional and to be exercised with caution (at para.32). Where there were pre-existing and apparently bona fide corporate entities, and no evidence that the defendant's assets had been transferred or its asset base diminished in order to avoid the enforcement of a judgment, an injunction against such third parties will be refused (*Linsen International Ltd v Humpuss Sea Transport Pte Ltd* [2011] EWHC 2339 (Comm); [2011] 2 Lloyd's Rep. 663 (Flaux J.), at [147] to [150]).

Evidence

Replace the third paragraph (beginning with "The claimant should"), with:

25.1.25.5
The claimant should depose to objective facts from which it may be inferred that the defendant is likely to move assets or dissipate them; unsupported statements or expressions of fear have little weight (*O'Regan v Iambic Productions* (1989) 139 N.L.J. 1378 (Sir Peter Pain); *Rosen v Rose* [2003] EWHC 309 (QB); 27 January 2003, unrep. (Fulford J)). Great care should be taken in the presentation of evidence to the court so that the court can see, not only whether the applicant has a good arguable case, but also whether there is a real risk of dissipation of assets. The applicant must show a real risk, supported by solid evidence, that a future judgment would not be met because of an unjustifiable disposition of assets. This is a binary threshold, not a sliding scale depending on the intrusiveness of the relief sought (*Holyoake v Candy* [2017] EWCA Civ 92, 28 February 2017, CA, unrep., at paras 39, 41 and 45). It is for the applicant to satisfy the threshold that there is a real risk of dissipation, and unless it has done so, the respondent is not obliged to provide any explanation (above at paras 50 and 51). The risk of dissipation must be established as against each respondent (above at para.54).

Varying, clarifying or revoking order

Replace the second paragraph with:

25.1.25.9
Applications to vary a freezing order may be made for a wide range of different purposes, and either by the claimant or by the defendant or by a person notified of the order. For example, in *Compagnie Noga d'Importation et d'Exportation SA v Australian and New Zealand Banking Group* [2006] EWHC 602 (Comm), March 24, 2006, unrep. (Christopher Clarke J.), principally on the ground it was not appropriate to make the variation sought because the interests of justice did not require it, the judge dismissed the application of one defendant for a variation to enable him to apply certain funds caught by a freezing order to putting up a bail bond for the brother of his business partner who had been charged with money laundering; in *Pacific Maritime (Asia) Ltd v Holystone Overseas Ltd* [2007] EWHC 2319 (Comm); [2008] 1 Lloyd's Rep. 371 (Christopher Clarke J.) the judge dismissed the defendant's application to reduce the freezing injunction sum and to increase the security that the claimant's had been ordered to give in respect of its undertaking in damages; in *Intercontinental Bank Plc v Akingbola* [2010] EWHC 35 (QB), January 6, 2010, unrep. (Holroyde J.) the defendant unsuccessfully sought a variation of the disclosure obligation so as to limit the persons to whom disclosure of the relevant assets had to be made; in *Abbey Forwarding Ltd v Hone* [2010] EWHC 1532 (Ch), May 14, 2010, unrep. (Morgan J.) the judge granted the application of two defendants, directors of a company in provisional liquidation, permitting them to make from frozen money a loan to another company in which they had an interest. In *Gangway Ltd v Caledonian Park Investments (Jersey) Ltd* [2001] 2 Lloyd's Rep. 715 (Colman J), the court granted the third party bank's application for permission to realise assets, which had been charged to it as security for the defendant's debts, and to exercise its rights of set off against the credit balance in the defendant's deposit account; in *Taylor v Van Dutch Marine Holding Ltd* [2017] EWHC 636 (Ch), 27 March 2017, unrep. (Mann J) it was explained (at paras 10 and 12) that, because the exercise of disposal rights by a security holder is not an act prohibited by the order, the need to obtain such permission is normally unnecessary.

Cross-undertaking in damages

To the end of the fifth paragraph, beginning with "The cross-undertaking should usually", before the last line, insert:

25.1.25.10   The difficulties in using an insurance policy as a means of providing fortification of a cross-undertaking in damages were considered in *Holyoake v Candy* [2017] EWCA Civ 92, 28 February 2017, CA, unrep.

Obligations of claimant after grant of freezing injunction

To the end of the first paragraph, add:

25.1.25.11   Where the claimant "warehouses" the proceedings (i.e. chooses, without the sanction of the court, not to progress them), that is a serious abuse of the process which may warrant striking out the claim (*Societe Generale v Goldas Kuyumculuk Sanayi Ithalat Ihracat A.S.* [2017] EWHC 667 (Comm), 3 April 2017, unrep. (Popplewell J), at [63]).

II.   Security for Costs

"A defendant to any claim may apply"

At the end of the first paragraph, replace "B (Infants), Re [1965] 1 W.L.R. 946; [1965] 2 All E.R. 651 (Note))." with:

25.12.4   *Taly NDC International NV v Terra Nova Insurance Co Ltd* [1985] 1 W.L.R. 1359 (which held that the claimants were not entitled to make an application for security for costs in respect of a defendant's application for specific discovery and interrogatories). It is wrong to assume that orders for security for costs can be made only against parties who commence legal proceedings by means of an originating process. The leading case here is *GFN SA v The Liquidators of Bancredit Cayman Limited (in official liquidation)* [2009] UKPC 39; [2010] Bus L.R. 587, which held that "the court must look at the substance of the application as opposed to its strict form" ([31]). Thus, in some cases an interlocutory application may be regarded as a free standing claim (see for example, *Bancredit* itself; in proceedings in which an order for the winding-up of a company had been made, the liquidators were entitled to seek security for costs against creditors who had made an interlocutory application in those proceedings seeking to challenge the liquidators' rejection of their proofs of debt). In other cases a new action may be commenced by parties in their role as defendants in earlier proceedings (for example, sometimes it is appropriate to take committal proceedings to enforce an injunction by way of a new action rather than by way of an interlocutory application in the original proceedings; the ability of an alleged contemnor to obtain security for costs of the committal application should be the same in both cases (*Bancredit* per Lord Scott at [23])).
   The action entitled *In the matter of Dalnyaya Step LLC (in liquidation)* [2017] EWHC 756 (Ch), concerned proceedings taken following the making of an order recognising an insolvency order made by a foreign court. The recognition order had been sought in order to obtain judicial assistance in the execution of the foreign order and had been obtained by means of a "without notice" application by N, who was the person named in the foreign order as the liquidator of a company being wound up. Rose J held that the applicants for an order setting aside the recognition order were also entitled to apply for security for costs against N. This was so even though the applicants had not been parties to the foreign proceedings or to N's application for the recognition order. A factor the learned judge relied upon in making her decision was that, when seeking the recognition order, N had not made full and frank disclosure of the consequences which the recognition order could have on persons who were not then before the court. N's main if not sole purpose in applying for the recognition order had been to seek relief against the applicants. It would be wrong to deprive the applicants of a right to apply for security simply because no reference had been made to them at the time of the "without notice" application.

Subsequent applications concerning security for costs

In the fourth paragraph (beginning with "In Holyoake v Candy"), replace "Holyoake v Candy [2016] EWHC 3065 (Ch), 29 November 2016, unrep." with:

25.12.11   *Holyoake v Candy* [2016] EWHC 3065 (Ch); [2016] 6 Costs L.R. 1157

Discretionary power to order security for costs

After the fifth paragraph (beginning with "A claimant who has"), add new paragraph:

25.13.1   Whilst ATE policies are often accepted as reliable sources of litigation funding, the same cannot be said of an indemnity given to a claimant company by its sole shareholder; there would be a real risk that the shareholder might procure the claimant company not to call upon the indemnity or might seek to resist enforcement of it (*Dunn Motor Traction Ltd v National Express Ltd* [2017] EWHC 228 (Comm)).

No discrimination against claimants resident in other States

In the last paragraph, replace "(Ras Al Khaimah Investment Authority v Bestfort Developments LLP [2016] EWCA Civ 1099, 8 November 2016, CA, unrep.;" with:

(*Ras Al Khaimah Investment Authority v Bestfort Developments LLP* [2016] EWCA Civ 1099; [2017] **25.13.6**
CP Rep 9;

Foreign and English co-claimants

In the last paragraph, replace "Holyoake v Candy [2016] EWHC 3065 (Ch), 29 November 2016, unrep. (Nugee J)" with:
    Holyoake v Candy [2016] EWHC 3065 (Ch); [2016] 6 Costs L.R. 1157 (Nugee J.)   **25.13.10**

Particular discretionary factors where condition (c) relied on

In the second paragraph, replace "Holyoake v Candy [2016] EWHC 3065 (Ch), 29 November 2016, unrep. (Nugee J)" with:
    Holyoake v Candy [2016] EWHC 3065 (Ch); [2016] 6 Costs L.R. 1157 (Nugee J.)   **25.13.13**

Proving insolvency or impecuniosity

In the last paragraph, replace "Premier Motorauctions Ltd v PricewaterhouseCoopers LLP [2016] EWHC 2610 (Ch)," with:
    Premier Motorauctions Ltd v PricewaterhouseCoopers LLP [2016] EWHC 2610 (Ch); [2017] Bus L.R. **25.13.14**
490; [2017] B.P.I.R. 182; [2017] Lloyd's Rep I.R. 186,

Add new paragraph at end:
    However, in *Newwatch Ltd v Bennett* (QBD) Carr J, 21 December 2016, unrep., on an application for security on ground (c), Carr J held that, on the basis of the evidence presented to her, the claimants would be unable to pay the defendants' costs without the ATE insurance cover. Having reached that conclusion, it was necessary to consider the terms of the insurance to decide whether it would provide adequate protection. The starting point should be that policies issued by reputable insurers and organised by reputable litigation solicitors (as in this case) are a reliable source of litigation funding. However, in this case, the limits of indemnity under the policies (£1.8 million) provided only partial cover at best. There were also risks that the insurers in this case would not pay if called upon to do so: the claimants were not named as beneficiaries of the policies and there were some uncertainties about the assignment of the policies to them; there were also a number of exclusion clauses that may be engaged. On the application for security of £3 million, security of £1.2 million was ordered.

Condition (f): nominal claimant

Replace with:
    Rule 25.13(2)(f) enables the court to order security for costs against a claimant who is acting as a **25.13.17**
nominal claimant other than as a representative claimant under Pt 19, and there is reason to believe that he will be unable to pay the defendant's costs if ordered to do so. Despite the use of the words "claimant" and "defendant's costs" this ground can also be used against a counterclaiming defendant (see para.25.12.3 above and see further, para.25.13.1.1, above).
    As to the meaning of the term "nominal", in *Chuku v Chuku* [2017] EWHC 541 (Ch), Newey J reviewed various authorities both pre- and post CPR and stated as follows:
    [26] In the light of these cases, it seems to me that:
      i)   A person with a significant interest in the outcome of a claim will rarely, if ever, be considered a "nominal claimant" within CPR 25.13(2)(f);
      ii)   A personal interest is not, however, essential. While a trustee, executor or personal representative will not be a "representative claimant under Part 19" merely because CPR 19.7A [representation of beneficiaries by trustees etc] is in point, he still will not ordinarily be a "nominal claimant", regardless of whether he is also a beneficiary;
      iii) At least typically, there "must be some element of deliberate duplicity or window-dressing" for a person to be a "nominal claimant".
    Ground (f) expressly excludes applications against claimants acting in a representative capacity under Pt 19 even if they would otherwise be regarded as nominal claimants. This exclusion applies to claimants appointed under r.19.6 (representative parties with the same interest), r.19.7 (representation of persons who cannot be ascertained etc), r.19.8 (death) and r.19.9 (derivative claims). The exception does not cover a litigation friend of a child or protected party (as to which, see r.21.2, above). However, as a matter of discretion, it seems unlikely that a litigation friend will be ordered to give security on an application made solely upon ground (f).
    In order to establish ground (f) the applicant is not required to prove that the respondent is insolvent or impecunious; it is sufficient to show that there is reason to believe that he will be unable to pay the respondent's costs if ordered to do so. However, the court must have regard to all the circumstances of the case when exercising its discretion under this rule. Unless insolvency or impecuniosity is proved (as to which, see para.25.13.14, above) the court may not be satisfied that it is just to make the order. See further, as to the discretionary nature of the court's power to order security for costs, para.25.13.1, above.

Applications for security may also be made under particular statutes which permit the court to require security for costs. Two such statutes merit mention here; County Courts Act s.49 (see Vol.2, para.9A-492; a trustee in bankruptcy who elects to continue a claim in the County Court which was commenced by the bankrupt, may be ordered to give security); and Postal Services Act 2000 s.92; the appointment of a person to bring proceedings under the Act in the name of the sender or ad-dressee of a postal packet may be made "upon such terms as to security, caution, costs, expenses and otherwise as the court considers appropriate" (and see further, r.19.7B, above)).

Scope of this rule

Replace the second paragraph with:

25.14.1   Rule 25.14 does not spell out the consequences if a person ordered to give security under this rule fails to do so. An order under this rule should not provide for the claim to be struck out if the order is not complied with since to do so would terminate the current claimant's claim. It would be wrong to impose upon a new claimant an obligation as to security for costs which could not otherwise be imposed upon them under other rules of court (*Investment Invoice Financing Ltd v Limehouse Board Mills Ltd* [2006] EWCA Civ 9; [2006] 1 W.L.R. 985; however, in that case the cur-rent claimant's claim was stayed until the payment of two adverse orders for costs which had been made against his predecessor in title; see further, para.3.4.8 above). In the group litigation proceed-ings entitled In the matter of *In the matter of RBS (Rights Issue Litigation)* [2017] EWHC 1217 (Ch), Hildyard J made an order under r.25.14 against one of the claimants' third party funders to provide security totalling £7.5 million in respect of costs incurred from December 2016, such sum to be paid into court or held securely by the claimants' solicitors. If the necessary consents were obtained, the security was to be funded by way of sums payable to the funder because of settle-ments that had been made by the defendants with other claimants some months previously (see [10] and [48]). The order under r.25.14 was made subject to the defendants giving a cross-undertaking in respect of any loss the provision of security may cause to the funder if, ultimately, no order for costs is made against the claimants (see further, the Commercial Court Guide, Ap-pendix 16; White Book, Vol.2 para.2A-185).

Replace fourth paragraph (beginning "For a recent case") with:

For a recent case illustration (in which it seems no application was made under r.25.14 expressly) see *Compagnie Noga d'Importation et Exportation SA v Australia and New Zealand Banking Group Ltd* [2004] EWHC 2601, (Comm), especially para.130 thereof. In the *RBS (Rights Issue Litigation)* case (noted above), the third party funders against whom applications under r.25.14 were made were added as parties for the purposes of the application; both being based outside England and Wales, permission was granted to serve them outside the jurisdiction (see [6]).

Disclosure in aid of applications under r.25.14

In the last paragraph, replace "(Wall v Royal Bank of Scotland [2016] EWHC 2460 (Comm); [2016] 5 Costs L.R. 943)." with:

25.14.6   (*Wall v Royal Bank of Scotland* [2016] EWHC 2460 (Comm); [2016] 5 Costs L.R. 943; [2017] 4 W.L.R. 2).

PART 26

CASE MANAGEMENT—PRELIMINARY STAGE

Effect of rule

To the end of the first paragraph, add:

26.4.1   Subject to Practice Direction 2E, an order extending the stay must be made by a judge. The extension will generally be for no more than four weeks unless clear reasons are given to justify a longer time. (PD26, para.3.2)

PART 27

THE SMALL CLAIMS TRACK

Costs where a party has behaved unreasonably (r.27.14(2)(g))

Replace with:
    There is no specific definition of unreasonable behaviour in the rules. In *Dammermann v Lanyon* **27.14.4**
Bowder LLP [2017] EWCA Civ 269 the Court of Appeal doubted whether useful general guidance
could be given to assist courts deciding whether a party had behaved unreasonably, as all cases are
fact sensitive. However, the court did suggest that the acid test from the wasted costs jurisdiction
(r.46.8) and the case of *Ridehalgh v Horsefield* [1994] Ch 205 at 232F should provide sufficient guidance to judges dealing with small claims. In other words courts should consider whether the
conduct complained of "permits of reasonable explanation". This guidance came with a warning
that litigants should not be too easily deterred from using the small claims track by risk of an
adverse costs order based on unreasonable behaviour. The Court of Appeal also concluded that the
failure to accept an offer might be supportive of a finding of unreasonable behaviour, but was not,
on its own, sufficient to satisfy the test".

PART 29

Add new Practice Note:

PRACTICE NOTE: CHANGES TO THE PROCEDURE FOR OBTAINING TRIAL LISTING APPOINTMENTS WITH THE QB JUDGES LISTING OFFICE

1. This note is intended to provide guidance for practitioners about the new **29PN.1**
arrangements coming into effect from 19 June 2017 for issuing Listing appointments for trial before judges of the High Court in London.
    2. The Queen's Bench Judges Listing Office (QBJL) are to take over
responsibility for setting trial listing appointments when the listing directions
are made, usually by the assigned QB Master. Instead of the claimant applying
for a listing appointment, the Queen's Bench Masters Listing Section (QBML)
will send a copy of the sealed order giving the listing directions direct to QBJL
when it sends the sealed order to the parties. QBJL will then send a listing appointment to the parties.
    3. This change in procedure has resulted in an amendment to the model
directions in Forms PF52 and PF52A (the latter for claims in the Mesothelioma
List) and PF53, (giving directions for separate trial of an issue).
    Paragraph 22 of PF52 and Paragraph 4 (b) (ii) of PF53 now read as follows:
    "A copy of this sealed order will be sent to the Queen's Bench Judges
    Listing Office who will notify all parties of a listing appointment for a trial
    date or period within the trial window, which will usually be six weeks
    from the date the order is sealed. If parties have any queries in relation to
    the listing appointment they should contact Queen's Bench Judges Listing
    on qbjudgeslistingoffice@hmcts.gsi.gov.uk"
    Paragraph 12(1) (b) of PF52A as follows:
    "A copy of this sealed order will be sent to the Queen's Bench Judges
    Listing Office who will notify all parties of a listing appointment for a trial
    date or period within the trial window, which will usually be three weeks
    from the date the order is sealed. If parties have any queries in relation to
    the listing appointment they should contact Queen's Bench Judges Listing
    on qbjudgeslistingoffice@hmcts.gsi.gov.uk"
    (The only difference being the shorter timescale for providing a listing ap-
pointment for mesothelioma trials (where liability is in issue) which need to be
listed urgently.)

4. It is intended that this change in procedure will reduce the in-built delay in requiring the claimant/parties to obtain a listing appointment and the problems that occur when the claimant/parties fail to obtain a listing appointment by the date specified. It will also provide more control over listing appointments by QBJL and allow greater flexibility in listing trial dates.

5. Parties are requested to use the amended wording in PF52 and PF52A when providing draft directions orders with Directions questionnaires and for Costs and Case Management Conferences.

6. Trial Listing arrangements before QB Masters will continue to be arranged by the QBML qbmasterslisting@hmcts.gsi.gov.uk.

The Honourable Mr Justice Foskett and the Senior Master
13 June 2017

PART 30

TRANSFER

Transfer of proceedings between the court and the Competition Appeal Tribunal

Add new paragraph at end:

30.1.1   Transfer of proceedings to the High Court from the UK Intellectual Property Office, following the Comptroller declining to deal with the matter under sections 8, 12, 37 or 61 of the Patents Act 1977 are not within the scope of this Part. See instead CPR r.63.11 and para.2F-12.1.

PART 31

DISCLOSURE AND INSPECTION OF DOCUMENTS

(c)   Legal professional privilege generally

Documents privileged on the ground that production would be injurious to the public interest

After the third paragraph (beginning with "In R. v Chief"), add new paragraph:

31.3.33   In *Re C (a child)* [2017] EWHC 692 (Fam) (sub nom *Tower Hamlets LBC v M, F and C (a child by his guardian ad litem)*) public interest immunity was claimed in relation to a disclosure order which had been made in care proceedings, on the ground that disclosure would constitute a real risk of damage to national security.

(d)   Other grounds of privilege

Without prejudice communications

In the seventh paragraph (beginning with "Muller v Linsley"), add at end:

31.3.40   Also see *EMW Law LLP v Halborg* [2017] EWHC 1014 (Ch)

Add new paragraph 31.3.40A:

Effect of communications being without prejudice

31.3.40A   In *EMW Law LLP v Halborg* [2017] EWHC 1014 (Ch) Newey J held that the application of the without prejudice rule means that a party may withhold communications from compulsory disclosure, but that does not mean that such documents can only be shown to a third party only if both parties to the negotiations agree. The parties to such negotiations are still able to show those documents to others if they chose to.

Disclosure in particular types of cases and circumstances

After the second paragraph, add new paragraph:

31.6.4   *Re RBS Rights Issue Litigation* [2017] EWHC 463 (Ch) the court held that it has the power to order disclosure of an after the event insurance policy on the basis that its disclosure was necessary to enable the court to exercise its case management function proportionately and efficiently. In the general case an after the event insurance policy would not be relevant, but there could be exceptions, such as in group litigation where claimants had the benefit of several liability. Legal professional privilege was unlikely to attach to such policies, other than for the redaction of passages that conveyed the legal advice which had been given. In the instant case the disclosure application was refused as it did not have case management as its primary objective. The court did nonetheless order disclosure of the names and addresses of the claimants' third party litigation funders.

Procedure for bringing a Norwich Pharmacal application

Replace the first paragraph with:

31.18.11 Whether or not it is thought that the application is likely to be uncontested, a first application should be made by claim form under Pt 7 or (in most cases) Pt 8 as appropriate, so that issues arising can be identified early and managed appropriately (*Santander Bank plc v National Westminster Bank* [2014] EWHC 2626 (Ch), 31 July 2014, unrep. (Birss J), paras 50 & 51; *Towergate Underwriting Group Ltd v Albaco Insurance Brokers Ltd* [2015] EWHC 2874 (Ch), 13 October 2015, unrep. (Master Matthews); see also Chancery Guide para.7.4 (Vol.2 para.1A-51)). In the Norwich Pharmacal case itself the application was brought by originating summons rather than by writ. An order can, exceptionally, be granted without notice (e.g. *Bankers Trust Co v Shapira* [1980] 1 W.L.R. 1274, CA). An order may also be made during an existing action.

PART 32

EVIDENCE

Effect of rule

Add new paragraph at end:

32.7.1 In *Republic of Djibouti v Boreh* [2015] EWHC 769 (Comm), 23 March 2015, unrep. (Flaux J), where the defendant (D) applied to set side a freezing order on the ground that the claimant (C) and its legal representatives deliberately and/or recklessly misled the court in the application for the order, C filed the written evidence of a solicitor (X), being the legal representative against whom D's allegations were exclusively directed. As C did not propose to tender X as a witness at the hearing of D's application, the judge granted D's application under r.32.7 for an order for his cross-examination.

Effect of rule

Replace paragraph with:

32.12.1 This rule follows from RSC Ord.38 r.2A(11) and CCR Ord.20 r.12A(11). The procedure for requiring parties to serve witness statements has the principal effect of alerting each party to what their opponent's witnesses are going to say at trial, in the event of there being a trial. (This has the advantages of promoting settlements and avoiding unfair surprise at trial.) If there is a trial and the evidence contained in a particular witness's statement is given in court, the evidence is in the public domain and certain legal consequences follow from that (e.g. any privilege is waived). However, if the case is settled without trial, or if there is a trial but the witness is not called (or their statement adduced in evidence under the hearsay provisions) the general rule is that no other party may make use of that statement subsequently. The difficulty which arises is whether a party upon whom a witness statement has been served may make any use of it before trial (or settlement), during the interlocutory stages of the proceedings. Rule 32.12(1) says a witness statement "may be used only for the purpose of the proceedings in which it is served". The exceptions in (a) and (b) of para.(2) of r.32.12 are obvious enough and follow the former rules. Paragraph (c) did not appear in the former rules and may go some way towards clarifying problems that had arisen as to the status of witness statements before they are deployed at trial (see further, r.39.2 (General rule—hearing to be in public)). The collateral use protections imposed by r.32.12 in relation to witness statements are similar to those imposed by r.31.22 in relation to disclosed documents. The scope of the protections in both contexts, and the meaning of "use" and "purpose", were explained in *Tchenguiz v Grant Thornton UK LLP* [2017] EWHC 310 (Comm), 22 February 2017, unrep. (Knowles J). Some of the relevant authorities were discussed in the context of r.31.22 (subsequent use of disclosed documents) in *Cassidy v Hawcroft*, July 27, 2000, unrep., CA (in defamation proceedings claimant entitled to production of letter by third party referred to in affidavit sworn for purposes of applicant for interim remedy in previous proceedings in which claimant and deponent (but not third party) were parties). Note also *Chase v News Group Newspapers Ltd* [2002] EWHC 1101 May 29, 2002, unrep., Eady J. (in defamation proceedings against defendant newspaper, claimant granted permission to use affidavit of his employer filed in successful application for interim injunction made earlier by employer (and in which employer claimed no privilege) to restrain further publication by defendants). It has been held that, where an expert is to be called, being a witness who had prepared a report for use in earlier proceedings, this rule does not prevent the court from ordering disclosure of that report (*L'Oréal v Bellure NV* [2006] EWHC 1503 (Ch), May 24, 2006, unrep. (Peter Smith J.) (disclosure ordered because it was relevant as it went to issue whether the expert's opinion should be accepted on the evidence he would adduce at trial)). In *Zambia v Meer Care & Desai* [2006] EWCA Civ 390; March 7, 2006, unrep., CA, an application was made to stay English civil proceedings pending the determination of foreign criminal proceedings in which some of the same parties were involved. In refusing a stay the judge made various orders to protect the position of those parties, including an order directing that witness statements used in the civil proceedings (and documents disclosed) should not be used in any foreign proceedings without the permission of the court ([2005] EWHC 2102, Ch). The refusal of a stay was upheld by the Court of Appeal.

Defects in affidavits

Add new paragraph at the beginning:

32.16.2   In *Haederle v Thomas* [2016] EWHC 3498 (Ch), 2 November 2016, unrep. (Nugee J), the claimant applied to commit a defendant (D) for making a false statement in an affidavit. D resisted that application by arguing that, because the jurat had not been completed and bore no signature, the document did not comply with the requirements set out in Practice Direction 32 (in particular para.5.2), and therefore was not an affidavit. In rejecting that submission the judge held (1) a document which sets out a witness's evidence which the witness has sworn to be his evidence is, in technical terms, an affidavit, (2) it is not the case that failure to comply with every requirement in Practice Direction 32 renders a document not an affidavit, (3) in particular, a failure to comply with the jurat requirements in para.5.2 does not mean that a document sworn by a witness was not an affidavit.

PART 33

Miscellaneous Rules about Evidence

Effect of rule

After the seventh paragraph (beginning with "In Tsavliris Russ"), add new paragraph:

33.4.1   In *Towry EJ Ltd v Bennett and others* [2012] EWHC 224 (QB) in which the Claimant alleged that its former employees had unlawfully solicited former clients, witness statements were served by the Claimant from its current employees which referred to conversations alleged to have taken place with the former clients relating to the activities of the individual defendants. Carr J acceded to the Defendants application to permit the former clients to be called for cross-examination and dismissed the suggestion that it would have been open to the Defendants to obtain witness statements direct from the former clients. In this case the extent of the contact between the former clients and Defendants went to the heart of the Claimant's allegations of unlawful solicitation. The Judge also observed that it was correct to say that pursuant to CPR 33.4 it was the Defendants who should be treated as calling the hearsay witnesses, albeit that they are permitted to cross-examine them as to their evidence, but held that the court had a discretion not to treat the Claimant as bound by the oral evidence given by the hearsay witnesses (see paras [24] and [25]).

The cases referred to above all assume that the relevant hearsay evidence is contained in a witness statement. In *Brown v Mujibal* 4 April 2017, unrep. (Judge Mark Gargan) it was held that the language of r.33.4 is not so restricted and applies to any hearsay statement. The judge gave permission to the defendant to cross examine a brain damaged claimant, who had not served a witness statement, on statements made to medical experts and contained in medical reports which were admitted in evidence. The judge permitted the use of an intermediary as a reasonable adjustment to assist the process. Although not referred to in the judgment this decision would seem to be in accordance with the wording of The Civil Evidence Act 1995 s.3.

PART 34

Witnesses, Depositions and Evidence for Foreign Courts

Attendance of witnesses

Replace the last paragraph with:

As to process for compelling attendance at High Court hearing of witness situated outside **34.0.2** England and Wales but within United Kingdom, see the Senior Courts Act 1981 s.36. It is clear from s.36 that a witness summons only runs in the United Kingdom. The court cannot compel a witness who is not subject to the jurisdiction to give evidence. However, temporary absence, for example on a holiday does not result in a person not being subject to the jurisdiction; see *Clavis Liberty Fund v Revenue and Customs* [2015] 1 W.L.R. 2949 (Warren J); applying *SSL International v TTK LIG Ltd* [2012] 1 W.L.R. 1842, CA. Accordingly, if a party wishes to obtain evidence from a witness who is resident out of the jurisdiction (and assuming that the witness will not attend voluntarily) that party must obtain a deposition from the witness either under r.34.23 (where the person to be examined is in another Regulation State) or under para.5 of the Practice Direction to Part 34 (where the Taking of Evidence Regulation does not apply).

I.   Witnesses and Depositions

Add new paragraph 34.3.1.1:

In *Richard v BBC and Chief Constable of South Yorkshire* (ChD), 3 April 2017, unrep. (Mann J), in **34.3.1.1** order to avoid making an overly-wide, onerous third party disclosure order, the court created an alternative mechanism for achieving disclosure of necessary information by granting the applicant (the BBC) permission to issue a witness summons but ordering it not to serve it if the third party provided a witness statement containing the necessary information within a certain period of time. There was a parallel to that mechanism in patent actions where a party could provide a product and process description. The third party (the Metropolitan Police) was not present at the hearing and was at liberty to apply if it objected to the technique or scope of the information sought. The BBC undertook to provide the Metropolitan Police with a transcript of the instant hearing, and to pay the costs reasonably incurred in complying with the witness summons/statement; see cf. r.31.17 and r.46.1.

"a witness summons is to be served by the court ..."

Replace the first paragraph with:

Rule 34.6 refers to service of witness summonses, either by the court or by the party on whose **34.6.1** behalf it is issued. The rule does not attempt to explain what is required to ensure that there is good service. Rules as to the service of documents other than claim forms, for example, witness summonses, whether within or without the jurisdiction, are found in CPR Pt 6 (in particular Sections III and IV thereof). Service of witness summonses within the U.K. are dealt with in r.6.20. As to service of witness summonses by post under that rule, see para.6.20.2 above.

The general rule is that a witness summons should be served at least seven days before the hearing (r.34.5(1)). If it is to be served by the court it should be issued in sufficient time to enable service to be effected within that period. Where the court is to effect service the money to be paid to the witness in accordance with r.34.7 must be deposited in court pursuant to r.34.6(2).

II.   Evidence for Foreign Courts

General principles for compliance with foreign request for evidence

After the third paragraph (beginning with "As a matter of discretion"), add new paragraph:

The decision of the Senior Master in *Microtechnologies LLC v Autonomy Systems Ltd* [2016] EWHC **34.21.2** 1942 (QB) was overruled by Morris J at [2016] EWHC 3268 (QB). The judge held that the Senior Master had erred in refusing to give effect to a letter of request requiring a witness to attend an examination to give evidence for the purposes of a forthcoming trial in the US. Insofar as the examination was alleged to be oppressive on the grounds of the privilege against self-incrimination, the witness's ability to rely on the Fifth Amendment privilege against self-incrimination would prevent any such oppression arising. The witness was also a Defendant in linked proceedings in the Chancery Division. The judge held that the order for examination would not infringe his rights under ECHR art.6. given his ability to rely on the 5th Amendment. The overall fairness of the Chancery proceedings was a matter for the trial judge in those proceedings to monitor and control not for the instant court.

PART 35

EXPERTS AND ASSESSORS

When an expert fails to comply with their duty

Other guidance

35.3.4   *In the last paragraph, replace "Liverpool Victoria Insurance Co Ltd v Khan QBD, Lawtel, 21 June 2016," with:*
Liverpool Victoria Insurance Co Ltd v Khan [2016] EWHC 2590 (QB),

PART 36

OFFERS TO SETTLE

I.   Part 36 Offers to Settle

Offers before the commencement of proceedings

In the first paragraph, replace "Wes Futures Ltd v Allen Wilson Construction Ltd [2016] EWHC 2863 (TCC), 10 November 2016, unrep." with:
36.7.1   Wes Futures Ltd v Allen Wilson Construction Ltd [2016] EWHC 2863 (TCC); [2016] 6 Costs L.R. 1083

Costs consequences of withdrawing or changing the terms of a Part 36 offer

After the first paragraph, add new paragraph:
36.10.4   In *Thakkar v Patel* [2017] EWCA Civ 117; [2017] 2 Costs L.R. 233, the trial judge ordered that the defendants pay 75% of the claimants' costs despite the defendants' having made and withdrawn a higher Part 36 offer on the basis that: (a) the offer was withdrawn before disclosure and exchange of statements so that the claimants had not been properly able to assess the overall value of the claim; and (b) while not amounting to an outright refusal to mediate, a real prospect of settlement was lost by the defendants' conduct in "dragging their feet." The Court of Appeal regarded the costs order to be "tough" but not so severe that it should interfere.

Defendant's offer (rr.36.17(1)(a) and 36.17(3))

Add new paragraph at end:
36.17.3   In *Marathon Asset Management LLP v Seddon* [2017] EWHC 479 (Comm); [2017] 2 Costs L.R. 255, Leggatt J observed that, unlike r.36.17(4)(c), r.36.17(3)(b) does not allow the court to award interest on costs in excess of a normal commercial rate. The provision is therefore largely otiose given the court's practice of routinely ordering interest on costs pursuant to r.44.2(6)(g).

Claimant's offer (rr.36.17(1)(b) and 36.17(4))

After the first paragraph, add new paragraph:
36.17.4   In *OMV Petrom SA v Glencore International AG* [2017] EWCA Civ 195; [2017] 2 Costs L.R. 287; The Times, 10 May 2017, the Court of Appeal clarified that the objective of r.36.17(4) is to encourage good practice and to create an incentive to encourage claimants to make, and defendants to accept, appropriate settlement offers. While preferring not to use the word "penal", Sir Geoffrey Vos C. observed that the culture of litigation had changed since the Woolf reforms and that Pt 36 was a regime of sanctions and rewards. Accordingly, it was wrong to regard the Pt 36 benefits as entirely compensatory.

Order for interest on sum of money awarded (r.36.17(4)(a))

Add new paragraph at end:
36.17.4.1   In *OMV Petrom SA v Glencore International AG* [2017] EWCA Civ 195; [2017] 2 Costs L.R. 287; The Times, 10 May 2017, the Court of Appeal clarified, however, that the court undoubtedly has a discretion to include a non-compensatory element in its award under r.36.17(4)(a), but that the level of interest awarded must be proportionate to, among other factors: (a) the length of time that had elapsed between the offer and judgment; (b) whether the defendant took entirely bad points or whether it behaved reasonably, despite the offer, in pursuing its defence; and (c) the general level of disruption caused to the claimant by a refusal to negotiate or to accept the Part 36 offer. *OMV*

was a high value fraud case in which the defence had been founded on lies. The Court of Appeal ordered interest at the full 10 per cent over base.

Interest on costs (r.36.17(4)(c))

Replace first paragraph with:

In *OMV Petrom SA v Glencore International AG* [2017] EWCA Civ 195; [2017] 2 Costs L.R. 287; **36.17.4.3**
The Times, May 10, 2017, the Court of Appeal clarified the basis on which interest is awarded on costs pursuant to r.36.17(4)(c). Judges had for many years treated the provision as essentially compensatory, amounting to what Chadwick LJ described in *McPhilemy v Times Newspapers Ltd (No.2)* [2001] EWCA Civ 933; [2002] 1 W.L.R. 934; [2001] 4 All E.R. 861, CA, as a "generous" allowance for the cost of money. In *McPhilemy*, Chadwick LJ awarded what subsequently became the conventional rate of four per cent over base. In *OMV*, while holding that the Court was bound by McPhilemy to decide that interest should be set so as to achieve a fairer result for the claimant, Sir Geoffrey Vos C. clarified that the award under r.36.17(4)(c) was not purely compensatory. Taking into account a number of factors, but principally the defendants' conduct in pursuing a dishonest and unreasonable defence in the face of a reasonable settlement offer, the Court of Appeal ordered interest at the maximum 10 per cent over base.

Interest should be awarded under r.36.17(4)(c) even where the claimant is publicly funded: *KR v Bryn Alyn Community (Holdings) Ltd* [2003] EWCA Civ 383; [2003] C.P. Rep. 39; [2003] P.I.Q.R. P30, CA.

PART 39

MISCELLANEOUS PROVISIONS RELATING TO HEARINGS

Recording of hearings

Replace paragraph with:

Paragraph 6 of Practice Direction 39A contains provisions about the recording of hearings and **39.0.6**
about the supply to any party or person of transcripts of recordings (see para.39APD.6 below). On 14 February 2014, the Lord Chief Justice issued Practice Direction (Audio Recordings of Proceedings: Access) [2014] 1 W.L.R. 632, Sen Cts, for the purpose of clarifying the practice and procedure governing access to CD or digital audio recordings of civil and family proceedings in all courts in England and Wales; for text of this practice direction, which should be read with para.6 of PD 39A, see para.B19–001 below. Paragraph 6 of the latter Practice Direction states that an application for permission to listen to or receive a copy of an audio recording will only be granted in exceptional circumstances, for example where there is cogent evidence that the transcript may have been wrongly transcribed. In *Bath v Escott* [2017] EWHC 1101 (Ch), 11 May 2017, unrep. (Judge Matthews), a party to High Court proceedings, having obtained a written transcript of the judgment of a district judge in those proceedings, and being of the opinion that the transcript did not accurately set out the judgment as delivered by the district judge orally, applied to a High Court judge for an order for the release to him of the recording of the oral judgment. The judge dismissed the application, principally on the ground that the applicant gave no particulars of the differences to which he was referring. In doing so the judge explained that it does not matter if the approved transcript adds to or differs from the actual words used by the judge at the time of giving judgment; what matters is only that it has been considered, revised if necessary, and then approved by the judge; there is no duty on the judge to approve a transcript limited to the exact terms of the words spoken on the day.

Add new paragraph 39.2.3.1:

"matters relating to national security" (r.39.2(3)(d))

The court may order that a hearing should be in private if it involves matters relating to national **39.2.3.1**
security. The case law relevant to this departure from the principle of open justice, and the principles to be derived from it, were stated by the Court of Appeal (Criminal Division) in the case of *In re Guardian News and Media Ltd* [2016] EWCA Crim 11; [2016] 1 W.L.R. 1767, CA. See also CPR Part 82 (Closed Material Procedure), in particular r.82.6 (Hearings in private).

Anonymity of party or witness (r.39.2(4))

After the second paragraph, add new paragraph:

The practice to be followed in variation of trust claims where initial applications are made to the **39.2.14**
court to preserve confidentiality, including applications for interim orders anonymising the proceedings, is stated in *Practice Note (Variation of Trusts: Confidentiality Orders Pending the Hearing of Application)*, 9 February 2017, unrep. (see para.64PN.1).

Add new paragraph 39.3.7.4:

Relief from sanctions (r.3.9) and applications under r.39.3(3)

39.3.7.4   An application under r.39.3(3) to set aside a judgment or order is an application "for relief from any sanction" within the meaning of r.3.9. The tests for the application of r.3.9 laid down in *Denton v TH White Ltd (Practice Note)* [2014] EWCA Civ 906; [2014] 1 W.L.R. 3926, CA, are therefore engaged (*Gentry v Miller (Practice Note)* [2016] EWCA Civ 141; [2016] 1 W.L.R. 2696, CA, at para.23 per Vos LJ). Any application for relief against sanctions involves considering (1) the seriousness and significance of the default, (2) the reason for it, and (3) all the circumstances of the case. At the third stage factors (a) and (b) in r.3.9 are of particular, but not paramount, importance. In the context of r.39.3(3) the sanction from which relief is sought is the order granted when the applicant failed to attend the trial, not the delay in applying to set aside the resulting judgment. When dealing with an application under r.39.3(3) the court must first consider the three mandatory requirements of r.39.3(5), before considering the question of whether relief from sanctions is appropriate applying the Denton tests; the promptness of the application is a pre-condition under r.39.3(5)(a) and is considered as part of all the circumstances under the third stage of the Denton tests (ibid at para.25). See further commentary on r.3.9 at para.3.9.5 above.

PART 40

JUDGMENTS, ORDERS, SALE OF LAND ETC.

I. Judgments and Orders

Entry of judgment in foreign currency

To the end of the last paragraph, add:

40.2.3   In *Elkamet Kunststofftechnik GmbH v. Saint Gobain Glass France SA* [2016] EWHC 3421 (Pat), 25 November 2016, unrep. (Arnold J), a patent validity and infringement claim in which both parties were foreign companies, in making an order for costs on summary assessment, the judge concluded (1) that the court has power to make an order for costs expressed in a foreign currency, and (2) that if the court decides to make a costs order in sterling, it may also make an award to compensate for any exchange rate loss. In doing so the judge rejected the submission (made by the paying party) that, as an order for costs is designed to compensate a party for costs incurred in litigating in England, as a matter of principle, a costs order should be expressed in sterling regardless of the source of the funds from which the costs are to be paid. In *MacInnes v Gross* [2017] EWHC 127 (QB), 3 February 2017, unrep. (Coulson J), the judge, whilst determining whether costs should be on the standard or indemnity basis and interest on costs, declined to further order that the receiving party should recover any additional sums that may be assessed to reflect currency fluctuations (doubting whether a court had power to make such an order).

PART 44

GENERAL RULES ABOUT COSTS

I. General

Successful defendant's costs payable by unsuccessful defendant (Sanderson and Bullock Orders)

Replace the last paragraph with:

44.2.8   Under CPR r.44.2, by adopting an issue-based approach in exercising its discretion as to costs, the court may make orders closely reflecting the success or lack of success of parties on particular issues arising in the proceedings and departing from the general rule that the unsuccessful party should pay the successful party's costs. In proceedings where claims are made against several defendants, the flexibility of those powers may be utilised to advantage in circumstances where alternatively, but perhaps less satisfactorily, Bullock orders or Sanderson orders might be made. In *Grizzly Business Ltd v Stena Drilling Ltd* [2017] EWCA Civ 94 the second defendant, but not the first defendant, was found liable to the claimant. The Court of Appeal declined to interfere with an order that the successful first defendant should pay 90 per cent of the claimant's costs in circumstances where the first defendant had controlled and funded the defences of both defendants. The reduction of 10 per cent reflected the fact that the first defendant had succeeded on the issue of which defendant was liable. The court drew a close analogy with non-party costs orders. In circumstances where a non-party costs order under s.51 of the Senior Courts Act 1981 would have been justified had the successful party not been a party, it would be wrong for that party to avoid liability for the costs simply because it had been joined as a party: *Threlfall v ECD Insight Ltd* [2013] EWCA Civ 1444.

PART 45

FIXED COSTS

IIIA. Claims Which No Longer Continue Under the RTA or EL/PL Pre-Action Protocols—Fixed Recoverable Costs

Add new paragraph 45.29H.2:

Pre-commencement disclosure
Applications for pre-commencement disclosure in claims which fall within Section IIIA are **45.29H.2** interim applications to which this rule applies and only the fixed costs provided by this rule will be payable: *Sharp v Leeds City Council* [2017] EWCA Civ 33.

PART 46

COSTS—SPECIAL CASES

I. Costs Payable by or to Particular Persons

Add new paragraph 46.1.4:

Fixed Costs
The costs of applications for pre-commencement disclosure in claims which fall within Section **46.1.4** IIIA of Part 45 (Claims which no longer continue under the RTA or EL/PL Pre-Action Protocols) are limited to those fixed by r.45.29H: *Sharp v Leeds City Council* [2017] EWCA Civ 33.

Solicitors acting on own account

After the third paragraph (beginning with "The Court of Appeal"), add new paragraph:
The principle was extended to work done by a solicitor on behalf of the claimant company of **46.5.6** which the solicitor was the sole shareholder. The claimant had instructed solicitors to act on its behalf. However the shareholder had carried out a significant amount of work and in consequence the claimant had suffered a loss. It was held that the claimant could recover costs in respect of the work done by the shareholder, save insofar as such work did not duplicate work done by the claimant's external solicitors: *Shackleton and Associates Ltd v Al Shamsi* [2017] EWHC 304 (Comm).

III. Costs on Allocation and Re-Allocation

Editorial note

Replace the second paragraph with:
The rules relating to small claims and fast track trial costs do not apply until a claim is allocated **46.11.2** to a particular track (see paras 7 and 8 of Practice Direction 46). Rule 46.13(1) provides that any costs orders made before a claim is allocated will not be affected by the allocation. See also note at para.44.4.3 (*Voice & Script International Ltd v Alghafar* [2003] EWCA Civ 736).

PART 48

Part 2 of the Legal Aid, Sentencing and Punishment of Offenders Act 2012 Relating to Civil Litigation Funding and Costs: Transitional Provision in Relation to Pre-Commencement Funding Arrangements

(a) Section 44 of the 2012 Act (success fees)

To the first paragraph, add:

48.0.2.2 Where a CFA entered into before 1 April 2013 was varied after that date the variation did not affect the recoverability of the success fee because it did not have the effect of discharging the original CFA and replacing it with a new agreement: *Plevin v Paragon Personal Finance Ltd* [2017] UKSC 23.

(b) Section 46 of the 2012 Act (insurance premiums)

Add new paragraph at end:

48.0.2.3 In *Plevin v Paragon Personal Finance Ltd* [2017] UKSC 23 the respondent had purchased an ATE policy before 1 April 2013 in respect of the proceedings up to trial and had topped up the cover after that date for the appeal to the Supreme Court. It was held that "proceedings" in s.46(3) covered both the trial and any appeal and accordingly that the respondent could recover the cost of the top up premium.

PART 44

[Before April 1, 2013] General Rules about Costs

Judicial review

To the end of the sixth paragraph (beginning with "The correct starting"), add:

44x.3.12 Where the court had concluded that a statutory appeal would have been unsuccessful, yet the respondent had agreed to withdraw its decision in the light of new evidence produced by the appellant (who had therefore obtained the practical result that she was seeking), the appropriate order was that the appellant should pay the respondent's costs: *London Borough of Croydon v Lopes* [2017] EWHC 33 (QB). The key factor was that the respondent would have been successful had the appeal not become academic

Rule 44.3(6)—types of order

Add new paragraph 44x.3.22.3:

44x.3.22.3 The effect of exchange rate losses—It has been held that if a foreign litigant entitled to costs has incurred additional costs as the result of exchange rate losses, an additional sum by way of costs should be awarded as compensation for those losses: *Elkamet Kunststofftechnik GmbH v Saint-Gobain Glass France SA* [2016] EWHC 3421 (Pat).

GENERAL PRINCIPLES AND CASE LAW RELATING TO COSTS AND THEIR ASSESSMENT

Arbitration costs of claims consultants

Add new paragraph at end:

48GP.60 In adjudication enforcement proceedings, costs incurred by claims consultants assisting a litigant in person will usually be recoverable in principle provided that the same consultants represented the party in the adjudication. The costs will usually fall within the meaning of disbursements in r.46.5(3)(a): *Octoesse LLP v Trak Special Projects Ltd* [2016] EWHC 3180 (TCC).

PART 52

Appeals

I. Scope and interpretation

High Court's jurisdiction under the Extradition Act 2003

Replace "Criminal Procedure Rules 2014 (SI 2014/1610)" with:
Criminal Procedure Rules 2015 (SI 2015/1490) **52.1.6**

II. Permission to Appeal—General

Obtaining permission to appeal

In the seventh paragraph (beginning with "Where an application"), replace the sentence beginning "There is nothing" with:
The application may be made at a later date than the hearing at which the decision to be ap- **52.3.6** pealed was made where the court, at that hearing, adjourns the application to a later date. A lower court has no jurisdiction to permit a retrospective application for permission to appeal (See *Monroe v Hopkins (Rev 1)* [2017] EWHC 645 (QB), 28 March 2017, unrep. (Warby J)).

Role of respondents in permission application

Add new paragraph at end:
Where a respondent attends a permission hearing the general rule is that they will not be **52.5.2** awarded costs except in the circumstances specified in Practice Direction 52B para.8.1. Where costs are sought under Practice Direction 52B para.8.1(b) *Mount Cook Land Ltd v Westminster City Council* [2003] EWCA Civ 1346; [2004] C.P. Rep. 12, CA, para.76 provides guidance on the question whether it would be just in all the circumstances to depart from the general rule. Relevant factors that could justify an award of costs are: the hopelessness of the claim; persistence in pursuit of the claim despite the appellant being aware of the facts and/or law demonstrating its hopelessness; and whether the respondent's attendance provides the court with the benefit of an early substantive hearing of the issues at the oral renewal hearing: see *Robert v Woodall* [2017] EWHC 436 (Ch), 7 March 2017, unrep.

Appeal from decision "which was itself made on appeal" (second appeal)

After the fifth paragraph (beginning with "In Smith International"), add new paragraph:
In *Secretary of State for the Home Department v Akbar* [2017] EWCA Civ 16, 19 January 2017, **52.7.2** unrep. (Arden and Macfarlane LJJ, Cranston J), an appeal to the County Court from a decision of the Secretary of State's Immigration Enforcement decision was a first appeal. As such the Court of Appeal affirmed any subsequent appeal from the County Court was a second appeal.

III. Permission to Appeal—Judicial Review Appeals, Planning Statutory Review Appeals and Appeals from the Employment Appeal Tribunal

Effect of rule

Replace the first paragraph with:
With effect from 3 October 2016, this rule replaced former r.52.15. Paras (3) to (6) of r.52.8 are **52.8.1** to the same effect as paras (2) to (4) of former r.52.15. Paras (1) and (2) of r.52.8 replace paras (1) and (1A) of former r.52x.15 in terms slightly amended. The rule deals with applications to the Court of Appeal for permission to appeal to the Court from decisions of the High Court refusing applications for permission to proceed with applications for judicial review.

PART 52

PRACTICE DIRECTION 52B—APPEALS IN THE COUNTY COURT AND HIGH COURT
This Practice Direction supplements Part 52

Section 8 Hearings

52BPD.9   *In the first column of Table A, on the same line as "Banbury", insert "South East":*

8.3   Skeleton arguments:

Table A: Table of Appeal Centres for each Circuit

Circuit	*Court*	*Appeal Centre*
South East	Banbury	Oxford

PART 53

PRACTICE DIRECTION 53—DEFAMATION CLAIMS

Pleading the meaning

In the last paragraph, replace "inference," with:

53PD.6   inference (see for instance *Monroe v Hopkins* [2017] EWHC 433 (QB) at [69]-[70]),

Ruling on meaning

Replace "Al Alaoui v Elaph Publishing Ltd [2015] EWHC 1084 (QB))" with:

53PD.32   *Al Alaoui v Elaph Publishing Ltd* [2017] EWCA Civ 29; [2017] E.M.L.R. 13)

Actions where jury trial has been ordered

To the end of the paragraph, add:

53PD.32.1   , except (so it would seem: see *Al Alaoui*, above) for the purpose of an application to strike out

PART 54

JUDICIAL REVIEW AND STATUTORY REVIEW

I.   Judicial Review

Against whom does judicial review lie

In the first paragraph, replace "R (Miller) v Secretary of State for Exiting the European Union [2016] EWHC 2768 (Admin)" with:

54.1.2   *R. (Miller) v Secretary of State for Exiting the European Union* [2017] UKSC 5; [2017] 1 W.L.R. 583

Time limits and delay

In the first paragraph, replace "Finn-Kelcey v Milton Keynes BC [2009] Env. L.R. 17)." with:

54.5.1   *Finn-Kelcey v Milton Keynes BC* [2009] Env. L.R. 17 and see *R. (Sustainable Development Capital LLP v Secretary of State for Business, Energy and Industrial Strategy* [2017] EWHC 771 (Admin)).

Challenges to new decisions

Replace "R (Hussain) v Secretary of State for the Home Department [2016] EWCA Civ 1111)." with:

54.6.4   *R. (Hussain) v Secretary of State for the Home Department* [2016] EWCA Civ 1111; [2017] 1 W.L.R. 761).

Reconsideration of a refusal of permission

In the second paragraph, replace "R (Wasif) v Secretary of State for the Home Department [2016] EWCA Civ 82, 9 February 2016, CA, unrep.," with:
    R. (Wasif) v Secretary of State for the Home Department [2016] EWCA Civ 82; [2016] 1 W.L.R. 2793, **54.12.1**

PART 55

POSSESSION CLAIMS

II. Accelerated Possession Claims of Property Let on an Assured Shorthold Tenancy

Claim form

Add new paragraph at end:
    Before a judge can make an order for possession under the accelerated procedure, the claimant **55.13.1** must establish that he is entitled to recover possession under section 21 of the 1988 Act. (r.55.16(2)(a) and PD55A para 8.1.). For tenancies commenced after 1 October 2015, the additional requirements prescribed by the Assured Shorthold Tenancy Notices and Prescribed Requirements (England) (Amendment) Regulations 2015 apply. They include confirmation that the tenant has "How to rent: the checklist for renting in England", as published by the Department for Communities and Local Government, an Energy performance certificate and a Gas safety certificate. However, the **Form N5B** in existence when Civil Procedure 2017 was published did not provide for reference to these requirements and, as a result, in some claims judges have refused to make possession orders under the accelerated procedure. It is understood that the Ministry of Justice is preparing an amended **Form N5B** which will incorporate the additional information.

PART 57

PROBATE, INHERITANCE AND PRESUMPTION OF DEATH

Related sources

Add to the end of the list: **57.1.2**
  •   CH30 Pronouncing for completed copy/torn up will

PART 64

ESTATES, TRUSTS AND CHARITIES

I. Claims Relating to the Administration of Estates and Trusts

Variation of Trusts Act 1958—r.64.2(c)

Add new paragraph at end:
    The practice concerning the way in which the initial stages of Variation of Trusts claims are **64.2.7** handled in the light of the decision in *V v T* [2014] EWHC 3432 (Ch), the change to Masters' jurisdiction in April 2015, and the guidance contained in paras 29.22 to 29.27 of the Chancery Guide (Vol.2 para.1A-246), is stated in Practice Note (Variation of Trusts: Confidentiality Orders Pending the Hearing of Application), 9 February 2017, unrep. (see para.64PN.1). The Practice Note is published on the *judiciary.gov* website. A draft confidentitality order is attached at Appendix A and also available (**CH 43**) on the *justice.gov* website.

Change title of document:

PRACTICE NOTE: VARIATION OF TRUSTS

Replace Practice Note where subtitle, date and Editorial Note have been inserted:

Confidentiality Orders Pending The Hearing Of The Application

64PN.1   This note sets out the practice concerning the way in which the initial stages of Variation of Trusts ("VoT") claims are handled in the light of:

i)   The decision in *V v T and A* [2014] EWHC 3432 (Ch);

ii)   The change to Masters' jurisdiction in April 2015;

iii) The guidance contained in paras 29.22 to 29.27 of the Chancery Guide [as amended].

The procedure set out below has been approved by the Chancellor with the agreement of the Chancery Bar Association.

Paragraph 30 of Morgan J's judgment in *V v T and A* makes suggestions for the future listing of VoT applications where there is a wish to preserve confidentiality. However, the guidance pre-dates the extension to the Masters' jurisdiction in April 2015. As from that date the Masters have had jurisdiction to make VoT orders and all VoT claims should in the first instance come before a Master.

When the parties are ready to issue VoT proceedings, they should attend before a Master in advance of the claim being issued (a) to consider whether orders should be made on an interim basis to preserve confidentiality pending the full hearing of the application and (b) to discuss whether the application is best suited for hearing by a Master or a judge. Whether a particular application is more suitably dealt with by a judge is decided on a case by case basis taking account of the complexity and scope of the application, whether there are novel legal issues, the parties involved and the parties' wishes. The draft Part 8 claim and the evidence in support should be lodged before the application is issued. It may be reviewed on paper but it is often more convenient for the claim to be discussed at an application without notice ("AWN") hearing. If the Master is satisfied, based on the evidence, that there is real prospect of the court being willing to direct that the main hearing should be in private and/or there should be reporting restrictions and/or access to the court file should be limited and/or the proceedings are anonymised then interim orders can be made to preserve confidentiality. An example of such an order is at Appendix A and is available at *http://hmctsformfinder.justice.gov.uk*, numbered CH 43.

Whether it is appropriate to make an interim order to restrict access to the claim form and evidence on the court file and to make the proceedings anonymous pending the disposal hearing will depend on the circumstances in each case. These orders are not automatic and the applicants will have to provide evidence which justifies the making of such an order. At the full hearing, in the light of more detailed consideration the court can decide whether these orders should be continued and whether the hearing should be in private.

Chief Master Marsh

9 February 2017

Editorial Note

For Variation of Trusts Act 1958, see para.64.2.7.

PART 68

References to the European Court

Applications for a preliminary ruling

Add new paragraph at end:

   In *Coal Staff Superannuation Scheme Trustees Ltd v The Commissioners for Her Majesty's Revenue and* **68.3.1**
Customs [2017] UKUT 137 (TCC) an unusual application was made by the Claimant Appellant for
a reference of certain questions to the European Court by the Upper Tribunal (UT). Article 267
TFEU gives jurisdiction to the CJEU to give preliminary rulings where a question is raised "..in a
case pending before a court or tribunal of a Member State against whose decisions there is no
judicial remedy under national law". It was accepted that s.13 of the Tribunals, Courts and
Enforcement Act 2007 provides for appeal from the UT to the CA. But it was argued that, because
of the notice served by HM government under Art.50(2) of the Treaty on European Union of the
UK's intention to withdraw from the EU, it appeared to be a core policy of HM government that
the exit of the UK from the EU will bring an end to the jurisdiction of the European Court in the
UK. The practical result, it was submitted, would be that any delay in referring to the European
Court any questions that arise in the case may result in the Claimant being deprived of its ability to
seek the assistance of the European Court in resolving the EU law based claim that had been made
in the proceedings, so that in the unprecedented circumstances arising from the service of the
Art.50 notice, the UT comes within the wording of Art.267, as set out above. Rose J dismissed that
argument, holding that the interrelationship between the two limbs of Art.267 and their application to the court system in the UK have been settled over many years and that is not changed by the
service of the Art.50 notice, nor does the triggering of Art.50 alter the test which the has hitherto
applied in deciding whether, as a matter of discretion, it should make a reference, citing *Capernwray
Missionary Fellowship of Torchbearers v HMRC* [2015] UKUT 368 and Lord Bingham's judgment (at
p.545) in *R. v International Stock Exchange of the United Kingdom and the Republic of Ireland Ltd ex parte
Else (1982) Ltd* [1993] Q.B. 534.

PART 73

Charging Orders, Stop Orders and Stop Notices

I. Charging Orders

Right to charging order where judgment debt payable by instalments

Add new paragraph at end:

   There is an important distinction between an order for payment of a specific sum by instalments **73.4.4**
and an order under which the amount to be paid has yet to be determined. Thus there is no power
to make a charging order in respect of costs which have not yet been assessed. Such unassessed
costs are not within the scope of s.1(1) of the Charging Orders Act 1979 as they are neither money
which the debtor is "required to pay" under an order, nor money "due or to become due" under an
order. Unassessed costs cannot be equated with future instalments under a quantified judgment or
order. (*Monte Developments Ltd v Court Management Consultants Ltd* [2010] EWHC 3071 (Ch): see also
Magiera v Magiera [2016] EWCA Civ 1292).

PART 74

ENFORCEMENT OF JUDGMENTS IN DIFFERENT JURISDICTIONS

I.   Enforcement in England and Wales of Judgments of Foreign Courts

Note

To the beginning of the paragraph, add:

74.4A.1   Note was added to reflect the simplified procedure for enforcement of a judgment under the recast Judgments Regulations, which applies to proceedings instituted, to authentic instruments formally drawn up or registered and to court settlements approved or concluded on or after

Fraud

Add new paragraph at end:

74.7.2   Although not a case of enforcement of a foreign judgment by registration, the decision in *Midtown Acquisitions LP v Essar Global Fund Ltd* [2017] EWHC 519 (Comm) is of relevance to reliance on fraud as a ground for opposing enforcement. It was held that conscious and deliberate dishonesty had to be established to make out a defence of fraud to the enforcement of a New York judgment in England.

V.   European Enforcement Orders

Add new paragraph 74.27.1:

74.27.1   In *Zulfikarpasic v Gajer (Case C-484/15)* (9 March 2017) the ECJ ruled that the concept of "court", "court proceedings" and "uncontested claim" under the EEO Regulation must be construed in accordance with the wording and objective of the Regulation. Thus, in Croatia, notaries, acting under powers conferred on them by national law in enforcement proceedings, who issued writs of execution based on an "authentic document", did not fall within the concept of "court" within the meaning of the Regulation, and the writs of execution could not be certified as an EEO.

The court noted that (i) there was no similar provision to that in the recast Brussels Regulation, where "court" was specified as encompassing not only judicial authorities but also any competent authority exercising judicial functions; and (ii) the principle of mutual recognition of judgments was based on the principle of mutual trust in the administration of justice between member states which required that judgments had been delivered in court proceedings offering guarantees of independence and impartiality and compliance with the principle of audi alteram partem (listening to the other side).

Enforcement costs following rescission of EEO in court of origin

Add new paragraph at end:

74.33.1   In *De La Hija v Lee* [2017] EWHC 634 (Ch) the EEO was issued after default judgement was granted by the Spanish court. The defendant successfully applied without notice in the English court for an order for a stay of enforcement of the EEO, then brought challenges in the Spanish court against the judgment and EEO. The claimant's application under CPR 3.1(7) to revoke that order was refused. It was held that although when the order for a stay was made, there was no subsisting challenge to the judgment or EEO in the Spanish courts, therefore the court had lacked jurisdiction to grant a stay under art.23 of the EEO Regulation, the EEO here was not capable of satisfying the enforcing court that the requirements of the EEO Regulation had been complied with (because the EEO was not fully completed). Therefore, the court had an inherent jurisdiction to stay its enforcement, but even if that was wrong, it would still not be right to exercise a discretion to revoke the order because the court had jurisdiction under Article 23 from the commencement of the challenges in the Spanish courts until final determination of those Spanish proceedings, and there were exceptional circumstances which justified the grant of a stay. The English court also held that although art.21(2) of the EEO Regulation provides that under no circumstances may the enforcing state review the judgment or its certification as an EEO, viewed in the context of the EEO Regulation, this referred to the formal act of considering a challenge to the judgment. If the court was wrong that it did not have jurisdiction under art.23, art.21 did not prevent the court from taking into account, as exceptional circumstances, the lack of merits of the claim and the manifest failure to comply with the service requirements in the EEO Regulation.

PART 81

APPLICATIONS AND PROCEEDINGS IN RELATION TO CONTEMPT OF COURT

VI.   Committal for making a false statement of truth (rule 32.14) or disclosure statement (rule 31.23)

Committal for knowingly swearing a false affidavit

To the end of the paragraph, add:

A deponent may be liable to committal for knowingly swearing a false affidavit where the af- **81.17.3**
fidavit is defective (*Haederle v Thomas* [2016] EWHC 3498 (Ch), 2 November 2016, unrep. (Nugee
J), where, though it could be proved that the witness had sworn the document, the jurat was not
completed

Effect of rule

Replace paragraph with:

This rule is supplemented by Practice Direction 81 para.5. Rule 81.18(3) is mandatory and not **81.18.1**
discretionary in its effect; a committal application "may be made only" by the Attorney General or
with the permission of a High Court judge. (In the FPR 2010 r.17.6(2) is to the same effect.) As to
committal applications made by (or referred by the court to) the Attorney General, see further
para.81.18.6 below.

VIII.   General rules about committal applications, orders for committal and writs of sequestration

Grounds and evidence relied on

To the end of the seventh paragraph (beginning with "In Otkritie International"), add:

On appeal, the Court of Appeal rejected X's submission that the judge erred in concluding that **81.28.4**
the allegations of contempt of court against her were established on the evidence beyond reasonable doubt (*Otkritie International Investment Ltd v Jemai* [2016] EWCA Civ 1316, 21 December 2016,
CA).

Hearing in absence of respondent

Replace first paragraph with:

The court's power to proceed with a trial in the absence of a party (CPR r.39.3) extends to the **81.28.6**
trial of committal applications, but to do so is an exceptional course (*Lamb v Lamb* [1984] F.L.R.
278, CA). In seeking to determine the applicable principles, in *JSC BTA Bank v Stepanov* [2010]
EWHC 794 (Ch), 31 March 2010, unrep. (Roth J), the judge noted that contempt proceedings are
quasi-criminal proceedings, and sought guidance from authorities on the circumstances in which a
court may proceed with a criminal trial in the absence of the defendant (para.12). In *JSC BTA Bank
v Solodchenko* [2011] EWHC 1613 (Ch), 17 May 2011, unrep. (Briggs J), the judge referred to the
principles derived by the judge in that case and ruled that in the case before him it was appropriate
to proceed with the hearing as the evidence showed that the respondent was deliberately concealing
his whereabouts and declining to respond, and added that in the event of a committal order being
made a short adjournment would be allowed before sentencing to give the respondent an opportunity to purge his contempt or to raise any relevant matters in mitigation (para.13). In *Sanchez
v Oboz* [2015] EWHC 235 (Fam); [2016] 1 F.L.R. 897 (Cobb J), the judge set out a check-list of
considerations for the court to have in mind (para.5); see also *Phonographic Performance Ltd v
Nightclub (London) Ltd* [2016] EWHC 892 (Ch), 21 April 2014, unrep. (Warren J); *Taylor v Van
Dutch Marine Holding Ltd* [2016] EWHC 2201 (Ch), 5 September 2016, unrep. (Warren J); *Hicken v
Ellison* [2016] EWHC 2791 (Ch), 8 November 2016, unrep. (Warren J); *Bunge SA v Huaya Maritime
Corp* [2017] EWHC 90 (Comm), 27 January 2017, unrep. (Cranston J). Where the court proceeds
in the respondent's absence, and imposes a custodial sentence, the court may consider it appropri-
ate to suspend the sentence for a very short period, even where the court is satisfied that the reason
for the non-attendance was not because the respondent was unaware of the proceedings, or unaware
of the consequences, but simply because he was determined not voluntarily to attend (see e.g.
Johnson v Argent [2016] EWHC 2978 (Ch), 13 September 2016, unrep. (Nugee J)).

Effect of rule

To the end of the second paragraph, add:

See further Vol.2 para.3C-91   **81.29.1**

After the second paragraph, add new paragraph:

As to the suspending of a committal order made where a debtor fails to attend at an adjourned hearing of an application for an attachment of earnings order, see r.89.9 (formerly CCR Ord. 27, r.7B).

PART 82

Closed Material Procedure

II. General Provisions

Add new paragraph 82.6.1:

Interests of national security

82.6.1   Paragraph (1) of s.11(1) of the 2013 Act states that rules of court must have regard to the need to secure that disclosures of information are not made where they would be damaging to the interests of national security (Vol.2 para.9B-147+). Paragraph (2)(e) of the section states that rules of court may make provision enabling the court to conduct proceedings in the absence of any person, including a party to the proceedings (or any legal representative of that party). For principles generally applicable to determination by a court of question whether it should sit in private to protect interests of national security, see *In re Guardian News and Media Ltd* [2016] EWCA Crim 11; [2016] 1 W.L.R. 1767, CA.

PART 83

Writs and Warrants—General Provisions

II. Writs and Warrants

Judgment over six years old—practice

In the last paragraph, replace "Society of LLoyds v Longtin [2005] EWHC 2471 (Comm)" with:

83.2.2   *Society of Lloyd's v Longtin* [2005] EWHC 2491 (Comm).

Schedule 2—CCR Provisions

CCR ORDER 28—JUDGMENT SUMMONSES

Order 27

Add new paragraph at end:

cc28.4.1   By SI 2016/234, r.7B of CCR Ord.27 was omitted from Schedule 2 of the CPR and in effect replaced by CPR r.89.9 (Suspended committal order). Rule 8 of the Order was omitted from Schedule 2 of the CPR by SI 2014/407 and in effect replaced by provisions in Part 33 of the Family Procedure Rules 2010, incorporating by reference (sometimes with modifications) various rules in the Order.

SECTION C   PRE-ACTION CONDUCT AND PROTOCOLS

Add new Pre-Action Protocol for Debt Claims:

The Protocol for Debt Claims

Editorial Introduction

This new Pre-Action Protocol has been a long time in preparation, being first proposed by the **C16A-001** Law Society in the late 1990's. The Jackson report revived the idea, which was taken forward by the Civil Justice Council in 2012, when a draft was sent to the Civil Procedure Rule Committee, who worked up the draft and consulted upon it. But the credit industry were not in favour. Some representatives of the industry (and of those advising debtors) were invited to become members of the CPRC Sub-Committee that prepared and consulted on a revised draft, which again produced critical responses from creditors and those that represent them. By December 2016 CPRC considered a further draft, which reduced the information that creditors had to provide with a letter of claim.

The Protocol comes into force on 1 October 2017. It applies to debts claimed by a business (which includes sole traders and public bodies) against individuals (that also includes sole traders). It does not apply to debt claims that are subject to other Pre-Action Protocols, including Construction, Mortgage and Rent Arrears, or to claims by HMRC for unpaid taxes which are governed by CPR PD7D. It is also subordinate to regulations set out in the Financial Conduct Authority's Handbook.

The main provisions are for the creditor's (or their assignee's) letter of claim to set out the details of the original agreement (the debtor may obtain a copy on request), explain any assignment of the debt, how it can be paid, attach an up-to-date statement of account, an information sheet (that includes details of some debt advice agencies), a reply form and a financial statement (of means) (templates for which are annexed to the protocol). If the debtor does not reply within 30 days the creditor may issue the claim. If the debtor is seeking advice or requires time to pay, the creditor must allow at least 30 days. If the debtor requests a document the creditor must provide it or explain why it is not available.

It is to be hoped that the Protocol will help to settle more debt claims, and that claims do not continue to be issued where no copy of the agreement can be found or reconstituted; where no default notice was sent or can't be found; and where there is no proof of the assignment or no notice of it has been sent to the debtor, which too frequently are discontinued, or are struck out or dismissed, and that defences do not continue to be filed simply denying the debt or the assignment, when there is evidence of both. These poorly prepared cases take up court time unnecessarily.

PRE-ACTION PROTOCOL FOR DEBT CLAIMS

Introduction

1.1 This Protocol applies to any business (including sole traders and public **C16-001** bodies) claiming payment of a debt from an individual (including a sole trader). The business will be referred to as the "creditor" and the individual will be referred to as the "debtor". This Protocol does not apply to business-to-business debts unless the debtor is a sole trader.

1.2 The Protocol describes the conduct the court will normally expect of those parties prior to the start of proceedings. It includes a template Information Sheet and Reply Form to be provided to debtors in all cases.

1.3 The Protocol is intended to complement any regulatory regime to which the creditor is subject. To the extent that compliance with this Protocol is inconsistent with a specific regulatory obligation (such as a principle, rule or guidance contained in the Financial Conduct Authority's Handbook) that regulatory obligation will take precedence. The Protocol should also be read in conjunction with industry and government guidance relating to good practice in the recovery of debt.

1.4 The Protocol does not apply:

(a) where the debt is covered by another Pre-Action Protocol such as Construction and Engineering or Mortgage Arrears; or

(b) to claims issued by Her Majesty's Revenue and Customs that are governed by Practice Direction 7D (Claims For The Recovery Of Taxes And Duties).

Aims of the Protocol

C16-002 **2.1** This Protocol's aims are to –

(a) encourage early engagement and communication between the parties, including early exchange of sufficient information about the matter to help clarify whether there are any issues in dispute;

(b) enable the parties to resolve the matter without the need to start court proceedings, including agreeing a reasonable repayment plan or considering using an Alternative Dispute Resolution (ADR) procedure;

(c) encourage the parties to act in a reasonable and proportionate manner in all dealings with one another (for example, avoiding running up costs which do not bear a reasonable relationship to the sums in issue);

(d) support the efficient management of proceedings that cannot be avoided.

Initial Information to be Provided by the Creditor

C16-003 **3.1** The creditor should send a Letter of Claim to the debtor before proceedings are started. The Letter of Claim should–

(a) contain the following information–

  (i) the amount of the debt;

  (ii) whether interest or other charges are continuing;

  (iii) where the debt arises from an oral agreement, who made the agreement, what was agreed (including, as far as possible, what words were used) and when and where it was agreed;

  (iv) where the debt arises from a written agreement, the date of the agreement, the parties to it and the fact that a copy of the written agreement can be requested from the creditor;

  (v) where the debt has been assigned, the details of the original debt and creditor, when it was assigned and to whom;

  (vi) if regular instalments are currently being offered by or on behalf of the debtor, or are being paid, an explanation of why the offer is not acceptable and why a court claim is still being considered;

  (vii) details of how the debt can be paid (for example, the method of and address for payment) and details of how to proceed if the debtor wishes to discuss payment options;

  (viii) the address to which the completed Reply Form should be sent;

(b) do one of the following–

  (i) enclose an up-to-date statement of account for the debt, which should include details of any interest and administrative or other charges added;

  (ii) enclose the most recent statement of account for the debt and state in the Letter of Claim the amount of interest incurred and any administrative or other charges imposed since that statement of account was issued, sufficient to bring it up to date; or

  (iii) where no statements have been provided for the debt, state in the Letter of Claim the amount of interest incurred and any administrative or other charges imposed since the debt was incurred;

(c) enclose a copy of the Information Sheet and the Reply Form at Annex 1 to this Protocol; and

(d) enclose a Financial Statement form (an example Financial Statement is provided in Annex 2 to this protocol).

3.2 The Letter of Claim should be clearly dated toward the top of the first page. It should be posted either on the day it is dated or, if that is not reasonably possible, the following day.

3.3 The Letter of Claim should be sent by post. If the creditor has additional contact details for the debtor, such as an email address, the creditor may also send the Letter of Claim using those details. If the debtor has made an explicit request that correspondence should not be sent by post, and has provided alternative contact details, the creditor should use those details when sending the Letter of Claim. (Note that a condition in a creditor's standard terms does not constitute an explicit request.)

3.4 If the debtor does not reply to the Letter of Claim within 30 days of the date at the top of the letter, the creditor may start court proceedings, subject to any remaining obligations the creditor may have to the debtor (for example, under the Financial Conduct Authority's Handbook). Account should be taken of the possibility that a reply was posted towards the end of the 30-day period.

Response by the Debtor

4.1 The debtor should use the Reply Form in Annex 1 for their response. **C16-004** The debtor should request copies of any documents they wish to see and enclose copies of any documents they consider relevant, such as details of payments made but not taken into account in the creditor's Letter of Claim.

4.2 If the debtor indicates that they are seeking debt advice, the creditor must allow the debtor a reasonable period for the advice to be obtained. In any event, the creditor should not start court proceedings less than 30 days from receipt of the completed Reply Form or 30 days from the creditor providing any documents requested by the debtor, whichever is the later.

4.3 If the debtor indicates in the Reply Form that they are seeking debt advice that cannot be obtained within 30 days of their reply, the debtor must provide details to the creditor as specified in the Reply Form. The creditor should allow reasonable extra time for the debtor to obtain that advice where it would be reasonable to do so in the circumstances.

4.4 Where a debtor indicates in the Reply Form that they require time to pay, the creditor and debtor should try to reach agreement for the debt to be paid by instalments, based on the debtor's income and expenditure. In trying to agree affordable sums for repayment, the creditor should have regard where appropriate to the provisions of the Standard Financial Statement or equivalent guidance. If the creditor does not agree to a debtor's proposal for repayment of the debt, they should give the debtor reasons in writing.

4.5 A partially completed Reply Form should be taken by the creditor as an attempt by the debtor to engage with the matter. The creditor should attempt to contact the debtor to discuss the Reply Form and obtain any further information needed to understand the debtor's position.

Disclosure of Documents

5.1 Early disclosure of documents and relevant information can help to **C16-005** clarify or resolve any issues in dispute. Where any aspect of the debt is disputed (including the amount, interest, charges, time for payment, or the creditor's compliance with relevant statutes and regulations), the parties should exchange information and disclose documents sufficient to enable them to understand each other's position.

5.2 If the debtor requests a document or information, the creditor must–

(a) provide the document or information; or

(b) explain why the document or information is unavailable,
within 30 days of receipt of the request.

Taking Steps to Settle the Matter and Alternative Dispute Resolution

C16-006   **6.1** If the parties still cannot agree about the existence, enforceability, amount or any other aspect of the debt, they should both take appropriate steps to resolve the dispute without starting court proceedings and, in particular, should consider the use of an appropriate form of Alternative Dispute Resolution (ADR).

6.2 ADR may simply take the form of discussion and negotiation, or it may involve some more formal process such as a complaint to the Financial Ombudsman Service where the dispute concerns a debt regulated under the Consumer Credit Act 1974.

6.3 In some cases, especially where the debt is large, mediation (a third party facilitating a resolution) might be appropriate. Details of registered mediation providers can be obtained from the Civil Mediation Provider Directory at *www.civilmediation.justice.gov.uk*. The potential costs of mediation should be considered in relation to the amount of the debt.

6.4 Where the parties reach agreement concerning the repayment of the debt, the creditor should not start court proceedings while the debtor complies with the agreement. Should the creditor wish to start court proceedings at a later date, they must send an updated Letter of Claim and comply with this Protocol afresh. If documentation was sent with a Letter of Claim in the preceding 6 months, that documentation need not be sent again unless it requires updating.

Compliance with this Protocol

C16-007   **7.1** If a matter proceeds to litigation, the court will expect the parties to have complied with this Protocol. The court will take into account non-compliance when giving directions for the management of proceedings. The court will consider whether all parties have complied in substance with the terms of the Protocol and is not likely to be concerned with minor or technical infringements, especially when the matter is urgent.

7.2 For further information about the court's approach to compliance, see Practice Direction – Pre-Action Conduct and Protocols (paragraphs 13 to 16).

Taking Stock

C16-008   **8.1** Where the procedure set out in this Protocol has not resolved the matter between the debtor and creditor, they should undertake a review of their respective positions to see if proceedings can be avoided and, at the least, to narrow the issues between them.

8.2 Where the debtor has responded to the Letter of Claim but agreement has not been reached, the creditor should give the debtor at least 14 days' notice of their intention to start court proceedings, unless there are exceptional circumstances in which urgent action is required (for example, because the limitation period is about to expire).

ANNEX 1

INFORMATION SHEET

You have received this notice because a business intends to take you to C16-009 court in relation to a debt. This notice tells you what to do next, including how to avoid court action. Please read it carefully.

What should I do now to make sure I am not taken to court unnecessarily?

Read the enclosed letter from the business very carefully. Think about whether you owe the debt and whether the amount is correct. The letter should provide information about how much money you owe and any interest and fees added to the debt. If it doesn't, ask the business for more information.

Once you have read the letter, consider the following options.

- **Seeking debt advice.** If you are in financial difficulty or need advice to help you work out whether you owe the debt, or how you might pay the debt, contact a debt advisor (particularly if you haven't been in contact with the business for a number of years).

  The following organisations offer free, impartial and non-judgemental advice:

Citizens Advice	03444 111 444 (England) 03444 772 020 (Wales)	*www.citizensadvice.org.uk*
Civil Legal Advice	0345 345 4345	*www.gov.uk/civil-legal-advice*
StepChange Debt Charity	0800 138 1111 (Freephone)	*www.stepchange.org*
National Debtline	0808 808 4000 (Freephone)	*www.nationaldebtline.org*
AdviceUK	0300 777 0107	*www.adviceuk.org.uk*
Christians Against Poverty	0800 328 0006 (Freephone)	*www.capuk.org*

  It is recommended that you get debt advice if you have any doubt about whether you owe the debt or whether you can pay it now.

  If you don't have a copy of the agreement (contract) between you and the business, and you need this to decide what to do next or to help you get debt advice, you can ask the business to provide you with a copy.

- **Speaking to the business.** If you agree you owe the debt and want to talk to the business about payment terms, or if you have any questions or concerns, get in touch with the business as soon as possible. Their contact details should be in the letter they sent you.

- **Filling in the Reply Form.** If you have not been able to resolve the matter by speaking to the business, you should fill in the Reply Form that was provided with the letter from the business, and then send it back to the business. You should complete the Reply Form with as much information as possible to avoid court action being taken against you.

How long do I have to fill in the Reply Form?

You only have **30 days** from the date at the top of the letter from the business to send back the Reply Form. If the business does not get your Reply Form within 30 days, it could **take you to court** in relation to the debt. Make sure you allow time for posting.

If a court orders you to pay an amount of money (called "having judgment entered against you"), details of the judgment will usually be entered on the Register of Judgments, Orders and Fines. Most entries stay on the Register for six years unless you pay the amount you owe within one month of the judgment.

Organisations such as banks, building societies and credit companies use the information on the Register when someone applies for credit, such as a loan or overdraft. It helps them decide whether or not that person would be able to pay off a debt.

What happens if I fill in and return the Reply Form in time?

If you return the Reply Form within 30 days, you and the business will have at least a further 30 days to discuss the debt, or for you to seek debt advice, before the business takes you to court. During that time you should discuss with the business how you can resolve the matter, ideally without going to court.

If you request more information in the Reply Form, the business must wait at least 30 days after it gives you that information before taking you to court.

Where can I find out more?

This Information Sheet is a summary of your rights and responsibilities under the Pre-Action Protocol for Debt Claims. Where a business and an individual disagree about a debt claim, the Protocol tells them what they should do before they go to court. If you want to know more, the full Protocol is available at: *https://www.justice.gov.uk/courts/procedure-rules/civil/protocol.*

Reply Form

C16-010   YOU HAVE 30 DAYS FROM THE DATE AT THE TOP OF THE EN-CLOSED LETTER TO FILL IN AND RETURN THIS FORM.

IF YOU DON'T, IT COULD RESULT IN COURT PROCEEDINGS.

If you have any questions or would like to discuss the debt, please call the business that sent you this form as soon as possible.

Full name: ....

Address and postcode: ....

Contact telephone numbers: ....

Email address: ....

Reference: ....

SECTION 1: Do you owe the debt?

Fill in one of the boxes in this section. Use more pages if you need to.

It is recommended that you get debt advice if you have any doubt about whether you owe the debt and whether you can pay it now, or if you want advice on any rights and protections you may have.

Box G below asks about debt advice.

☐ **BOX A**   **I agree I owe the debt.**   *Tick this box if you agree you owe the debt and agree the amount of the debt is correct.*   IF YOU WILL PAY THE DEBT, GO TO SECTION 2.   IF YOU NEED DEBT OR LEGAL ADVICE, GO TO SECTION 3.
☐ **BOX B**   **I owe some of the debt, but not all of it.**   *Tick this box if you agree you owe some of the debt, but not all of it, for example if you think too much interest has been added or you haven't been credited for payments you made in the past.*

The amount of debt I owe to you is £..........
Say how much you think you owe.
I don't owe any more than this because ....
Explain on a separate piece of paper why you don't owe all of the debt. Give as much detail as possible and provide copies of any supporting documents.
IF YOU WILL PAY THE PART OF THE DEBT YOU OWE, GO TO SECTION 2.
IF YOU NEED DEBT OR LEGAL ADVICE, GO TO SECTION 3.
OTHERWISE, GO TO SECTION 4.

☐ **BOX C**
I don't know whether I owe the debt.
Tick this box if you're not sure whether you owe the debt and/or you need help from a debt adviser to work out whether you should pay.
NOW GO TO SECTION 3.

☐ **BOX D**
I dispute the debt.
Tick this box if you don't owe the debt, for example because the debt should be paid by someone else, because you have already paid it, or because there is a legal problem with the credit agreement.
I dispute the debt because ....
Explain on a separate piece of paper why you dispute the debt. Give as much detail as possible and provide copies of any supporting documents.
NOW GO TO SECTION 4.

SECTION 2: How will you pay?

Only complete this section if you ticked Box A or Box B in Section 1 and you want to pay now.
The letter from the business will tell you how to pay. Keep a record of the payments you make.

☐ **BOX E**
I will pay what I owe now.
Tick this box if you agree that you owe all or part of the debt and you are able to pay what you owe now. You should pay using the payment details in the letter from the business. Keep a copy of any proof of payment you receive.

☐ **BOX F**
I will pay, but I need time to pay.
Tick this box if you agree that you owe all or part of the debt, but you can't pay right now.
If you offer to make repayments, you must be able to afford them. You should consider getting debt advice about how much you can afford to repay. If you are seeking debt advice, complete Section 3.
My proposals for repayment are ....
Explain on a separate piece of paper how you intend to pay the debt. Say how much you could pay now and how you will pay the remainder. For example, say how much you could pay each week, fortnight or month and when your first payment would be made.
I have provided a Financial Statement showing my current financial situation:
Yes ☐ No ☐
To help the business ensure you can afford your proposed repayments, fill out the Financial Statement that is attached to this form. You should also attach a copy of any budget or financial statement that a debt advice organisation has helped you prepare.

SECTION 3: Do you intend to get, or are you already getting, debt advice?

Only complete this section if you are getting debt advice about whether you owe the debt or whether you can afford to pay.

☐ **BOX G**
I am getting or intend to get debt advice.
I am getting advice from ....
....
Insert the name and contact details of the person or organisation giving you advice.
I am getting advice about ....
Explain on a separate piece of paper what you are getting advice about, for example whether you owe the debt or how you could pay.
I have an appointment with an adviser on ....
....
If you have an appointment with a debt adviser, give the appointment date and time.
I can't obtain advice within 30 days of returning this Reply Form because ....
If it will take you longer than 30 days to get debt advice, explain on a separate piece of paper the reason for the delay and when you expect advice will be available.
NOW COMPLETE SECTION 4.

SECTION 4: What documents are you sending with this form? What information do you need?

Complete the boxes below if you want to provide or get more information.

☐ **BOX H**
I have provided documents.
Tick this box if you want to provide documents about the debt, for example you might want to provide a letter showing you have an appointment for debt advice or a receipt showing you paid some of the debt.
I have enclosed the following documents ....
Describe on a separate piece of paper the documents you have provided and why they are important.

☐ **BOX I**
I need more documents or information.
Tick this box if you need more information, such as copies of documents you don't currently have.
I need a copy of ....
....
....
Additional documents or information that you might need could include:
- *A copy of the written contract for the debt*
- *A full statement of account, including details of all interest and charges included on the outstanding balance of the debt, explaining how they have been calculated, and any payments already made toward the debt*
- *A calculation of the interest claimed*
- *The annual or daily rate of interest*
- *A description of the nature and amount of any administrative charges included in the debt*
- *A copy of the notice of assignment of the debt*

Signature .... **Date**........../.........../..........
  Print name ....

Sign and date this Reply Form once you've filled it in. Then send it to the address given in the letter from the business.

Make sure you keep a copy of this form for reference in the future.

If your circumstances change, please update the business as soon as possible.

ANNEX 2

STANDARD FINANCIAL STATEMENT

C16-011

Name:
D.O.B.:
Application: ▣ Single ▣ Joint
Partner: (if applicable):
Partner D.O.B. (if applicable):
Address:

Contact/team name:
Agency:
Agency address:

Dependent children: Under 16   16-18:
Other dependants:
Number in household:
Number of vehicles in household:
Housing tenure: ▣ Owner ▣ Mortgage ▣ Tenant – private ▣ Tenant – social ▣ Living with parents ▣ Other

Membership code number:
Case reference number:
Date of statement
Date of review (if applicable):
Employment: ▣ Full-time ▣ Part-time ▣ Unemployed ▣ Not working due to illness / disability ▣ Self-employed ▣ Retired ▣ Carer ▣ Student ▣ Other

Please confirm you have considered (or discussed with an adviser) the use of any assets to make lump sum payments   Tick to confirm ✔ ☐

Partner's employment: ▣ Full-time ▣ Part-time ▣ Unemployed ▣ Not working due to illness / disability ▣ Self-employed ▣ Retired ▣ Carer ▣ Student ▣ Other

Overview	Amount (£)	Additional notes (e.g. reasons for debt, circumstances, temporary situations)
Total income		
Total outgoings		e.g. Made redundant in June 2014 and was out of work for 6 months
(Income – outgoings)		
(Savings contribution)		e.g. Communications and leisure: Mobile phone – client has multiple family members abroad
Debt admin fee (if applicable):		
Total available for priority creditors		
Total available for non-priority creditors		
Monthly Income		
Earnings		
Benefits and tax credits		
Pensions		
Other income		
Total income		
Monthly Outgoings: Fixed Costs		
Home and contents		
Utilities		
Water		
Care and health costs		
Transport and travel		
School costs		
Pensions and insurances		
Professional costs		
Other essential costs		
Total fixed costs		
Monthly Outgoings: Flexible Costs		
Communications and leisure		
Food and housekeeping		
Personal costs		
Total flexible costs		
Total monthly outgoings (fixed and flexible)		
Savings		

Please confirm that a monthly contribution to savings has been considered (or discussed with an adviser)   Tick to confirm ✔ ☐

Version 1.0

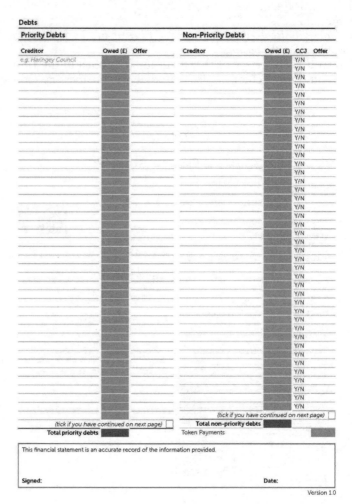

Summary version

Debts *(continued)*

Priority Debts			Non-Priority Debts			
Creditor	Owed (£)	Offer	Creditor	Owed (£)	CCJ	Offer
					Y/N	
					Y/N	
					Y/N	
					Y/N	
					Y/N	
					Y/N	
					Y/N	
					Y/N	
					Y/N	
					Y/N	
					Y/N	
					Y/N	
					Y/N	
					Y/N	
					Y/N	
					Y/N	
					Y/N	
					Y/N	
					Y/N	
					Y/N	
					Y/N	
					Y/N	
					Y/N	
					Y/N	
					Y/N	
					Y/N	
					Y/N	
					Y/N	
					Y/N	
					Y/N	
					Y/N	
					Y/N	
					Y/N	
Total priority debts			**Total non-priority debts**			

Version 1.0

Additional notes (e.g. reasons for debt, circumstances, temporary situations)

e.g. *Made redundant in June 2014 and was out of work for 6 months*

e.g. **Communications and leisure:** *Mobile phone – client has multiple family members abroad*

This financial statement is an accurate record of the information provided.

Signed: Date:

Version 1.0

Reproduced with permission of the Money Advice Service

VOLUME 2

SECTION 1   COURT GUIDES

SECTION 1A   CHANCERY GUIDE

Editorial introduction

In the first paragraph, after "correct as of", replace "1 November 2016." with:
25 April 2017.

CHAPTER 1 INTRODUCTION

ABOUT THIS GUIDE

Replace paragraph 1.11 with:
1.11 The aim of this Guide is to provide practical information and should be used in conjunc- tion with the Civil Procedure Rules (CPR). It is not the function of the Guide to summarise the CPR or the Practice Directions ("PD's"), nor should it be regarded as a substitute for them. However, there are a number of aspects of practice in the Chancery Division which differ from other courts and specialist jurisdictions due to the nature of the work carried out. The Rules, PD's, pre-action protocols and forms are [published by the Stationery Office] and are on the gov.uk website: *https://www.gov.uk/courts-tribunals/chancery-division-of-the-high-court* (and for forms *http://hmctsformfinder.justice.gov.uk/HMCTS/FormFinder.do*). In addition, a number of standard forms of order which are specifically for use in the Chancery Division, including case management directions, may be found at *http://hmctsformfinder.justice.gov.uk/HMCTS/GetForms.do?court_forms_num=&court_forms_title=&court_forms_category=Chancery.*

Replace paragraph 1.14 with:
1.14 Between the publication of the previous Guide in 2013 and of this Guide in 2016 there were major changes in procedure and practice. These included the cost management reforms to the CPR introduced by Jackson LJ, the changes introduced following the Chancery Modernisation Review ("CMR") published by Briggs LJ on 17th December 2013, the introduction of the CE-file on 1st October 2014 and of electronic filing on 16th November 2015, changes to the production and service of orders with effect from 2nd January 2015 and the changes to PD 2B, with effect from 6th April 2015, which removed most of the restrictions on the types of relief a Master might grant and permitted Masters to try Part 7 cases without the consent of the parties, thus making Chancery Masters' jurisdiction, subject to certain exceptions, very similar to that of the Judge. These changes are all covered in this Guide. There have also been many changes since this Guide came out in its original form. These have all been included in ongoing amendments to the Guide. The most recent among them, is the mandatory use of electronic filing for professional users of the court in all cases from 25th April 2017. This is a major change of great importance. Details are given in Chapter 6.

Replace paragraph 1.15 with:
1.15 The text of the Guide is published, together with other useful information concerning the administration of justice in the Chancery Division, on the.gov.uk website (*https://www.gov.uk/courts-tribunals/chancery-division-of-the-high-court*) and on the Judiciary website (*https://www.judiciary.gov.uk/*). The Guide will continue to be kept under review in the light of practical experience and of changes to the rules and PD's and amendments will be made on the website from time to time as necessary. References to amendments are listed on the front cover. The Guide is printed in the main procedural reference books. It is no longer printed separately in hard copy.

Chapter 2 Contact details

IN THE ROLLS BUILDING

THE JUDGES

Replace table with:

High Court Judges' Clerks

1A-3

Judge	Clerk	Telephone	Email
Chancellor of the High Court, the Rt Hon Sir Geoffrey Vos	Jessie Davidson, Clerk Adam David, SPS Vannina Ettori, Private/Legal Secretary		jessie.davidson@hmcts.gsi.gov.uk adam.davis@ejudiciary.gsi.gov.uk vannina.ettori@judiciary.gsi.gov.uk
Mr Justice Peter Smith	Supriya Saleem	7379	supriya.saleem@hmcts.gsi.gov.uk
Mr Justice Mann	Susan Woolley	7964	susan.woolley@hmcts.gsi.gov.uk
Mr Justice Warren	Amanda Collins	7260	amanda.collins@hmcts.gsi.gov.uk
Mr Justice Morgan	Heather Watson	6419	heather.watson@hmcts.gsi.gov.uk
Mr Justice Norris	Adham Harker	7073 1728	adham.harker@hmcts.gsi.gov.uk
Mr Justice Barling	Helen Trout	6675	helen.trout@hmcts.gsi.gov.uk
Mrs Justice Proudman	Amanda Collins	7260	amanda.collins@hmcts.gsi.gov.uk
Mr Justice Arnold	Pauline Drewett	7073 1789	pauline.drewett@hmcts.gsi.gov.uk
Mr Justice Roth	Jessie Davidson *(Based at*	7071 5694 *Competition*	jessie.davidson@hmcts.gsi.gov.uk *Appeal Tribunal)*
Mr Justice Newey	Cathy Johnson	7467	cathy.johnson@hmcts.gsi.gov.uk
Mr Justice Hildyard	Jasjit Marway	6039	jasjit.marway@hmcts.gsi.gov.uk
Mrs Justice Asplin	Chris Ellis	6589	chris.ellis@hmcts.gsi.gov.uk
Mr Justice Birss	Supriya Saleem	7379	supriya.saleem@hmcts.gsi.gov.uk
Mrs Justice Rose	Rebecca Sigrist	5694	rebecca.sigrist@hmcts.gsi.gov.uk
Mr Justice Nugee	Gary Clark	7200	gary.clark@hmcts.gsi.gov.uk
Mr Justice Snowden	Wendy Simpson	7073 0304	wendy.Simpson@hmcts.gsi.gov.uk
Mr Justice Henry Carr	Jas Kahlon	6339	jas.kahlon@hmcts.gsi.gov.uk
Mr Justice Marcus Smith	Steven Brilliant	7767	steven.brilliant@hmcts.gsi.gov.uk

IPEC

Replace table with:

Chancery Masters' Clerks

1A-6

Chief Master Marsh	Hearing room 2	Beth Gilligan	beth.gilligan@hmcts.gsi.gov.uk
Master Bowles	Hearing room 4	Frances Schwarzkopf	frances.schwarzkopf@hmcts.gsi.gov.uk

Master Price	Hearing room 1	Nichola Pierce	nichola.pierce@hmcts.gsi.gov.uk
Master Teverson	Hearing room 5	Sherrina Thomas	sherrina.thomas@hmcts.gsi.gov.uk
Master Clark	Hearing room 6	Mohammed Choudhury	mohammed.choudhury5@hmcts.gsi.gov.uk
Vacant	Hearing Room 3	Salim Patel	chancery.mastersappointments@hmcts.gsi.gov.uk

OUTSIDE LONDON

Replace with:

See Chapter 30 for the court addresses, telephone and email addresses of the courts at which **1A-21** there are regular Chancery sittings outside London.

CHAPTER 3 USERS COMMITTEES AND SUGGESTIONS FOR IMPROVEMENT

FINANCIAL LIST USERS' COMMITTEE

Replace paragraph 3.5 with:

3.5 This users' committee is a joint Chancery-Commercial Court enterprise, as the Financial **1A-26** List is composed of judges from both of those jurisdictions. The members of the committee include members from the Bar, solicitors, representatives from legal or financial professional associations, and general counsel or chief executive officers from financial institutions. Meetings are held twice a year and more often if necessary. Suggestions for points to be considered by the committee should be sent to the Secretary to the Committee, Vannina Ettori, at Vannina.ettori@judiciary.gsi.gov.uk.

Replace title with: **1A-31**

COURT USERS' COMMITTEES OUTSIDE LONDON: SEE CHAPTER 30

Delete paragraph 3.11.

CHAPTER 6 THE COURT FILE

CE-FILE AND ELECTRONIC FILING

Replace paragraph 6.1 with:

6.1 The Chancery Division in London has been using the new CE-File electronic court file **1A-44** since 1 October 2014. This means that the court does not hold a paper file for claims issued from that date. This has important practical consequences for dealing with the court. Under the Electronic Working pilot scheme court users may file documents electronically, direct to the court file, in all the Rolls Building Courts, including the Chancery Division. As from 25th April 2017, electronic filing is mandatory for professional court users in all cases, although not for litigants in person at present.

CE-FILE

Replace paragraph 6.3 with:

6.3 All claims issued are allocated a "new style" number. The Master with responsibility for **1A-45** each claim is allocated in rotation on a random basis and the claim form is stamped with the Master's name. Claims issued prior to 1st October 2014 ("Old Claims") were given a new style claim number in place of the existing number on the first occasion a document is filed after 30th September 2014. Old claims where no document has been filed after that date will retain their old number, with the Masters identified by a letter of the alphabet. The old claim number will not be recognised by CE-File.

Replace paragraph 6.5 with:

6.5 New claims are managed from the electronic file. All documents lodged with the court are held on the electronic file, and routine case management is generally carried out using that file unless the volume of documents makes it impractical. If paper copies are required by the court a direction will be given to lodge further paper copies, usually in the form of a bundle (see below). The parties may be asked on occasions to file a pdf version of long documents to assist the court.

Replace paragraph 6.6 with:

6.6 No paper file is maintained for new claims. Paper documents lodged with the court, after having been scanned to the file, are retained in day files for a period of 6 months. They will be available only in the event that scanning errors need to be corrected. They are destroyed at the end of the period.

Replace paragraph 6.7 with:

6.7 The only exception is original documents (see 6.18 below) which are required to be lodged with the court pursuant to an order or a provision of the CPR (such as original wills). Original documents are retained in a separate secure storage area. Original documents must be clearly marked as such with a front sheet marked in a font of not less than 14 point, as follows:

"**CLAIM NO. XXXXXX**
ORIGINAL DOCUMENT – NOT TO BE DESTROYED"

ELECTRONIC FILING

Replace paragraph 6.9 with:

1A-46 **6.9** The Electronic Working Pilot Scheme initially went live on 16th November 2015, enabling parties to commence proceedings and file documents online. As from 25th April 2017 it is mandatory for all professional court users to use the scheme. Therefore legal representatives must file all documents (apart from original documents), in all courts in the Rolls Building, using Electronic Working. This applies to commencing proceedings and to filing documents in existing cases. Litigants in person are encouraged to use e-filing wherever possible but they still have the option of filing documents in hard copy at present.

Replace paragraph 6.10 with:

6.10 Electronic Working is used to start, or continue, Part 7, Part 8 and Part 20 claims and pre-action applications. Also, other parties to proceedings are able to inspect electronically all documents on the file which are available to them under CPR 5.4B once they have been granted access to the system.

Replace paragraph 6.11 with:

6.11 Details of how the system works are set out in Practice Direction 51O and there is more information on the Government website *www.gov.uk/guidance/ce-file-system-information-and-support-advice*. There are considerable advantages both for court users and the court in this system being used. The system can be used 24 hours a day, every day, including out of normal court office hours and at weekends and bank holidays. The filing party will know at once, from an electronic confirmation, that the court has received the document and will subsequently receive further confirmation, after it has been reviewed by the court, that it has been accepted.

Replace paragraph 6.13 with:

6.13 It is important to note that where documents are filed and payment of a fee is not required the date and time of filing will be the date and time of issue for all claim forms and the date and time of filing for all other documents for the purposes of any direction under the CPR or of complying with a court order. Where a fee is required the date and time of filing will be deemed to be the date and time at which payment of the court fee is made using Electronic Working. Fees relating to any filing may be paid using the PBA system (details may be obtained from the PBA Support Team, telephone 01633 652125) FeeAccountPayments@hmcts.gsi.gov.uk; LiberataRecDD@justice.gsi.gov.uk; Liberata UK Ltd, PO Box 736, Newport, NP20 9FN; DX134282, Cleppa Park 2 or by credit or debit card.

Replace paragraph 6.15 with:

6.15 Parties filing documents using Electronic Working should not also file the documents by another means unless required to do so, for example bundles for applications hearings, directions hearings (including case and costs management) or trials.

Replace paragraph 6.18 with:

6.18 Where an original document, for example a will, is to be lodged it cannot be filed using electronic working but must be filed physically with the court. If an original document is required to be filed at the same time as issue of the claim form, the court will accept an electronic copy of the document but the original will or other document must then be lodged with the court within 48 hours.

Replace paragraph 6.19 with:

6.19 Users wishing to apply for a fee remission should contact the court initially.

ONLINE PUBLIC SEARCH

Replace paragraph 6.20 with:

1A-47 **6.20** Online public search went live in May 2016 and office copy request functionality in

August 2016. A court user registered as an "E-Filer" will automatically have access to this function and should use it where possible. A court user who is not an E-Filer, but wishes to use this function should register for an account on the Electronic Working website *www.ce-file.uk*. Once approved, parties will be able, upon payment of the relevant fee, to carry out a search of the Rolls Buildings Register of Claims as permitted under PD 5.4B and request office copies. A non-party may make a request for copies of documents to which they are entitled as set out in. PD 5.4C. In addition, in due course parties and nonparties will be able to inspect the electronic record on one of the terminals being installed in the Rolls Building.

OTHER COMMUNICATIONS WITH THE COURT

Replace paragraph 6.21 with:
   6.21 There have recently been some important changes in the use of emails to the court where **1A-48** electronic working is used. On 3 October 2016 PD51O was amended, as a step towards the increased use of electronic working by court users, and PD 5B (which enables parties to file certain documents by email and to use email to communicate with the court), was disapplied for all Rolls Building courts. the following sub-paragraph was added to paragraph 3.4 of PD51O:

Replace the second paragraph of para.6.22 with:
   This wording proved however to be unduly restrictive and has now been re-amended.

Replace the third paragraph of para.6.22 with:
   The new wording of paragraph 3.4, which came into effect on 1st April 2017, is as follows:
   (1)   The court may refuse to convert documents to PDF format where those documents were originally submitted by other means.
   (2)   In relation to any document required by the Rules, any Practice Direction or any order of the court to be filed, the court will not accept that document for filing if submitted by e-mail and any such document must be filed through Electronic Working (unless submitted on paper); but if a judge, Master or Registrar has requested or permitted the submission of such a document by email then it must be so submitted as well as being filed through Electronic Working (or on paper).

Replace paragraph 6.23 with:
   6.23 The effect of this amendment is that "submissions", that is all documents which are required by the rules or any practice direction to be filed on the court file, need to be filed using Electronic Working, but such documents may also to be sent via email if the judge, Master or Registrar requests or permits. The practice in the Chancery division should be as follows.

Replace paragraph 6.24 with:
   6.24 Normal day to day communications with the court, such as dealing with routine case management issues, do not generally need to be filed and will be accepted by email, as may documents such as skeleton arguments and chronologies which are submitted for any hearing or paper application.

Replace paragraph 6.25 with:
   6.25 If the court considers that an email (which is not in itself a submission – see paragraph 6.23 above) contains information that should be placed on the electronic file then the clerk will either file the email or will request the party to do so. The document filed will then be treated as a submission.

Replace paragraph 6.27 with:
   6.27 As from 25th April 2017 legal representatives must issue all claims and file all documents using Electronic Filing. Documents accepted in paper form will in general be restricted to hearing and trial bundles, bundles of authorities and original documents such as wills.

CHAPTER 14 JUDGES/MASTERS

INTRODUCTION: CHANGES IN JURISDICTION

Replace paragraph 14.2 with:
   14.2 Since April 2015, when PD 2B was amended, there is a greater overlap between the **1A-80** responsibilities of High Court Judges and Masters. The revision of PD2B removed most of the restrictions on the types of relief a Master may grant and Masters may try Part 7 cases without the consent of the parties. The main restriction in the CPR which remains concerns applications for freezing and search orders which are the exclusive preserve of High Court Judges. Applications for other types of interim injunction may be granted by a Master but in practice most interim injunctions are granted by High Court Judges in the Applications Court. Below is a summary of what Masters may or may not do. It should not be regarded as definitive. The full position is largely set out in CPR PD2B.

Add new paragraph 14.2.1:
14.2.1 MASTERS' JURISDICTION

1.	**Excluded claims:**
	Masters may not deal with:
	Claims in the Financial List
	Arbitration Appeals
	Other appeals
	Committal for contempt
	Claims in the Patents Court other than extensions of time, permission to serve out of the jurisdiction, security for costs and consent orders dealing with procedural matters. Masters may not approve settlements of the whole claim.
2.	**Excluded orders:**
	Masters may not make the following orders:
	Freezing orders
	Search orders
	Extended civil restraint orders
	Indemnity for costs out of the assets of a company in a derivative claim
	All Part 24 or strike out applications will be released to the Judge.
3.	**Non-excluded matters**
	Injunctions (typically in a Part 24 application in an IP claim but also in possession claims etc) Masters will not normally grant interim injunctions of the type granted in the applications court but have power to do so.
	Specific performance
	Declarations
	Rectification
	Approval of compromises
	Trustee approvals
	Variation of Trusts
	Beddoe orders
	Trials – Part 7 (including IP claims) and Part 8, and Shorter trials list
	Pre-action disclosure
	Norwich Pharmacal/Bankers Books
	Possession claims (including special procedure for dealing urgently with squatters)
	Land Charges Act
	Land Registration Act

Replace paragraph 14.3 with:

14.3 Other types of application, whether for case management, interim relief or disposal should normally be listed before a Master. If it is considered that exceptionally the application should be heard by a High Court Judge the Master should be requested to release it. Masters may (and should) deal with urgent applications before a trial including applications to vacate the trial date unless properly brought at a PTR.

CHAPTER 17 CASE AND COSTS MANAGEMENT

THE COSTS AND CASE MANAGEMENT CONFERENCE

Replace paragraph 17.17 with:

1A-117 **17.17** At the CCMC the court will normally deal with directions first and costs management afterwards. However the directions are likely to be informed by the budgets. The court will wish to form an overall view about proportionality taking into account the factors in CPR 44.3(5) and may wish to be addressed on this subject before considering the disputed budget phases. The court may not manage costs which have been incurred and the power to make comments about incurred costs is likely to be used sparingly. It is made clear in changes to Part 3 and 3E PD made in April 2017 that the court is approving or the parties are agreeing only the prospective costs. The result of costs budgeting should be a figure for each phase in respect of the future costs only. However, if the court considers that the incurred costs are outside the range of reasonable and proportionate costs it may proceed on the assumption that of such incurred costs only those which are reasonable and proportionate will be allowed on detailed assessment (see *Various Claimants v McAlpine http://www.bailii.org/ew/cases/EWHC/QB/2015/3543.html* at para 30).

CHAPTER 25 THE BANKRUPTCY AND COMPANIES COURTS

Add new paragraph 1A–226.1:

COURT-TO-COURT COMMUNICATIONS IN CROSS-BORDER INSOLVENCY CASES

25.30 There is increasing international recognition that communication between courts in dif- **1A-226.1** ferent jurisdictions may be of assistance in the efficient conduct of cross-border insolvency cases. Improved communication may lead to a co-ordinated approach between the courts and maximisation of benefit for all stakeholders of financially troubled enterprises.

25.31 There are, at present, three principal sets of guidelines for court-to-court communications which might be adopted, with appropriate modifications, in such cases. These are the American Law Institute/International Insolvency Institute Guidelines Applicable to Court-to-Court Communications in Cross-Border Cases; the EU Cross-Border Insolvency Court-to-Court Communications Guidelines; and The Judicial Insolvency Network Guidelines for Communication and Cooperation between Courts in Cross-Border Insolvency Matters. The ALI/III Guidelines are available at *https://www.iiiglobal.org/sites/default/files/media/_1000_Guidelines_English.pdf*. The EU Guidelines are available at *http://www.tri-leiden.eu/uploads/files/eu-cross-border-insolvency-court-to-court-cooperation-principlespdf.pdf*. The JIN Guidelines (with minor amendments for use in England and Wales) are available at *https://www.gov.uk/government/uploads/system/uploads/attachment_data/file/612376/JIN_Guidelines.pdf*.

25.32 In a cross-border insolvency case, the insolvency practitioner involved, together with any other interested parties, should consider, at an early stage in the proceedings, whether the Companies Court should be invited to adopt one of these sets of guidelines for use in the proceedings, with such modifications as the circumstances of the case may require.

CHAPTER 30 CHANCERY BUSINESS OUTSIDE LONDON

Add new paragraph 30.13: **1A-281**

Court Users' Committees

30.13 There are several Court Users' Committees relating to chancery work outside London, as follows:

The Northern Circuit Chancery Court Users' Committees and the North-Eastern Region Court Users' Committees: the Northern Region Chancery Court Users' Committee, which meets in Manchester; the Leeds Chancery and Mercantile Court Users' Committee; and the Newcastle Joint Chancery Mercantile and TCC Court Users' Committee. Each of these meets two or three times a year, and has a membership including judges, court staff, barristers and solicitors. The Vice-Chancellor of the County Palatine of Lancaster chairs these three Committees, and the Vice-Chancellor's clerk acts as secretary to each Committee. All communications should be to the clerk.

The Western Region, Wales and Midland Region Court Users' Committees: these committees normally meet three or four times per year. They have a membership including judges, court staff, barristers and solicitors.

Western Region: Judge McCahill QC chairs the committee in Bristol (or Mr Justice Newey when there), Mrs Liz Bodman acts as secretary. All communications should be addressed to her at Bristol Civil Justice Centre, 2 Redcliff Street, Bristol BS1 6GR.

Wales: Judge Jarman QC chairs the committee in Cardiff (or Mr Justice Newey when there), the diary manager, Annette Parsons acts as secretary. All communications should be addressed to her at Cardiff Civil Justice Centre, 2 Park Street, Cardiff CF1 1ET.

Midland Region: Judge Purle QC chairs the committee in Birmingham (or Mr Justice Newey when there), the Chancery Listing Officer acts as secretary. All communications should be addressed to her at Chancery Listing Section, Birmingham Civil Justice Centre, 33 Bull Street, Birmingham B4 6DS.

SECTION 1B   QUEEN'S BENCH GUIDE

QUEEN'S BENCH GUIDE

20.   LISTING BEFORE JUDGES

20.1   RESPONSIBILITY FOR LISTING

Replace paragraph 20.1.1 with:

1B-85   **20.1.1**   At the case management conference the Master will order a "trial window", i.e. a period of time within which the Queen's Bench Judges' Listing Officer (formerly known as the Clerk of the Lists) is to arrange for the trial to take place. The window may be a period defined by reference to certain named dates or months, or defined by reference to a stated Law Term. The trial window will be no longer than three months, unless for good reason the court considers that a longer trial window is required, in which case directions will be given for a trial window no longer than four months. The Master will not generally order a fixed trial date without first consulting the Listing Officer.

Replace paragraph 20.1.2 with:

   20.1.2   The Queen's Bench Judges Listing Office will then notify all parties of a listing appointment for a trial date or period within the trial window. The listing appointment will usually be about six weeks from the date the directions order is sealed, save in the case of claims in the Mesothelioma list, where the listing appointment will generally be about three weeks from the date the order is sealed. If parties have any queries in relation to the listing appointment they should contact Queen's Bench Judges Listing on qbjudgeslistingoffice@hmcts.gsi.gov.uk. The Listing Office will also generally agree to an agreed listing appointment date from the parties. Parties should notify any agreed date by email to qbjudgeslistingoffice@hmcts.gsi.gov.uk as soon as possible.

Replace paragraph 20.1.3 with:

   20.1.3   The Listing Officer is in general responsible for listing. All applications relating to listing should in the first instance be made to the Listing Officem. Any party dissatisfied with any decision by them may, on one day's notice to all other parties, apply to the Judge in charge of the relevant list. Any such application should be made within 7 days of the decision of the Listing Officer.

Replace paragraph 20.1.4 with:

   20.1.4   It should be emphasised that, once a Master has ordered that a trial should take place within a particular trial window, all listing matters are thenceforth under the control and supervision of the Judge in charge of the Queen's Bench Civil List or, where relevant, the Judge in charge of the Media and Communications List. It follows that any requested change to the trial window, whether by consent or otherwise, will not be dealt with by a Master, but will be considered by the Judge in charge of the Queen's Bench Civil List or, as appropriate, the Judge in charge of the Media and Communications List or by a judge nominated by them. Any practice that may have existed in the past of the parties simply placing a consent order providing for the change of trial window before a Master no longer obtains. Any application for such an order will simply be transferred by the Master to the Judge in charge of the Queen's Bench Civil List or, as appropriate, the Judge in charge of the Media and Communications List, for consideration by them or by a judge nominated by them. Accordingly, to avoid delay, any application, whether by consent or otherwise, to extend, or change a trial window of whatever duration as set by order of a Master or which will affect the choice of date within that period or the listing of a fixed trial must be lodged in the QB Listing office with a view to being considered by the relevant judge.

Replace paragraph 20.1.5 with:

   20.1.5   Parties must understand that merely because the diary commitments of witnesses (expert or otherwise) are such as apparently to preclude their attendance at a trial within the trial window ordered by a Master, this will not necessarily be treated as a reason for altering the trial window. When the non-availability of witnesses during the trial window is relied upon in support of an application to extend or alter the trial window, full details must be given of which witnesses are unavailable, why their evidence is important and what steps have been taken to overcome the problem, including why reception of the evidence by video-link may not be appropriate. Until this information is provided in sufficient detail the QB Listing Office will not forward the application for judicial consideration. Parties must also understand that, whilst efforts to accommodate the convenience of Counsel are made, that factor cannot be determinative of when a trial is listed.

20.3   THE JURY LIST

Replace paragraph 20.3.4 with:

1B-87   **20.3.4**   Furthermore, in substantial claims likely to take more than 10 days to try, the Master will probably have directed a pre-trial review to be heard. The Listing Officer will list the date for the PTR at the trial listing appointment.

Replace the first paragraph of para.20.3.7 with:

20.3.7 Applications for directions and other applications in jury actions within the Master's jurisdiction should firstly be made to a Master unless:

(1)   a listing appointment has been given for the arranging of a trial date or period, or

(2)   a date has been fixed or a period given for the trial.

20.4   THE NON-JURY LIST

Replace paragraph 20.4.5 with:

20.4.5 The arrangements for the listing appointment and for listing a trial date or trial period **1B-88** are set out in 20.1.2 and 20.1.3 above.

Delete paragraph 20.4.6.

Delete paragraph 20.4.7.

SECTION 2   SPECIALIST PROCEEDINGS

SECTION 2A   COMMERCIAL COURT

ADMIRALTY AND COMMERCIAL COURTS GUIDE

Replace the Table of Contents with:

A. PRELIMINARY

A1 THE PROCEDURAL FRAMEWORK

Replace paragraph A1.9 with:

2A-40   **A1.9** On 1 April 2009 the Commercial Court started an electronic working pilot scheme under PD Electronic Working Pilot Scheme. On 1 April 2010 the pilot scheme was replaced with the Electronic Working Scheme as set out in Practice Direction 5C. The Scheme may be used to start claims pursuant to Part 7, Part 8 and Part 20 and also Arbitration claims and Admiralty proceedings as appropriate in the Admiralty and Commercial Court . Full details of the scheme and the text of the Practice Direction can be found at Appendix 18. Information about the scheme can also be found on the Commercial Court website, *www.gov.uk/courts-tribunals/commercial-court.*

B. COMMENCEMENT, TRANSFER AND REMOVAL

B2 STARTING A CASE IN THE COMMERCIAL COURT

Replace paragraph B2.4 with:

2A-45   **B2.4** A request for the issue of a Part 7 or a Part 8 claim form may be made by fax at certain times when the Registry is closed to the public: PD58 2.2. The procedure is set out in Appendix 3.

Further details may be obtained from the Commercial Court website (*www.gov.uk/courts-tribunals/commercial-court*) or from the Registry. The fax number is 0870 761 7725.

F. Applications

F5 ORDINARY APPLICATIONS

Replace paragraph F5.5 with:
F5.5 Save in very short and simple cases, skeleton arguments must be provided by all parties. **2A-89** These must be lodged with the Listing Office and served on the advocates for all other parties to the application by 1 p.m. on the day before the date fixed for the hearing (i.e. the immediately preceding day). Advocates should note:
(1) The skeleton should include an estimate of the reading time likely to be required by the court and a suggested reading list.
(2) Skeletons should not without good reason be more than 15 pages (font minimum 11 point) in length.
(3) Guidelines on the preparation of skeleton arguments are set out in Part 1 of Appendix 9.

Replace paragraph F5.6 with:
F5.6 Thus for an application estimated for a half day or less and due to be heard on a Friday:
(i) the application bundle and case management bundle must be lodged by 1 p.m. on Wednesday; and
(ii) skeleton arguments must be lodged by 1 p.m. on Thursday.

H. Evidence for Trial

H1 WITNESSES OF FACT

PREPARATION AND FORM OF WITNESS STATEMENTS

Replace paragraph H1.1 with:
H1.1 Witness statements must comply with the requirements of PD32. The following points are **2A-103** also emphasised
(i) the function of a witness statement is to set out in writing the evidence in chief of the witness; as far as possible, therefore, the statement should be in the witness's own words;
(ii) it should be as concise as the circumstances of the case allow without omitting any significant matters;
(iii) it should not contain lengthy quotations from documents;
(iv) it is seldom necessary to exhibit documents to a witness statement;
(v) it should not engage in (legal or other) argument;
(vi) it must indicate which of the statements made in it are made from the witness's own knowledge and which are made on information or belief, giving the source for any statement made on information or belief;
(vii) it must contain a statement by the witness that he believes the matters stated in it are true; proceedings for contempt of court may be brought against a person if he makes, or causes to be made, a false statement in a witness statement without an honest belief in its truth: rule 32.14(1).
(viii) it must comply with any direction of the court about its length. Unless the court directs otherwise, witness statements should be no more than 30 pages in length.

J. Trial

J5 READING LISTS, AUTHORITIES AND TRIAL TIMETABLE

Replace paragraph J5.4 with:
J5.4 Cases which are unreported and which are also not included in the index of Judgments of **2A-111** the Commercial Court and Admiralty Court of England and Wales should normally only be cited where the advocate is ready to give an assurance that the transcript contains a statement of some relevant principle of law of which the substance, as distinct from some mere choice of phraseology, is not to be found in any judgment that has appeared in one of the general or specialised series of law reports. The index of Judgments of the Commercial Court and Admiralty Court of England and Wales can be found at *www.bailii.org*.

N.   Admiralty

N5   THE EARLY STAGES OF A COLLISION CLAIM

Add new paragraph N5.0:

2A-133   **N5.0**   Any party, or potential party, to a collision claim, who has in its control any electronic track data (as defined in rule 61.1(1)(m)[1]) recording the tracks of the vessels involved leading up to the collision, should have regard to Appendix 20 ('Electronic Track Data in Collision Claims'), which contains provisions relating to (i) the preservation, pre-action disclosure and inspection, and early disclosure and inspection, of electronic track data, and (ii) the case management of collision claims where electronic track data is available. (See also rule 61.4(4A) and PD61 §4.7.)

N7   ISSUE OF DOCUMENTS WHEN THE REGISTRY IS CLOSED

Replace paragraph N7.1 with:

2A-135   **N7.1**   When the Registry is closed (and only when it is closed) an Admiralty claim form may be issued on the following designated fax machine: 0870 761 7725 and only on that machine.

Replace paragraph N7.4 with:

   N7.4   When the Registry is closed (and only when it is closed) a notice requesting a caution against release may be filed on the following designated fax machine: 0870 761 7725 and only on that machine. This machine is manned 24 hours a day by court security staff (telephone 020 7947 6260).

N8   CASE MANAGEMENT

Replace paragraph N8.1 with:

2A-136   **N8.1**   The case management provisions of the Guide apply to Admiralty claims save that
   (i)   In Admiralty claims the case management provisions of the Guide are supplemented by PD61 § § 2.1-2.3 which make provision for the early classification and streaming of cases;
   (ii)   In a collision case the claimant should apply for a case management conference within 7 days after the last Collision Statement of Case is filed: PD61 §4.6;
   (iii)   In a limitation claim where the right to limit is not admitted and the claimant seeks a general limitation decree, the claimant must, within 7 days after the date of the filing of the defence of the defendant last served or the expiry of the time for doing so, apply to the Admiralty Registrar for a case management conference: PD61 § 10.7;
   (iv)   In a collision claim (PD61 §4.6) or a limitation claim a mandatory case management conference will normally take place on the first available date 5 weeks after the date when the claimant is required to take steps to fix a date for the case management conference;
   (v)   In a limitation claim, case management directions are initially given by the Registrar: PD61 § 10.8;
   (vi)   In the Admiralty Court, the Case Management Information Sheet should be in the form in Appendix 6 of this Guide but should also include the following questions
      1.   Do any of the issues contained in the List of Issues involve questions of navigation or other particular matters of an essentially Admiralty nature which require the trial to be before the Admiralty Judge?
      2.   Is the case suitable to be tried before a Deputy Judge nominated by the Admiralty Judge?
      3.   Do you consider that the court should sit with nautical or other assessors? If you intend to ask that the court sit with one or more assessors who is not a Trinity Master, please state the reasons for such an application.
   (vii)   In a collision claim where electronic track data is available the court will seek to adopt fast track procedures for the determination of issues of liability as part of its duty actively to manage cases in accordance with the overriding objective, which may include making one or more of the directions listed in PD61 §4.7: see also section N5.0 and Appendix 20 ('Electronic Track Data in Collision Claims');
   (viii) In a collision claim, the Case Management Information Sheet should also include the following question:
      4.   Do you or any other party have in their control electronic track data (as defined in rule 61.1(1)(m)[2]) recording the tracks of the vessels involved leading up to the collision? If so, would it be appropriate for the court to make one or more of the directions listed in PD61 §4.7 (or other similar directions)? Please state reasons.

---

[1] This reference should be to CPR 61.1(2)(m)
[2] This reference should be to CPR 61.1(2)(m)

P.   Miscellaneous

P2   INDEX OF DECISIONS OF THE COMMERCIAL AND ADMIRALTY COURTS

Replace paragraph P2.3 with:
P2.3 The index of Judgments of Commercial Court and Admiralty Court of England and **2A-154**
Wales is available to all Internet users and can be found at *www.bailii.org.*

Appendix 13

Pre-Trial Checklist

Replace the third paragraph with:
[**Note:** this checklist should normally be completed with the involvement of the advocate(s) **2A-171**
instructed for trial.]
1.   Have you completed preparation of trial bundles in accordance with Appendix 10 to the
     Commercial Court Guide?
2.   If not, when will the preparation of the trial bundles be completed?
3.   Which witnesses of fact do you intend to call?
4.   Which expert witness(es) do you intend to call (if directions for expert evidence have been
     given)?
5.   Will an interpreter be required for any witness and if so, have any necessary directions
     already been given?
6.   Have directions been given for any witness to give evidence by video link? If so, have all
     necessary arrangements been made?
7.   What are the advocates' confirmed estimates of (i) the minimum and maximum lengths of
     the trial (ii) the pre-reading time likely to be required for the judge? (A confirmed estimate
     of length signed by the advocates should be attached).
8.   What is your estimate of costs already incurred and to be incurred at trial for the purposes
     of section 46 of the Practice Direction supplementing CPR Part 43? (If the trial is not
     expected to last more than *one day* the estimate should be substantially in the form of a
     statement of costs as illustrated in Form H of the Schedule of Costs Forms annexed to the
     Practice Direction).

Appendix 14

Video Conferencing Guidance (Annex 3 to PD32)

Editorial note

Replace with:
The Video Conferencing Guidance contained in this Appendix reproduces the Guidance in An- **2A-172**
nex 3 of Practice Direction—Evidence, which can be found at: *http://www.justice.gov.uk/courts/
procedure-rules/civil/rules/pd_part32.*

Appendix 19

Guidance on practical steps for transferring cases to the Mercantile Courts

Replace the entry for 'London Mercantile Court' with:

London Mercantile Court   **2A-214**
020 7947 6826
E-mail: comct.listing@hmcourts-service.gsi.gov.uk

Add new "Appendix 20" at paragraph 2A–215:

Appendix 20

Electronic Track Data in Collision Claims

INTRODUCTION

1. In many collision cases, the tracks of the vessels involved leading up to the collision(s) are **2A-215**
captured electronically or digitally by, for example, ship or shore-based AIS, ECDIS, or voyage data

recorders (such track data, and any associated visual or audio recordings, being referred to herein as "Electronic Track Data"; see Rule 61.1(1)(m)[1]). The availability of such Electronic Track Data can greatly aid the quick and efficient disposal of disputes over liability for the collision.

2. Where such Electronic Track Data is available, it may therefore be possible, and desirable, to modify or dispense with various aspects of the normal procedure in a Collision Claim. (The normal procedure in a Collision Claim is set out in Rule 61.4,PD61 §§4.1-4.6, and Sections N.5, N.8, N.9 and N.14 of the Guide.)

PRESERVATION OF ELECTRONIC TRACK DATA

3. Electronic Track Data will almost certainly be of great importance in any Collision Claim in which liability might be in dispute. A party to an anticipated Collision Claim should therefore take all reasonable steps promptly to preserve and/or procure the original and/or copies of any Electronic Track Data in its control. (Rule 31.6(2)[2] provides that a party has a document "in his control" if (a) it is in his physical possession, (b) he has a right to possession of it, or (c) he has a right to inspect or take copies of it.)

PRE-ACTION DISCLOSURE & INSPECTION OF ELECTRONIC TRACK DATA

4. It is to be expected that the early disclosure, and provision or inspection, of Electronic Track Data will enable the rapid and cost-effective resolution of many disputes, or potential disputes, concerning liability for collisions without recourse to formal proceedings.

5. Therefore, each party to an anticipated Collision Claim will generally be expected to
a.   disclose to one another any Electronic Track Data, which is or has been in its control, and
b.   if each party has Electronic Track Data in its control, thereafter exchange copies of and/or permit reciprocal inspection of such Electronic Track Data,
during the course of pre-action correspondence. A failure by one party so to disclose, exchange copies of, or permit reciprocal inspection of, Electronic Track Data at the request of another party to an anticipated Collision Claim prior to the commencement of proceedings without good reason is likely to attract a costs sanction from the Court.

6. Furthermore, an application under Rule 31.16 by a person likely to be a party to a subsequent Collision Claim for mutual or reciprocal disclosure and/or inspection of Electronic Track Data by another person likely to be a party to that action before proceedings have started is likely to be considered favorably by the Court if each such person has Electronic Track Data in its control.

EARLY DISCLOSURE & INSPECTION OF ELECTRONIC TRACK DATA

7. Rule 61.4(4A) requires every party in a collision claim to give early disclosure of any electronic track data, which is or has been in their control, within either (a) 21 days after the defendant files their acknowledgment of service, or (b) where the defendant makes an unsuccessful application under Part 11, within 21 days after the defendant files their further acknowledgment of service. Where every party has electronic track data in its control, each party must provide copies, or permit inspection of, that electronic track data within 7 days of a request by another party to do so: Rule 61.4(4A).

8. The parties should then file at Court completed Collision Statements of Case in the usual way in accordance with Rule 61.4. The time limits set out in Rule 61.4 should not normally require extension because of the provision of Electronic Track Data pursuant to the paragraph above. (Rule 61.4 requires the parties to file at Court completed Collision Statements of Case (a) within 2 months after the defendant files his acknowledgment of service, or (b) where the defendant unsuccessfully applies under Part 11 to dispute the Court's jurisdiction, within 2 months after the defendant files his further acknowledgment of service.)

CASE MANAGEMENT WHEN ELECTRONIC TRACK DATA IS AVAILABLE

9. In accordance with PD61 §4.6, and paragraphs N8.1(ii) and (iv) of the Guide, the claimant should apply for a mandatory case management conference within 7 days after the last Collision Statement of Case is filed, which mandatory case management conference will normally take place on the first available date 5 weeks thereafter.

10. The availability of Electronic Track Data is likely to enable the Court to adopt fast track procedures for the determination of issues of liability in a Collision Claim. The Court will seek to adopt such fast track procedures as part of its duty actively to manage cases in accordance with the overriding objective, and will give due consideration to making one or more of the directions listed in PD61 §4.7. (See also paragraphs N8.1(vii), N9.1 and N14.1 of the Guide.)

11. The parties should give careful consideration to the possibility of adopting such (or other)

---

[1] This reference should be to CPR 61.1(2)(m)
[2] This reference should be to CPR 31.8(2)

fast track procedures when completing their case management information sheets prior to the case management conference: see paragraph N8.1(viii). Parties are reminded of their obligation to help the Court to further the overriding objective. While the Court will always be astute to manage each particular Collision Claim to meet the demands of justice and the overriding objective, in making directions for the proper management of the case, the Court will give due consideration to any agreement made by the parties designed to dispose of the claim in a swift and cost-efficient manner. (For example, reference is made to the Fast Track Procedure form of agreement prepared by the Admiralty Solicitors Group for use in Collision Claims where Electronic Track Data is available.)

ADDRESSES AND CONTACT DETAILS

Move 'Addresses and Contact Details' from paragraph 2A-215 to 2A-216 and replace details as follows:
The individual telephone and fax numbers are as follows:

2A-216

The Admiralty Marshal:
Tel: 020 7947 7111
Fax: 0870 761 7725

The Admiralty & Commercial Registry:
Tel: 020 7947 6112
Fax: 0870 761 7725
DX 160040 Strand 4

The Admiralty & Commercial Court Listing Office:
Tel: 020 7947 6826
DX 160040 Strand 4

The Secretary to the Commercial Court Committee:
Mr James Kelly
Tel: 020 7947 6826
DX 160040 Strand 4[1]

Fax number for the procedure undersections B3.11 and B4.4 of the Guide for the issue of claim forms when the Registry is closed: 0870 761 7725.

SECTION 2E ARBITRATION PROCEEDINGS

PART 62—ARBITRATION CLAIMS

I. Claims under the 1996 Act

Note

To the end of the paragraph, add:
Followed in *Cruz City 1 Mauritius Holdings v Unitech Ltd* [2014] EWHC 3704 (Comm); [2015] 1 **2E-13**
All E.R. (Comm) 305; [2015] 1 Lloyd's Rep. 191 and *Dtek Trading SA v Morozov* [2017] EWHC 94 (Comm); [2017] Bus. L.R. 628; [2017] 1 Lloyd's Rep. 126.

Arbitration Act 1996

Exercise of court's powers

Replace with:
In a case under s.10 of the 1950 Act it was held that the court had power to appoint a single **2E-137**
arbitrator in respect of two arbitrations, and it is highly desirable to do so to avoid the danger of inconsistent findings, where disputes involve interrelated and also separate issues of fact and law in both arbitrations (see *Abu Dhabi Gas Liquefaction Co Ltd v Eastern Bechtel Corp* [1982] Com.L.R. 215; [1982] 2 Lloyd's Rep. 425, CA). In *Shagang South-Asia (Hong Kong) Trading Co Ltd v Daewoo Logistics*

---

[1] The Secretary to the Commercial Court Committee is now Joseph Quinn. Contact details are unchanged.

[2015] EWHC 194 (Comm); [2015] 1 All E.R. (Comm) 545; [2015] 1 Lloyd's Rep. 504 Hamblen J held that where an arbitrator had been appointed without any attempt to follow the procedures set out in s.16(3) and without recourse to the court under this section, the appointment made was invalid. In *Silver Dry Bulk Co Ltd v Homer Hulbert Maritime Co Ltd* [2017] EWHC 44 (Comm) Males J held that the court had no power to make a direction under the Arbitration Act 1996 s.18(3) concerning the appointment of an arbitrator where an arbitration clause agreed between the parties had operated as intended, albeit that one of the parties had failed to cooperate; the clause had made provision for non-cooperation.

Add new paragraph 2E–149.1:

Disclosure in aid of application

2E-149.1   In *P v Q* [2017] EWHC 148 (Comm) Popplewell J held that an application for disclosure in support of an application under this section could only be granted where the removal application had a real prospect of success and the disclosure sought was strictly necessary to resolve it, and only in a wholly exceptional case would it be appropriate to grant disclosure of an arbitral tribunal's internal communications.

Add new paragraph 2E–197.1:

Orders against Third Parties

2E-197.1   The power of the Court to grant orders under ss.44(2)(b) and (c) is limited to orders against parties to the arbitration: *Cruz City 1 Mauritius Holdings v Unitech Ltd* [2014] EWHC 3704 (Comm); [2015] 1 All E.R. (Comm) 305; [2015] 1 Lloyd's Rep. 191 (Males J) and *Dtek Trading SA v Morozov* [2017] EWHC 94 (Comm); [2017] Bus. L.R. 628; [2017] 1 Lloyd's Rep. 126 (Sara Cockerill QC).

Note

Replace "Essar Oilfield Services v Norscot Rig Management Pvt [2016] EWHC 2361 (Comm)" with:

2E-230.1   *Essar Oilfield Services v Norscot Rig Management Pvt Ltd* [2016] EWHC 2361 (Comm); [2016] 2 Lloyd's Rep. 481

"On the ground of serious irregularity"

In the fifth paragraph, replace "Essar Oilfield Services v Norscot Rig Management Pvt [2016] EWHC 2361 (Comm)" with:

2E-262   *Essar Oilfield Services v Norscot Rig Management Pvt Ltd* [2016] EWHC 2361 (Comm); [2016] 2 Lloyd's Rep. 481

Replace the ninth paragraph with:

Where an award is challenged on the ground that the serious irregularity affecting the award in that it was obtained by fraud (s.68(2)(g)), it is not enough to show that one party inadvertently misled the other, however carelessly (*Cuflet Chartering v Carousel Shipping Co Ltd (The Marie H)* [2001] 1 All E.R. (Comm) 398; [2001] 1 Lloyd's Rep 707 (Moore-Bick J)). The relevant law was explained in *Double K Oil & Products Ltd v Neste Oil OYJ* [2010] EWHC 3380 (Comm); [2010] 1 Lloyd's Rep. 141 (Blair J). It will normally be necessary to satisfy the court that some form of reprehensible or unconscionable conduct has contributed in a substantial way to the obtaining of the award. A challenge to an award cannot, therefore, be made on the grounds of an innocent failure to give proper disclosure (*Profilati Italia SRL v PaineWebber Inc* [2001] 1 Lloyd's Rep. 715; [2001] All E.R. (Comm) 1065; [2001] CLC 672 (Moore-Bick J)), or the innocent production of false evidence (*Elektrim SA v Vivendi Universal SA* [2007] EWHC 11 (Comm); [2007] 2 All E.R. (Comm) 365; [2007] 1 Lloyd's Rep. 693 (Aikens J)). A failure to disclose correspondence that related to a significant issue in the case which was misleading and deliberate and had led to substantial injustice was however sufficient: *Celtic Bioenergy Ltd v Knowles Ltd* [2017] EWHC 472 (TCC), Jefford J. Where the allegation is fraud in the production of evidence, the onus is on the applicant to make good the allegation by cogent evidence (*Cuflet* at [12], *Elektrim* at [81]). The applicant must show that the new evidence relied upon to demonstrate the fraud was not available at the time of the arbitration and would have had an important influence on the result (*Westacre Investments Inc v Jugoimport-SDPR Holding Co Ltd* [2000] Q.B. 288, CA; [1999] 3 All E.R. 864; [1999] 2 Lloyd's Rep. 65; see also *Thyssen Canada Ltd v Mariana Maritime SA* [2005] EWHC 219 (Comm); [2005] 1 Lloyd's Rep. 640 (Cooke J), and *DDT Trucks of North America Ltd v DDT Holdings Ltd* [2007] EWHC 1542 (Comm); [2007] 2 Lloyd's Rep 213 (Cooke J) *Chantiers de L'Atlantique SA v Gaztransport & Technigaz SAS* [2011] EWHC 3383 (Comm) (Flaux J)). The latter point (important influence on the result) takes effect within the statutory requirement that the irregularity has caused or will cause substantial injustice to the applicant (*Thyssen* at [65]).

Subsection (5)

At the end of the paragraph, replace "Dowans Holdings SA v Tanzania Electric Supply Co Ltd [2011] EWHC 1957 (Comm); [2012] 1 All E.R. (Comm) 820; [2011] 2 Lloyd's Rep. 475 and IPCO (Nigeria) v Nigerian National Petroleum [2015] EWCA Civ 1144; [2016] 1 Lloyd's Rep. 5 where the Court of Appeal considered the circumstances in which a decision to adjourn an enforcement decision in the face of allegations of fraud will be made. In a supplementary judgment [2015] EWCA Civ 1145; [2016] 1 Lloyd's Rep. 36 the Court rejected the argument that there was no application for security on the facts and the court therefore lacked jurisdiction." with:

    Dowans Holdings SA v Tanzania Electric Supply Co Ltd [2011] EWHC 1957 (Comm); [2012] 1 All **2E-361** E.R. (Comm) 820; [2011] 2 Lloyd's Rep. 475.

After the first paragraph, add new paragraph:

    In *IPCO (Nigeria) v Nigerian National Petroleum Corp* [2017] UKSC 16; [2017] 1 W.L.R. 970 the Supreme Court held that that in contrast with s.103(5) of the Arbitration Act 1996, which specifically provided that security might be ordered where there was an adjournment within its terms, there was nothing in s.103(3) which provided that an enforcing court could make the decision of an issue raised under that subsection conditional on the provision of security in respect of the award; that a delay in making a decision was only in the nature of "an adjournment" for the purposes of s.103(5) where a court adjourned its decision on enforcement while an application for setting aside or suspension of the award was pending in a foreign court. It followed that once the Court of Appeal had held that the issue whether fraud was an answer to enforcement should be decided by the English courts, there ceased to be an "adjournment" for the purposes of s.103(5). Accordingly, the order for security was not within the scope of any jurisdiction or power conferred by s.103; it could not be justified by reference to general English procedural rules, since the conditions for recognition and enforcement set out in the New York Convention constituted a code relating to security for an award when the issue was enforcement or adjournment, and the code excluded requiring security for an award in the face of a properly arguable challenge. Followed: *Eastern European Engineering Ltd v Vijay Construction (Proprietary) Ltd* [2017] EWHC 797 (Comm), Andrew Baker J.

SECTION 2F   INTELLECTUAL PROPERTY PROCEEDINGS

Part 63—Intellectual Property Claims

I. Patents and Registered Designs

Add new paragraph 2F–12.1:

When Comptroller should decline to deal in favour of the High Court

    In *NGPOD Global Ltd v Aspirate N Go Ltd* [2016] EWHC 3124 (Pat), Mann J heard an appeal **2F-12.1** from a decision of a UKIPO hearing officer in the context of entitlement proceedings. The defendant had by an application principally under s.37(8) of the Patents Act 1977 invited the hearing officer to decline to hear the entitlement claim, and to direct that it be heard in the High Court. The hearing officer refused the defendant's application; Mann J heard the appeal from that refusal.

    The judge cited Warren J's review of the factors going to the assessment under s.37(8), set out in *Luxim Corp v Ceravision Ltd* [2007] EWHC 1624 (Ch); [2007] R.P.C. 33. In NGPOD, Mann J summarised them as follows (with parenthetical references to paragraphs in *Luxim*):

(a)   The fact that a different costs regime applied before the hearing officer—in the court full adverse costs orders could be made against a losing party, but far lower adverse costs are payable in the IPO (para.49).

(b)   Technical issues—ordinarily a hearing officer would be equipped to deal with those (para.55(a), implicitly adopting the submissions of counsel).

(c)   Factual issues unrelated to technical issues. "Factual issues unrelated to technical issues: these are bread-and-butter matters for a judge. Of themselves, they may not merit a referral to the court. But the issues may be seen to be sufficiently complex to merit a transfer, especially, I would observe, if findings of fraud or breach of fiduciary duty are to be found against a party or a witness, a factor which, whilst not by itself conclusive, one might normally expect to be more appropriate for a judge" (para.55(b)).

(d)   Patent law issues—normally the hearing officer would be expected to deal with those (para.55(c)).

(e)   Non-patent law issues—these would normally be regarded as the province of the judge, but that did not mean that any case which involved such an issue would be more properly dealt with by a judge. This struck Warren J as an important factor (para.55(d)).

(f)   The test was not whether a matter could be described as "highly complex"; nor was the jurisdiction one which should be exercised cautiously, or with great caution or sparingly (para.65).

(g)   All relevant factors must be weighed in the balance (para.66).

In light of a review of the relevant factors, Mann J upheld the appeal, and directed that—particularly in light of the complexity of the issues in the case—the case should be heard by the High Court.

V.   Intellectual Property Enterprise Court

Sub-rule (2)

Replace the first paragraph with:

2F-17.13.2   The particulars must state whether the pre-action steps therein set out have been complied with. This is not a requirement to comply, but merely to state whether or not a party has complied. This affects the timing of any defence. There would not appear to be any reason why a party's compliance (or failure to comply) may not also be taken into account when considering the question of costs in the usual way.

SECTION 2FA   FINANCIAL LIST

PART 63A—FINANCIAL LIST

Editorial introduction

To the end of the first paragraph, add:

2FA-1.1   From June 2017, the Financial List will form part of the new Business and Property Courts that act as a single umbrella for business specialist courts across England and Wales.

The objectives of the Financial List

Replace the second paragraph with:

2FA-1.2   The Judiciary's website dedicated to the Financial List also explains that the Financial List compliments arbitration and mediation, working together harmoniously to enrich dispute resolution. Further, that the initiative is part of a continuing response of commercial parties selecting English Law and UK dispute resolution to "ensure a business-relevant law", which requires "keeping up to date with the business field". The Lord Chief Justice Lord Thomas of Cwmgiedd expressed similar sentiments in the 2016 Mansion House speech. The speech confirmed the introduction of a Standing International Forum of Commercial Courts, which will unite specialist commercial courts across the world. The objective is to develop better ways of upholding the rule of law in international markets and commerce. It is anticipated that the first meeting of the Forum will be held in London in May 2017.

Financial List claims

In the second paragraph, after "on public information,", replace "an estimated 25 cases have been issued or transferred into the Financial List, with seven cases leading to judgment although certain cases are now subject to appeal." with:

2FA-2.1   over 30 cases have been issued or transferred into the Financial List.

In the fifth paragraph (beginning with "Mr Justice Blair handed down"), after "The Court of Appeal dismissed an appeal from the judgment in December 2016", add:
(see *Banco Santander Totta SA v Companhia Carris De Ferro De Lisboa SA* [2016] EWCA Civ 1267). The Court of Appeal decision also disapproved of the decision in *Dexia Crediop SpA v Comune di Prato* [2015] EWHC 1746 (Comm).

From the start of the seventh paragraph, delete "When Financial List claims start to lead to a wider body of published judgments, it should provide further clarification on the types of cases that are suitable for determination in the Financial List.".

Replace the eighth paragraph with:
The Judiciary intends to use the Claims Information Form to be completed by claimants issuing Financial List claims to gather statistics on Financial List Claims to improve the Financial List

(Financial List Guide at para.10.2). The Judiciary may also publish this information to provide guidance to users. In the interim, parties have the opportunity to raise queries by writing to the Financial List Users' Committee (Committee), which will provide a forum in which the High Court will listen and respond to matters raised by litigators and others concerned with the financial markets (Financial List Guide at para.4.1). Anyone having views concerning the improvement of financial markets litigation is invited to make his or her views known to the Committee, preferably through the relevant professional representative on the Committee or its secretary. The Committee held its first meeting in early 2016 and held its second meeting in early 2017. The dates for future meetings, when fixed, will be published on the Financial List website. The matters discussed at the meetings included the types of cases suitable for determination using the Financial Markets Test Case Scheme introduced under Practice Direction 51M and ensuring the expedited determination of Financial List claims. The introduction of the Committee reflects the Judiciary's commitment to listen to users so as to improve the Financial List where possible. An aim endorsed by the comments of the Lord Chief Justice Lord Thomas, who has been at the vanguard of the Financial List, at the official launch event on 20 October 2015 who explained that the procedure would be kept under review and that "I do hope this initial experiment will work and we will try and improve it wherever possible" (reported at (2015) 6 LS Gaz, 26 Oct.). Similarly, Mr Justice Blair in a speech to the Commercial Litigators Forum in November 2016, noted that the Users Committee meetings are not closed, and users and potential uses of the List will be welcome to attend to provide feedback.

Effect of rule

The Financial List judges

Replace the first paragraph with:

2FA-5.1

The Financial List bridges the expertise of the judges sitting in the Chancery Division and Commercial Court. With the Chancellor and the Judge in Charge of the Commercial Court jointly responsible for appointing Financial List judges from the Chancery Division or Commercial Court to hear a particular case. As well as the head of the two Courts, the Financial List judges then comprise up to five judges from the Chancery Division and up to five judges from the Commercial Court. The number and identity of the judges nominated for the Financial List is likely to change from time to time, in accordance with demand and to respect other judicial responsibilities.

Delete "Mr Justice Flaux;".

SECTION 3   OTHER PROCEEDINGS

SECTION 3A   HOUSING

Protection from Eviction Act 1977

Excluded tenancies and licences

Replace s.3A(1)(a) with:

3A-77

(a)   the council of a county, county borough, district or London Borough, the Common Council of the City of London, the Council of the Isles of Scilly, the Inner London Education Authority, a fire and rescue authority created by an order under section 4A of the Fire and Rescue Services Act 2004, the London Fire and Emergency Planning Authority, a joint authority within the meaning of the Local Government Act 1985 or a residuary body within the meaning of that Act;

Note

To the end of the paragraph, add:

3A-78

Subsection (8)(a) amended by the Policing and Crime Act 2017 Sch.1(2) para.39, with effect from 3 April 2017.

Rent Act 1977

Protected tenants and tenancies

To the end of the last paragraph, add:

3A-92   and *Watts v Stewart* [2016] EWCA Civ 1247, 8 December 2016.

Landlord's interest belonging to local authority, etc.

Replace s.14(1) with:

3A-142   (1)   A tenancy shall not be a protected tenancy at any time when the interest of the landlord under that tenancy belongs to—

    (a)   the council of a county or county borough;

    (b)   the council of a district or, in the application of this Act to the Isles of Scilly, the Council of the Isles of Scilly;

   (bb) the Broads Authority;

   (bc) a National Park Authority;

    (c)   the council of a London borough or the Common Council of the City of London;

   (ca) [...]

  (caa) a police authority established under section 3 of the Police Act 1996;

 (caaa) [...]

  (cba) [...]

  (cbb) an economic prosperity board established under section 88 of the Local Democracy, Economic Development and Construction Act 2009;

  (cbc) a combined authority established under section 103 of that Act;

  (cb) a joint authority established by Part IV of the Local Government Act 1985;

  (cc) the London Fire and Emergency Planning Authority;

  (cd) a fire and rescue authority created by an order under section 4A of the Fire and Rescue Services Act 2004;

   (d) the English new towns residuary body;

   (e) a development corporation established by an order made, or having effect as if made, under the New Towns Act 1981; or

   (f) [...]

   (g) an urban development corporation within the meaning of Part XVI of the Local Government, Planning and Land Act 1980;

  (ga) a Mayoral development corporation;

   (h) a housing action trust established under Part III of the Housing Act 1988;

   (i) the Residuary Body of Wales (Corff Gweddilliol Cymru);

nor shall a person at any time be a statutory tenant of a dwelling-house if the interest of his immediate landlord would belong at that time to any of those bodies.

Note

To the end of the paragraph, add:

3A-143   ; and the Policing and Crime Act 2017 Sch.1 para.38, with effect from 3 April 2017.

Housing Act 1985

Replace s.4(1)(e) with:

OTHER AUTHORITIES AND BODIES

Other descriptions of authority

(e) "local authority" means a county, county borough, district or **3A-317** London borough council, the Common Council of the City of London or the Council of the Isles of Scilly, in sections 43, 44 and 232 includes the Broads Authority, in sections 438, 441, 442, 443, and 458 includes the Broads Authority, a joint authority established by Part IV of the Local Government Act 1985, an economic prosperity board, a combined authority, a fire and rescue authority created by an order under section 4A of the Fire and Rescue Services Act 2004, and the London Fire and Emergency Planning Authority, and in sections 45(2)(b), 50(2), 51(6), 80(1), 157(1), 171(2), 573(1), paragraph 2(1) of Schedule 1, grounds 7 and 12 in Schedule 2, ground 5 in Schedule 3, paragraph 7(1) of Schedule 4, paragraph 5(1)(b) of Schedule 5 and Schedule 16 includes the Broads Authority, a police and crime commissioner, [...] a joint authority established by Part IV of the Local Government Act 1985, an economic prosperity board, a combined authority, a fire and rescue authority created by an order under section 4A of the Fire and Rescue Services Act 2004, and the London Fire and Emergency Planning Authority.

Note

To the end of the paragraph, add:
; and the Policing and Crime Act 2017 Sch.1 para.49, with effect from 3 April 2017. **3A-318**

The tenant condition

In the first paragraph, after "(the Housing Act 1985 s.93).", add:
There are two parts to the question of what amounts to occupation of a dwelling as an only or **3A-342** principal home, namely (a) does the person in question occupy the dwelling as a home and (b) if so, does he or she occupy it as his or her only or principal home? (*Dove v Havering LBC* [2017] EWCA Civ 156; 22 March 2017.)

Note

After the first paragraph, add new paragraph:
The amendments made by the Localism Act 2011 only apply in respect of tenancies where the **3A-395.2** secure tenant referred to in s.90(1) died on or after 1 April 2012.

Persons qualified to succeed tenant in England

After the first paragraph, add new paragraph:
ECHR Article 8 may provide a defence to a possession claim for an occupant who falls outside **3A-395.6** the categories of persons qualified to succeed, but see *Thurrock BC v West* [2012] EWCA Civ 1435; [2013] H.L.R. 5 and *Holley v Hillingdon LBC* [2016] EWCA Civ 1052, 1 November 2016. In the latter case, Briggs LJ stated that local authorities usually seek eviction as a proportionate means of achieving a legitimate aim because they will thereby vindicate their own unencumbered property rights, and be able to comply with their duties in relation to the distribution and management of scarce social housing stock. He continued: "[An occupant] seeking to rely on article 8 will need to demonstrate a minimum length of residence in order to show that the property in question is their home, so that article 8 is engaged. Secondly, the period of residence, however long, will not on its own be sufficient to found an article 8 proportionality defence in the second succession context because, if it would, then it is hard to see how the English statutory prohibition of second succession could be compatible with the convention" (para.15).

Persons qualified to succeed tenant

To the end of the first paragraph, add:

3A-402   The purpose of imposing the twelve-month condition is that a reasonably long period of living together might be taken to demonstrate the same element of permanence and constancy in the relevant relationship. That aim is legitimate. It does not breach ECHR Article 14 (*R. (Turley) v Wandsworth LBC* [2017] EWCA Civ 189; 24 March 2017).

Housing Act 1988

3A-953   *Replace paragraph 12(2) of Sch.1 with:*

SECTION 1

SCHEDULE 1

Tenancies Which Cannot be Assured Tenancies

Part I

The Tenancies

Local authority tenancies etc.

(2)   The following are local authorities for the purposes of sub-paragraph (1)(a) above—
  (a)   the council of a county, county borough, district or London borough;
  (b)   the Common Council of the City of London;
  (c)   the Council of the Isles of Scilly;
  (d)   the Broads Authority;
  (da) a National Park authority;
  (e)   the Inner London Education Authority; and
  (ea) a fire and rescue authority created by an order under section 4A of the Fire and Rescue Services Act 2004;
  (f)   a joint authority, within the meaning of the Local Government Act 1985.
  (g)   a police authority established under section 3 of the Police Act 1964.

Note

To the end of the paragraph, add:

3A-958   ; and the Policing and Crime Act 2017 Sch.1 para.58, with effect from 3 April 2017.

Housing Act 1996

Introductory tenancies

To the end of the fourth paragraph (beginning with "Landlords may only bring introductory tenancies"), add

3A-1070   As there is no prescribed form for a s.128 notice, the starting point is whether the document or documents relied on can reasonably be described as a notice. To do so, they have to give the tenant notice of the intended proceedings in compliance with s.128(1). To comply with the section the notice must contain the other information which s.128 prescribes. There is nothing in s.128 which limits the notice to a single page or a single document. No such restriction can be spelt out of the statute. It is therefore a question of objective fact in every case whether the documents relied on do or do not form part of the notice. (*Islington LBC v Dyer* [2017] EWCA Civ 150; 22 March 2017, where, looked at objectively, two documents functioned together as the notice for the purposes of s.128 even though only one of them was in fact called the 'Notice'.)

They are satisfied that the accommodation is suitable (s.193(7F))

Replace the second paragraph with:

3A-1373   The Order also sets out the circumstances in which a private rented sector offer is not to be regarded as suitable. For comments on the inter-relationship between the duty to secure that accommodation which is suitable is available and the public sector equality duty under Equality Act 2010 s.149, see *Hackney LBC v Haque* [2017] EWCA Civ 4, 17 January 2017.

Housing Act 2004

Replace s.212 with:

PART 6

OTHER PROVISIONS ABOUT HOUSING

CHAPTER 4

TENANCY DEPOSIT SCHEMES

Tenancy deposit schemes

212.—(1) The appropriate national authority must make arrangements for **3A-1612** securing that one or more tenancy deposit schemes are available for the purpose of safeguarding tenancy deposits paid in connection with shorthold tenancies.

(2) For the purposes of this Chapter a "tenancy deposit scheme" is a scheme which—

    (a) is made for the purpose of safeguarding tenancy deposits paid in connection with shorthold tenancies and facilitating the resolution of disputes arising in connection with such deposits, and

    (b) complies with the requirements of Schedule 10.

(3) Arrangements under subsection (1) must be arrangements made with any body or person under which the body or person ("the scheme administrator") undertakes to establish and maintain a tenancy deposit scheme of a description specified in the arrangements.

(4) The appropriate national authority may—

    (a) give financial assistance to the scheme administrator;

    (b) make payments to the scheme administrator (otherwise than as financial assistance) in pursuance of arrangements under subsection (1).

(5) The appropriate national authority may, in such manner and on such terms as it thinks fit, guarantee the discharge of any financial obligation incurred by the scheme administrator in connection with arrangements under subsection (1).

(6) Arrangements under subsection (1) must require the scheme administrator to give the appropriate national authority, in such manner and at such times as it may specify, such information and facilities for obtaining information as it may specify.

(6A) For further provision about what must be included in the arrangements, see section 212A.

(7) The appropriate national authority may make regulations conferring or imposing—

    (a) on scheme administrators, or

    (b) on scheme administrators of any description specified in the regulations,

such powers or duties in connection with arrangements under subsection (1) as are so specified.

(8) In this Chapter—

    "authorised", in relation to a tenancy deposit scheme, means that the scheme is in force in accordance with arrangements under subsection (1);

    "custodial scheme" and "insurance scheme" have the meaning given by paragraph 1(2) and (3) of Schedule 10);

    "money" means money in the form of cash or otherwise;

    "shorthold tenancy" means an assured shorthold tenancy within the meaning of Chapter 2 of Part 1 of the Housing Act 1988 (c. 50);

    "tenancy deposit", in relation to a shorthold tenancy, means any money intended to be held (by the landlord or otherwise) as security for—

(a)   the performance of any obligations of the tenant, or

(b)   the discharge of any liability of his, arising under or in connection with the tenancy.

(9)   In this Chapter—

(a)   references to a landlord or landlords in relation to any shorthold tenancy or tenancies include references to a person or persons acting on his or their behalf in relation to the tenancy or tenancies, and

(b)   references to a tenancy deposit being held in accordance with a scheme include, in the case of a custodial scheme, references to an amount representing the deposit being held in accordance with the scheme.

Note

After the first paragraph, add new paragraph:

3A-1613   Subsection (6A) inserted by the Housing and Planning Act 2016 s.128(2), with effect from 6 April 2017.

Add new paragraphs 3A-1617.1 and 3A-1617.2:

Provision of information to local authorities

3A-1617.1   212A.—(1)   Arrangements under section 212(1) made by the Secretary of State must require the scheme administrator—

(a)   to give a local housing authority in England any specified information that they request, or

(b)   to provide facilities for the sharing of specified information with a local housing authority in England.

(2)   In subsection (1) "specified information" means information, of a description specified in the arrangements, that relates to a tenancy of premises in the local housing authority's area.

(3)   Arrangements made by virtue of this section may make the requirement to provide information or facilities to a local housing authority conditional on the payment of a fee.

(4)   Arrangements made by virtue of this section may include supplementary provision, for example about—

(a)   the form or manner in which any information is to be provided,

(b)   the time or times at which it is to be provided, and

(c)   the notification of anyone to whom the information relates.

(5)   Information obtained by a local housing authority by virtue of this section may be used only—

(a)   for a purpose connected with the exercise of the authority's functions under any of Parts 1 to 4 in relation to any premises, or

(b)   for the purpose of investigating whether an offence has been committed under any of those Parts in relation to any premises.

(6)   Information obtained by a local housing authority by virtue of this section may be supplied to a person providing services to the authority for a purpose listed in subsection (5).

(7)   The Secretary of State may by regulations amend the list of purposes in subsection (5).

3A-1617.2   Note —Inserted by the Housing and Planning Act 2016 s.128(3), with effect from 6 April 2017.

Anti-social Behaviour, Crime and Policing Act 2014

Sentences for breach of injunctions

Replace the first paragraph with:

3A-1782   An application for an order committing a person to prison or attaching a power of arrest to an injunction or remanding a person pursuant to Part 1 of the Anti-social Behaviour, Crime and Polic-ing Act 2014 may be listed before a district judge (Practice Direction 2B—Allocation of Cases to Levels of Judiciary para.8.3). Any sentence imposed for breach of an injunction should reflect the culpability of the offender and the harm caused by the particular breach. In *Wolverhampton CC v Green* [2017] EWHC 96 (QB), 20 January 2017, Holroyde J stated (at para.19), "When determining the appropriate sanction for an admitted breach of injunction of this kind, the court has a number of objectives. First, the sanction is intended to ensure compliance in the future with the court's order. Secondly, it is intended to protect the public who would be affected by future breaches and who have been affected by past breaches. Thirdly, it is intended as a punishment to those who have breached the order, to bring home to them the seriousness of breaching a court's injunction." (Sentences of four months and three months detention in a young offender institution imposed for breach of an injunction preventing car cruising.)

After the first paragraph, add new paragraph:
Guidance as to the appropriate range of sentence can be gleaned from cases decided under Housing Act 1996 s.153A which this Act replaced.

SECTION 3B   BUSINESS TENANCIES

Landlord and Tenant Act 1927

Introduction

In the second paragraph, after "substantially reduced to take account of the uncertainty.", add:
In *Car Giant Ltd v Hammersmith and Fulham LBC* [2017] EWHC 197 (TCC) the cost of the **3B-67.1** limited works actually carried out by the landlord was the best evidence of diminution of the value of the reversion. The landlord was unable to recover the cost of carrying out the remaining repairs as it had not put forward any evidence to show that it intended to undertake those works, nor that its reversion had diminished by an amount equivalent to their cost.

Landlord and Tenant Act 1954

"tenant's request"

Replace with:
Section 26 does not apply where (i) the landlord has already served a s.25 notice; (ii) the tenant **3B-139** has already given notice to quit; (iii) or the tenant has already given a s.27 notice to avoid continu-ance under the Act. The exercise by a landlord of its break right allowed a tenant validly to request a new tenancy, which commenced before the original expiry date of the lease. In such circumstances the proviso in s.26(2) does not apply. The proviso to s.26 was designed to ensure that a tenant can-not bring a lease to an end early by applying for a new lease to commence before the expiry of the contractual term. However, this did not apply where the original lease had been brought to an end earlier than the term expiry date by the landlord's own actions (*Fast Drinks Ltd v Cetyl International Group Inc* [2016] EWHC 3501 (QB)).

If there are joint tenants, all must join in the request, unless they are partners (see s.41A). The request must be served upon the competent landlord or the landlord's authorised agent and set out the tenant's proposals as to the new tenancy. The request brings the existing tenancy to an end, but an interim continuation tenancy then comes into being (s.26(2)). Within two months of receipt the landlord may give a counter-notice stating that the grant of a new tenancy will be opposed on one of the s.30 grounds. Failure to give a counternotice during the prescribed period prevents the landlord form opposing the grant of a new tenancy. There is no prescribed form for a landlord's counter-notice. As to contents, see *Marks (Morris) v British Waterways Board* [1963] 1 W.L.R. 1008; [1963] 3 All E.R. 28, CA.

"rent"

Replace the last paragraph with:
The High Court was entitled to refuse to admit fresh evidence on an appeal about a new rent. **3B-207** The fact that the relevant date for the purposes of determining the terms of the new tenancy was the appeal date rather than the trial date did not mean that the court had little alternative but to admit fresh evidence. (*Clear Call Ltd v Central London Investments Ltd* [2016] EWCA Civ 1231; *Davy's of London (Wine Merchants) Ltd v City of London Corp* [2004] EWHC 2224 (Ch) distinguished.)

Interpretation

Replace s.69(1) with:

3B-289   (1)   In this Act the following expressions have the meanings hereby assigned to them respectively, that is to say—

"agricultural holding" has the same meaning as in the Agricultural Holdings Act 1986;

"development corporation" has the same meaning as in the New Towns Act 1946;

"farm business tenancy" has the same meaning as in the Agricultural Tenancies Act 1995;

"local authority" means any local authority within the meaning of the Town and Country Planning Act 1990, any National Park authority, the Broads Authority[, the London Fire and Emergency Planning Authority, a joint authority established by Part 4 of the Local Government Act 1985, an economic prosperity board established under section 88 of the Local Democracy, Economic Development and Construction Act 2009, a combined authority established under section 103 of that Act or a fire and rescue authority created by an order under section 4A of the Fire and Rescue Services Act 2004;]

"mortgage" includes a charge or lien and "mortgagor" and "mortgagee" shall be construed accordingly;

"notice to quit" means a notice to terminate a tenancy (whether a periodical tenancy or a tenancy for a term of years certain) given in accordance with the provisions (whether express or implied) of that tenancy;

"repairs" includes any work of maintenance, decoration or restoration, and references to repairing, to keeping or yielding up in repair and to state of repair shall be construed accordingly;

"statutory undertakers" has the same meaning as in the Town and Country Planning Act 1971;

"tenancy" means a tenancy created either immediately or derivatively out of the freehold, whether by a lease or underlease, by an agreement for a lease or underlease or by a tenancy agreement or in pursuance of any enactment (including this Act), but does not include a mortgage term or any interest arising in favour of a mortgagor by his attorning tenant to his mortgagee, and references to the granting of a tenancy and to demised property shall be construed accordingly;

"terms", in relation to a tenancy, includes conditions.

Note

To the end of the paragraph, add:
3B-290   ; and the Policing and Crime Act 2017 Sch.1 para.15, with effect from 3 April 2017.

SECTION 3C   CONTEMPT OF COURT

C. Contempt of Court Act 1981

Add new paragraph 3C–70.1:

Source of information
3C-70.1   The scope of s.10 was examined in *Hourani v Thomson* [2017] EWHC 173 (QB), 6 February 2017, unrep. (Warby J), where an individual brought a claim against several defendants for libel and harassment and against one other defendant (D) for harassment only, in respect of their al-

leged roles in a campaign involving street demonstrations, online publications, and the distribution of stickers promoting the impression that C had been involved in a serious crime. D did not dispute his engagement in the activities of which C complained but pleaded a statutory defence provided by s.1(3) of the Protection from Harassment Act 1997. It was conceded that D was not acting of his own initiative, but had been engaged to do so and funded by others unknown (X). By application under CPR r.18.1, C sought the identity of X and information about D's dealings with them. In resisting this application (made to the trial judge) D submitted that the order sought would represent an unjustified interference with the rights to source protection under s.10 of the 1981 Act and under Article 10 of the Convention. The judge dismissed C's application, holding that the disclosure order sought would not represent a justified interference with those rights in s.10 as it was not "necessary" within the meaning of that section. On the question whether X were "the source of information" within s.10 the judge rejected C's submission that they were not because they were not "journalistic sources" engaged in the reporting of matters of public interest in good faith. The judge ruled that the word "source" should be given its ordinary meaning as it would be unsatisfactory for the court to adopt an approach to the meaning of the word which distinguished between different categories or classes of person who, as a matter of fact, provide information to others with a view to that information being published to the public or a section of the public; such an approach would tend to undermine legal certainty (para.33).

Suspension of order

Replace with:

3C-91   CPR r.81.29(1) states that the court making the committal order may also order that its execution will be suspended for such period or on such terms or conditions as it may specify. Section 14(1) requires the "period of committal", by which is meant the term of imprisonment, to be for a fixed term not exceeding two years. Where the effect of an order suspending the committal order is that the period of suspension exceeds two years there is no infringement of s.14(1), as that provision neither defines nor confines the period and terms of suspension of the committal order; *Griffin v Griffin* [2000] 2 F.L.R. 44, CA; *Christie v Birmingham City Council* [2016] EWCA Civ 1339, 14 December 2016, CA, unrep. See further Vol.1 para.81.29.1.

SECTION 3E   INSOLVENCY PROCEEDINGS

Insolvency proceedings

Replace the first paragraph with:

3E-21.3   The substantive law relating to insolvency is found primarily in the Insolvency Act 1986 (as amended) and the Insolvency Rules 1986 (as amended) (SI 1986/1925). With effect from 6 April 2017, the Insolvency Rules 1986 will be replaced by the Insolvency (England and Wales) Rules 2016 (SI 2016/1024), which were laid before Parliament on 25 October 2016. For transitional provisions see Sch.2 to the 2016 rules. Note in particular Sch.2 para.14(1), which provides:

> "Where an application to court is filed or a petition is presented under the Act or under the 1986 Rules before the commencement date and the court remains seised of that application or petition on the commencement date, the 1986 rules continue to apply to that application or petition."

For the purposes of this edition dual references are included. See too the Insolvency (England and Wales) (Amendment) Rules 2017 (SI 2017/366) and the Insolvency (England and Wales) Rules 2016 (Consequential Amendments and Savings) Rules 2017 (SI 2017/369). The law governing the insolvency of partnerships is to be found in the Insolvent Partnerships Order 1994 (SI 1994/2421) as amended (see most recently the amendments effected by the Deregulation Act 2015 and Small Business, Enterprise and Employment Act 2015 (Consequential Amendments) (Savings) Regulations 2017 (SI 2017/540) Sch.2, paras 2 to 11) and that governing the insolvency of limited liability partnerships may be found in the Limited Liability Partnerships Act 2000 and related secondary legislation (in particular the Limited Liability Partnerships Regulations 2001 (SI 2001/1090)). The administration of the estates of deceased insolvent individuals is governed by the Administration of Insolvent Estates of Deceased Persons Order 1986 (SI 1986/1999), as most recently amended by the Deregulation Act 2015 and Small Business, Enterprise and Employment Act 2015 (Consequential Amendments) (Savings) Regulations 2017 (SI 2017/540) Sch.2 para.1.

SECTION 3F PERSONAL INJURY

Damages Act 1996

The Lord Chancellor's discount rate

3F-41
Replace the first paragraph with:
    The *Damages (Personal Injury) Order 2017 (SI 2017/206)*. In force from *20 March 2017*. On 27 February 2017, under power provided by s.1 of the Damages Act 1996, the Lord Chancellor announced the modification of the personal injury discount rate for compensation for future financial loss. The modification is set out in the Damages (Personal Injury) Order 2017. From 1 March 2017 the discount rate will be minus 0.75 per cent (-0.75%). The previous rate which had been in force since 2001 was 2.5 per cent (2.5%).

Replace the second paragraph with:
    In practice the manner in which practitioners approach the calculation of future pecuniary loss in a straightforward case making use of the applicable percentage rate is to consult the applicable percentage discount rate column within the Ogden tables, at the row representing the period of time over which the loss will occur. That provides a multiplier for the loss which takes into account normal likelihood of death (other than where there is a particular raised chance of death over and above normal mortality levels) and takes into account the accelerated or reduced recovery due to the investment grown or loss arising from the rate set by the SI on the lump sum whilst drawing down on the capital over the number of years specified as the loss period.

Replace the fourth paragraph with:
    Prior to the announcement of the original 2.5 per cent rate in 2001 (later varied in 2017 as noted above) by the Lord Chancellor the prevailing rate was set by common law in the absence of any order under s.1. In *Wells v Wells; Thomas v Brighton Health Authority; Page v Sheerness Steel Co Plc* [1999] 1 A.C. 345 the House of Lords set a guideline rate of 3 per cent based on the average rate of return of Index Linked Government Securities, the House stressing that it was not in their view appropriate to assume a higher rate based on a premise that injured parties will invest in more hazardous forms of investment, per Lord Steyn:
        "The premise that plaintiffs, who have perhaps been very seriously injured, are in the same position as ordinary investors is not one that I can accept. Such plaintiffs have not chosen to invest: the tort and its consequences compel them to do so. For plaintiffs an investment in equities is inherently risky, notably in regard to the timing of the investment...
        Typically, by investing in equities an ordinary investor takes a calculated risk which he can bear in order to improve his financial position. On the other hand, the typical plaintiff requires the return from an award of damages to provide the necessities of life. For such a plaintiff it is not possible to cut back on medical and nursing care as well as other essential services. His objective must be to ensure that the damages awarded do not run out. It is money that he cannot afford to lose ... It is therefore unrealistic to treat such a plaintiff as an ordinary investor. It seems to me entirely reasonable for such a plaintiff to be cautious and conservative ... it seems to me difficult to say that an investment in index-linked securities by plaintiffs would be unreasonable."

In the fifth paragraph (beginning with "The analysis of the underlying principles"), replace "a 2.5 per cent" with:
    different rate in 2001 and again in 2017

Replace the sixth paragraph with:
    The *Damages (Personal Injury) Order 2017 (SI 2017/206)*, in force from *20 March 2017* sets the "discount rate" which the courts had to take into account when awarding damages for future pecuniary loss in personal injury cases, under s.1 of the Damages Act 1996. Its predecessor from 2001 onwards was the Damages (Personal Injury) Order 2001 (SI 2001/2301). Prior to the making of this Order the rate in use was fixed by Common Law at 3 per cent following the case of *Wells v Wells; Thomas v Brighton Health Authority; Page v Sheerness Steel Co Plc* [1999] 1 A.C. 345; [1998] 3 All E.R. 481 HL. The 2001 Order sets the rate at 2.5 per cent with effect from 28 June 2001.

Basis for the Lord Chancellor's decision to set the rate

3F-42 *Add new sub-heading under the main heading for this paragraph:*

The 2.5% rate from 28 June 2001 to 19 March 2017

Add new paragraph 3F–42.1:

3F-42.1 *The -0.75% rate from 20 March 2017–*The Lord Chancellor gave the following reasons for setting the discount rate at -0.75% from 20 March 2017:

"*Discount rate: statement placed by The Rt Hon Elizabeth Truss MP, Lord Chancellor, in the libraries of the Houses of Parliament on 27 February 2017*

1. As Lord Chancellor, I have power pursuant to section 1 of the Damages Act 1996 from time to time to set the discount rate applied to personal injury awards covering future pecuniary losses. In November 2010 my predecessors began a review of the discount rate for personal injury damages awards. On 27 January this year I indicated my intention to complete the review in February 2017.

2. In the course of my review, I have considered all the material available to me, including the responses to a Ministry of Justice public consultation in 2012, the report of an expert panel in 2015 (which reached majority and minority conclusions) and the responses of statutory consultees, HM Treasury and the Government Actuary. The process of review has been lengthy, and extraordinarily thorough. That process reflects the complexity and importance of the subject matter.

3. This statement sets out the decision I have reached as a result of this exercise and a summary of my reasons for that decision. I am also separately publishing today the Response to the 2012 public consultation.

Decision

4. I have concluded that a discount rate of minus 0.75% is the appropriate rate.

Reasons

5. I emphasise at the outset that the approach to the exercise of setting the discount rate is inevitably relatively broad brush. It is not a simple arithmetical exercise leading to a single, correct answer. It involves making judgements at various stages of the consideration of the issues, some of which are finely balanced and some of which involve making predictions about the future which are inherently uncertain.

6. I have noted the object of the award of damages set out by the House of Lords in *Wells v Wells* [1999] 1 A.C. 345, per Lord Hope of Craighead (page 390A-B): "... the object of the award of damages for future expenditure is to place the injured party as nearly as possible in the same financial position he or she would have been in but for the accident. The aim is to award such a sum of money as will amount to no more, and at the same time no less, than the net loss ..."

7. I have approached the setting of the discount rate on the basis that the governing principle is as identified by Lord Hope in that case: "[The discount rate] is the rate of interest to be expected where the investment is without risk, there being no question about the availability of the money when the investor requires repayment of the capital and there being no question of loss due to inflation."

8. The principles in *Wells v Wells* [1999] 1 A.C. 345 lead me to base the discount rate on the investment portfolio that offers the least risk to investors in protecting an award of damages against inflation and against market risk. I take the view that a portfolio that contains 100% index-linked gilts (ILGs) best meets this criterion at the current time. A portfolio of ILGs, comprising stocks spread across a range of redemption dates guarantees the investor an inflation-adjusted income, known with certainty at the time of the award. Basing the discount rate on the real redemption yield of ILGs is consistent with the approach taken by the House of Lords in *Wells v Wells* and by the then Lord Chancellor, Lord Irvine, when he last set the rate in the Damages (Personal Injury) Order 2001 (S.I. 2001/2301).

9. I am aware that issues have been raised as to whether ILGs (or a portfolio containing 100% ILGs) continues to represent a realistic or the appropriate basis for arriving at the discount rate, in part because changed economic circumstances have had an impact on the demand for ILGs. In particular, the case has been made by a number of respondents to the consultation exercises that it might be more appropriate and realistic to use a 'mixed portfolio' approach (in which other securities feature). I acknowledge that those arguments have some merit. However, I am not persuaded by them. I consider that a faithful application of the principles in *Wells v Wells* leads to the 100% ILGs approach as the best way, in the current markets, of ensuring that there is "no question about the availability of the money when the investor requires repayment of the capital and there being no question of loss due to inflation." The mixed portfolio approach in contrast runs counter to these principles by requiring the assumption by the investor of a greater degree of risk.

10. have specifically considered whether the 100% ILGs approach might create different risks such as the risk of not being able to meet unexpected capital needs. I recognise that point. However, I consider that those risks should be capable of effective management and that they are outweighed by the risks associated with the 'mixed portfolio' approach.

11. In a statement laid before Parliament on 27 July 2001, Lord Irvine recommended that the approach to setting the discount rate should respect the following general principles, which I have adopted.

    a. There should be a single, fixed rate to cover all cases. This accords with the solution adopted by the House of Lords in Wells v Wells. It eliminates argument about the applicable rate at court and avoids the complexity and extra costs that a formula would entail.

b. The rate should be one which is easy for all parties and their lawyers to apply in practice and which reflects the fact that the rate is bound to be applied in a range of different circumstances over a period of time. Given the uncertainties and imprecisions involved in the process of setting the discount rate, a rounded rate is preferable. Accordingly, I have decided to round to the nearest 0.25%. Ogden tables, applied by the courts to adjust awards according to a given discount rate, are currently published for rates at intervals of 0.5%. However, they can readily and swiftly be adapted to an intermediate rate.

12. In his 2001 decision, Lord Irvine obtained a discount rate by taking the average gross real redemption yields on ILGs across all maturity dates. He averaged real yield over the previous three years and rounded after making allowances for various factors. Lord Irvine noted that Lord Hope in Wells v Wells had regard to an average of gross redemption yields on ILGs with more than five years to maturity. Lord Irvine decided, however, to include all stocks in his calculations on the basis that some claimants, whose losses extend over periods of about 5 years or less, would have to purchase all or most of their ILGs in this category of stock. However, real yields on ILGs vary according to the maturity dates of stocks. I consider that it is the real yields of long- dated stocks that should be given more weighting when setting the discount rate according to real ILGs yields. This is because awards intended to cover the longest periods are most sensitive to any discrepancy between the discount rate set and the real yield obtained at the date of the award. Indeed, many awards are for the long term, quite often decades.

13. To weight long term stocks in a simple and transparent way, I have taken a simple average of gross real redemption yields across all ILGs and, in line with Wells v Wells, have excluded stocks with less than five years to maturity. This is not to deny the need for some or, indeed, all claimants to receive an income in the first few years of their award but to account, in a simple way, for the effect that short-dated stocks can have on real redemption yield as a representative discount rate for claimants as a whole. The real yield data on which I have obtained an average are those published by the Debt Management Office (DMO).

14. Regarding the period over which the real redemption yield is averaged, I have followed the majority view from Wells v Wells and the practice adopted by Lord Irvine in 2001, namely to average over the three years to a convenient date (in this instance, 30 December, the last trading day of 2016). I note that real yields have witnessed steady decline since 2001 and there may be a case for changing the averaging period to limit the influence of historical trends. However, I am reluctant to depart from earlier practice on this occasion.

15. The three year simple average gross real redemption yield on ILGs is minus 0.83% as of 30 December 2016 excluding ILGs with less than 5 years to maturity. As noted above, it would be appropriate to round this figure to acknowledge the inherent uncertainties and imprecisions involved in setting a representative discount rate and I am persuaded that rounding to the nearest 0.25% points is adequate. This would lead to a discount rate of minus 0.75%. The only reason to round down to minus 1.00% would be to account for claimant costs, in particular taxation and management fees. However, the case for such adjustment is not strong and has weakened in recent years. Because of the steady issuance of new ILGs with lower coupons (and, therefore lower taxation), it is not unreasonable that an adjustment for tax should be lower now than when Lord Irvine determined the discount rate in 2001; and investment management costs are relatively modest for ILGs.

16. For all of these reasons, I have decided that the discount rate should be minus 0.75%.

The Rt Hon Elizabeth Truss MP Lord Chancellor, 27 February 2017"

3F-43 *Change title of paragraph 3F–43:*

Court's discretion to depart from the Lord Chancellor's discount rate

Add new paragraph 3F–43A:

Controversy over the discount rate from March 2017 and subsequent consultation

3F-43A Following criticism in the media by insurance industry and defendant lawyers about the impact of the changed rate upon multipliers in personal injury claims such that the revised values of such claims would be expected to increases very significantly, a consultation was launched by the Lord Chancellor on 30 March 2016 details of which can be found at *https://consult.justice.gov.uk/digital-communications/personal-injury-discount-rate/*.

For examples of criticisms and of discussion in the media at the time in relation to the impact of the changed rate see, e.g.:

http://www.blmlaw.com/discountrate and

http://www.devereuxchambers.co.uk/resources/blog/personal-injury/view/the-discount-rate-whatever-next.

The scope of the consultation was described as follows:

"This consultation forms part of the review of the framework under which the personal injury discount rate is set.

The paper considers possibilities for how, when and by whom the discount rate should be set, but does not make specific proposals.

The core issues examined in the consultation paper are:

- what principles should guide how the rate is set?
- how often should the rate be set?
- who should set the discount rate?

The paper also considers whether sufficient use is being made of periodical payment orders. The consultation is aimed at people and organisations with an interest in personal injury claims and damages in the UK."

SECTION 3G   THE DATA PROTECTION ACT 1998

INTRODUCTION

Replace the first paragraph with:

3G-1 The Data Protection Act ("the Act" or "DPA") was passed to implement Directive 95/46 of 24 October 1995 on the protection of individuals with regard to the processing of personal data and the free movement of such data ("Directive 95/46"). It repealed the Data Protection Act 1984 which had been passed to enable the UK to ratify the Convention for the Protection of Individuals with regard to automatic processing of Personal Data ("Treaty 108"). Directive 95/46 will be replaced by the General Data Protection Regulation (Reg.2016/679) and the accompanying Directive applicable to personal data in the criminal justice system (Dir.2016/680). Both instruments were approved in April 2016, and will be operational by 25 May 2018. The UK Government confirmed on 24 October 2016 that the legislation would become applicable in the UK. The UK courts have referred to the Directive, Treaty 108 and the Convention Rights under the European Convention on Human Rights and Fundamental Freedoms, particularly art.8, in interpreting cases on the Act. In case law since the Act came into force the courts have tended to consider the tort of misuse of private information and rights under art.8 in conjunction with the Act. The CJEU has increasingly referred to the European Union Charter of Fundamental Rights when considering data protection cases. Further specific rights in relation to telecommunications services and electronic marketing are contained in the Privacy and Electronic Communications (EC Directive) Regulations 2003 (see para.3G-17). That Directive has been under review. On 20 January 2017 the Commission issued a proposal for a regulation to replace the Directive. Retention of personal data derived from public telecommunications services was mandated by Directive 2006/24 EC. That directive was ruled to be invalid by the CJEU in April 2014 because it breaches Articles 7 and 8 of the EU Charter of Fundamental Rights, in joined cases C-293/12 and C-594/12. The UK has enacted the Data Retention and Investigatory Powers Act 2014 (DRIPA) to replace its earlier legislation. DRIPA is currently subject to legal challenge in the UK courts. The Court of Appeal referred questions on the law to the CJEU in April 2016. In case C-203/15 the CJEU held that the provisions were not compatible with arts 7, 8, 11 and 52(1) of the Charter Rights.

Data Protection Act 1998

Exemptions

To the end of the first paragraph, add:

3G-11 In *Dawson-Damer v Taylor Wessing LLP* [2017] EWCA Civ 74 the court held that the exemption is limited to a claim of LPP in respect of proceedings under UK law.

Editorial note

Replace the first paragraph with:

3G-13 "Disproportionate effort"—*R. (Lord) v SSHD* held s.8(2)(a) cannot justify withholding information in the form in which the data subject would otherwise be entitled to receive it para.155. The term was considered in *Dawson-Damer v Taylor Wessing LLP* [2017] EWCA Civ 74 and *Ittihadieh v 5-11 Cheyne Gardens RTM Co Ltd* [2017] EWCA Civ 121 and *Deer v Oxford University* [2017] EWCA Civ 121. The final view of the Court of Appeal was that s.8(2) does not apply to the obligation to carry out a search in order to respond to a subject access request. Nevertheless the implied obligation to search is limited to a reasonable and proportionate search applying the general principle of proportionality.

Editorial note

3G-21

After the sixth paragraph (beginning with "In Abayomi Sofola v Lloyds TSB Bank"), add new paragraph:
   In *Axon v Ministry of Defence* [2016] EWHC 787 (QB) Nichol J considered the possibility that an employer could be vicariously liable for a disclosure made by a "rogue" employee, although on the facts of the case no such liability arose.

The eighth principle

3G-62.0.24

At the end of the paragraph, replace "has been subject to criticism and subsequent revision. However in May the EU authorised the signing of an EU/US agreement on data protection in law enforcement exchanges (Decision 8505/16) which may resolve some areas of difficulty. The final authorisation has not been given for this replacement arrangement but is expected by the end of 2016." with:
   was subject to criticism and subsequent revision. However the agreement was successfully concluded and on 12 July 2016 the European Commission made an adequacy determination on the basis of the Shield (c/2016/4176). In May the EU authorised the signing of an EU/US agreement on data protection in law enforcement exchanges (Decision 8505/16) (the Umbrella Agreement) which resolved a further area of tension in transatlantic data exchange.

SECTION 3H   CONSUMER CREDIT AND CONSUMER LAW

Consumer Credit Act 1974

Form and content of agreements

3H-84

Add new paragraph at end:
   See *Home Credit Slovakia AS v Biroova* (C-42/15) EU:C:2016:842. This case concerned Directive 2008/48/EC on the interpretation of the expressions "on paper" and "durable medium"–required information. This was a reference to the Third Chamber of the Court to interpret the meaning of Art.10(1) and (2) of the directive.

Unfair relationships

3H-329

Add new paragraph at end:
   See *Nelmes v NRAM Plc* [2016] EWCA Civ 491. This case concerned a portfolio of buy to let properties where it was found that non-disclosure of a procuration fee (brokers commission) amounted to a breach of s.140A thereby requiring that commission to be credited back to the borrower by the lender.

Package Travel, Package Holidays and Package Tours Regulations 1992

"Proper performance of the contract"

3H-865

Add new paragraph at end:
   See *Wood v TUI Travel Plc (t/a First Choice)* [2017] EWCA Civ 11. Although the claimants failed to establish a breach of reg.15 in this case they went on to succeed under s.4(2) of the Supply of Goods and Services Act 1982 for breach of the implied term as to satisfactory quality. See note at para.3H-764.1+.

Consumer Rights Act 2015

Replace Part 1 of the Arrangement of Sections with:

ARRANGEMENT OF SECTIONS

PART 1

CONSUMER CONTRACTS FOR GOODS, DIGITAL CONTENT AND SERVICES

CHAPTER 1

INTRODUCTION

Replace s.48 with the following, and add para.3H–1058.1:

Part 1

Consumer Contracts for Goods, Digital Content and Services

Chapter 4

Services

What services contracts are covered?

Contracts covered by this Chapter

48.—(1)   This Chapter applies to a contract for a trader to supply a service to **3H-1058** a consumer.

(2)   That does not include a contract of employment or apprenticeship.

(3)   In relation to Scotland, this Chapter does not apply to a gratuitous contract.

(3A)   This Chapter does not apply to anything that is governed by Regulation (EU) No 181/2011 of the European Parliament and of the Council of 16 February 2011 concerning the rights of passengers in bus and coach transport and amending Regulation (EC) No 2006/2004.

(4)   A contract to which this Chapter applies is referred to in this Part as a "contract to supply a service".

(5)   The Secretary of State may by order made by statutory instrument provide that a provision of this Chapter does not apply in relation to a service of a description specified in the order.

(6)   The power in subsection (5) includes power to provide that a provision of this Chapter does not apply in relation to a service of a description specified in the order in the circumstances so specified.

(7)   An order under subsection (5) may contain transitional or transitory provision or savings.

(8)   No order may be made under subsection (5) unless a draft of the statutory instrument containing it has been laid before, and approved by a resolution of, each House of Parliament.

3H-1058.1   *Note* —Subsection (3A) inserted by the Rights of Passengers in Bus and Coach Transport (Exemptions and Enforcement) (Amendment) Regulations 2017 (SI 2017/99) reg.3, with effect from 1 March 2017.

Replace paragraph 10 of Sch.5 Pt 2 with:

SECTION 77

SCHEDULE 5

INVESTIGATORY POWERS ETC.

PART 2

THE ENFORCER'S LEGISLATION

Enforcer's legislation: duties and powers mentioned in paragraph 9(1)(a)

3H-1106   10.   The duties and powers mentioned in paragraph 9(1)(a) are those arising under any of the following provisions—

section 26(1) or 40(1)(b) of the Trade Descriptions Act 1968 (including as applied by regulation 8(3) of the Crystal Glass (Descriptions) Regulations 1973 (SI 1973/1952) and regulation 10(2) of the Footwear (Indication of Composition) Labelling Regulations 1995 (SI 1995/2489));

section 9(1) or (6) of the Hallmarking Act 1973;

paragraph 6 of the Schedule to the Prices Act 1974 (including as read with paragraph 14(1) of that Schedule);

section 161(1) of the Consumer Credit Act 1974;

section 26(1) of the Estate Agents Act 1979;

Article 39 of the Weights and Measures (Northern Ireland) Order 1981 (SI 1981/231 (NI 10));

section 16A(1) or (4) of the Video Recordings Act 1984;

section 27(1) of the Consumer Protection Act 1987 (including as applied by section 12(1) of the Fireworks Act 2003 to fireworks regulations under that Act);

section 215(1) of the Education Reform Act 1988;

section 107A(1) or (3) or 198A(1) or (3) of the Copyright, Designs and Patents Act 1988;

paragraph 3(a) of Schedule 5 to the Simple Pressure Vessels (Safety) Regulations 1991 (SI 1991/2749);

paragraph 1 of Schedule 3 to the Package Travel, Package Holidays and Package Tours Regulations 1992 (SI 1992/3288);

section 30(4) or (7) or 31(4)(a) of the Clean Air Act 1993;

paragraph 1 of Schedule 2 to the Sunday Trading Act 1994;

section 93(1) or (3) of the Trade Marks Act 1994;

section 8A(1) or (3) of the Olympic Symbol etc (Protection) Act 1995;

paragraph 2(a) or 3(1) of Schedule 15 to the Lifts Regulations 1997 (SI 1997/831);

paragraph 2(a) or 3(3)(a) of Schedule 8 to the Pressure Equipment Regulations 1999 (SI 1999/2001);

regulation 5C(5) of the Motor Fuel (Composition and Content) Regulations 1999 (SI 1999/3107);

paragraph 1(1)(b) or (2)(b) or 2 of Schedule 9 to the Radio Equipment and Telecommunications Terminal Equipment Regulations 2000 (SI 2000/730);

paragraph 1(a) of Schedule 10 to the Personal Protective Equipment Regulations 2002 (SI 2002/1144);

section 3(1) of the Christmas Day Trading Act 2004;

regulation 10(1) of the General Product Safety Regulations 2005 (SI 2005/1803);

regulation 10(1) of the Weights and Measures (Packaged Goods) Regulations 2006 (SI 2006/659);

regulation 17 of the Measuring Instruments (Automatic Discontinuous Totalisers) Regulations 2006 (SI 2006/1255);

regulation 18 of the Measuring Instruments (Automatic Railweighbridges) Regulations 2006 (SI 2006/1256);

regulation 20 of the Measuring Instruments (Automatic Catchweighers) Regulations 2006 (SI 2006/1257);

regulation 18 of the Measuring Instruments (Automatic Gravimetric Filling Instruments) Regulations 2006 (SI 2006/1258);

regulation 18 of the Measuring Instruments (Beltweighers) Regulations 2006 (SI 2006/1259);

regulation 16 of the Measuring Instruments (Capacity Serving Measures) Regulations 2006 (SI 2006/1264);

regulation 17 of the Measuring Instruments (Liquid Fuel and Lubricants) Regulations 2006 (SI 2006/1266);

regulation 16 of the Measuring Instruments (Material Measures of Length) Regulations 2006 (SI 2006/1267);

regulation 17 of the Measuring Instruments (Cold-water Meters) Regulations 2006 (SI 2006/1268);

regulation 18 of the Measuring Instruments (Liquid Fuel delivered from Road Tankers) Regulations 2006 (SI 2006/1269);

regulation 37(1)(a)(ii) or (b)(ii) of the Electromagnetic Compatibility Regulations 2006 (SI 2006/3418);

regulation 13(1) or (1A) of the Business Protection from Misleading Marketing Regulations 2008 (SI 2008/1276);

regulation 19(1) or (1A) of the Consumer Protection from Unfair Trading Regulations 2008 (SI 2008/1277);

paragraph 2 or 5 of Schedule 5 to the Supply of Machinery (Safety) Regulations 2008 (SI 2008/1597);

section A11(7)(a) of the Apprenticeships, Skills, Children and Learning Act 2009;

regulation 32(2) or (3) of the Timeshare, Holiday Products, Resale and Exchange Contracts Regulations 2010 (SI 2010/2960);

regulation 10(1) of the Weights and Measures (Packaged Goods) Regulations (Northern Ireland) 2011 (SR 2011/331);

regulation 11 of the Textile Products (Labelling and Fibre Composition) Regulations 2012 (SI 2012/1102);

regulation 6(1) of the Cosmetic Products Enforcement Regulations 2013 (SI 2013/1478);

regulation 23(1) of the Consumer Contracts (Information, Cancellation and Additional Charges) Regulations 2013 (SI 2013/3134);

section 87(1) of this Act;

section 93(1) or (2) of this Act;

regulation 7(1) of the Packaging (Essential Requirements) Regulations 2015.

Note

To the end of the second paragraph, add:
    ; and the Enterprise Act 2016 s.25(2), with effect from 1 April 2017   **3H-1111**

SECTION 3J   DIRECTORS DISQUALIFICATION PROCEEDINGS

PRACTICE DIRECTION—DIRECTORS DISQUALIFICATION PROCEEDINGS

Editorial note

Application of the CPR

Replace with:
    In a number of places the Practice Direction makes specific provision that a certain aspect of the **3J-2** CPR shall or shall not apply. This can be a trap for the unwary. It should be emphasised that the rules which primarily govern disqualification proceedings are the Insolvent Companies (Disqualification of Unfit Directors) Rules 1987 (as subsequently amended) (as amended, "the Disqualification Rules"), which were made under the rule-making power contained in s.21 of the Act and s.411 of the Insolvency Act 1986. By r.2(1), the CPR and any relevant practice directions are applied to disqualification proceedings, "except where these Rules make provision to inconsistent effect". This is equivalent to the position in relation to proceedings under the Insolvency Act 1986: see r.7.51A of the Insolvency Rules 1986 (now r.12.1(1) of the Insolvency (England and Wales) Rules 2016 ("the Insolvency Rules 2016"). Thus, for example, service out of the jurisdiction under r.5(2) of the Disqualification Rules is not subject to the regime set out in Pt 6 of the CPR (though the court may in its discretion apply parts of it by analogy): see *Re Seagull Manufacturing Co Ltd (No.2)* [1994] Ch. 91.

Service out of the jurisdiction

Replace with:
    As indicated above (see 3J-2, Application of the CPR), service out of the jurisdiction is governed **3J-19**

by the discretion given to the court under r.5(2) of the Disqualification Rules (repeated as para.6.4 of the Practice Direction), rather than the provisions now found in CPR Pt 6. It should be noted that when the Disqualification Rules were brought into effect, in this respect they reflected the approach in r.12.12 of the Insolvency Rules 1986. Rule 12.12 was revoked and replaced with r.12A.20, and now with para.1 of Sch.4 to the Insolvency Rules 2016, which applies CPR Pt 6 to service of insolvency proceedings. The position on service out of the jurisdiction in disqualification proceedings is therefore now out of step with insolvency proceedings generally.

Appeals

After the first paragraph, add new paragraph:

3J-63   With the introduction of the Insolvency Rules 2016, para.32 now needs to be recast. Rule 12.58 of the new Insolvency Rules simply provides: "CPR Pt 52 (appeals) applies to appeals under this Chapter as varied by any applicable Practice Direction". At the time of writing, the Insolvency Proceedings Practice Direction has not been updated for the introduction of the Insolvency Rules 2016. Instead, a Practice Note has been issued on 7 April 2017 to the effect that pending the making of a revised Insolvency Proceedings Practice Direction, (a) the Insolvency Rules 2016 should be given effect, and (b) the existing Insolvency Rules Practice Direction is to be treated as not in effect where it contradicts the new rules, but the practices set out in it may continue to be followed as sound guidance to the extent possible.

In the second paragraph, after "that appeals are", delete "now".

SECTION 30   EMPLOYMENT

Employment Tribunals Extension of Jurisdiction (England and Wales) Order 1994

Other areas of overlapping jurisdiction between courts and employment tribunals

Wages

Add new paragraph at end:

30-0.15   The EAT's decision in *Agarwal v Cardiff University* UKEAT/0210/16, 22 March 2017, postulated a further limitation on the wages jurisdiction of Employment Tribunals. This was that, if the question of whether a claimant is contractually entitled to the wages that she claims, turns on a disputed issue of construction of the express terms of her contract, or a dispute as to the application of an implied term, then the Tribunal would have no jurisdiction to entertain the claim under Pt II of the 1996 Act. However, shortly after, in *Weatherilt v Cathay Pacific Airways Ltd* UKEAT/0333/16, 25 April 2017, a different division of the EAT disagreed. In *Weatherilt* it was noted that in *Agarwal* the point had been agreed, and there was no adversarial argument. Further, two relevant Court of Appeal authorities had not been drawn to the EAT's attention in *Agarwal*. Relying on those binding authorities, the EAT in *Weatherilt* held that Tribunals do, when determining a wages claim, have the power to (and must) resolve any dispute about the amount "properly payable" to the worker, whether concerning an express or an implied term. That said, the EAT noted that such jurisdiction will be concurrent with that of the civil courts; and the Tribunal, could, if justified, stay a wages claim to enable the civil court to resolve an important issue.

Employment Tribunals (Constitution and Rules of Procedure) Regulations 2013

Amount of a costs order

To the end of the paragraph, add:

30-5.1   It is an error to assess the combined means of the paying party's family, instead of those of the paying party himself; but in an appropriate case the tribunal may, in assessing the paying party's means, have regard to evidence of his ability to call on the financial support of family members or other third parties. See: *Abaya v Leeds Teaching Hospital NHS Trust* UKEAT/0258/16, 1 March 2017.

Effect of a Deposit Order on Costs

At the start of the fourth paragraph, replace "Finally, note" with:

30-12.1   Note

Add new paragraph at end:

The decision of the EAT in *H v Ishmail* [2017] I.R.L.R. 228 emphasises that, when a deposit order is made, proper account must be taken of the paying party's means, so that the level of deposit required does not act as a barrier to access to justice, or back-door strike-out. However, the decision also throws the spotlight on the foregoing costs implications. The EAT states that the legitimate purpose of deposit orders is to highlight, at an early stage, claims which have little prospect of success, and to discourage their pursuit, including by the enhanced costs risk created by the making of a deposit order, should the claim ultimately fail at trial.

SECTION 4 SUPREME COURT OF THE UNITED KINGDOM AND JUDICIAL COMMITTEE OF THE PRIVY COUNCIL

SECTION 4A SUPREME COURT OF THE UNITED KINGDOM APPEALS

Supreme Court Rules 2009

Complying with r.18(2)

In the first paragraph, after "the terms of r.18 are re-stated and it is explained that", delete "the original and". **4A-20.3**

Effect of rule

Add new paragraph at end:

An example of a decision on costs being appealed to a single Justice under r.53, which is then **4A-53.1** referred by that Justice to a panel of Justices under r.53(2), is *Plevin v Paragon Personal Finance Ltd* [2017] UKSC 23; [2017] 1 W.L.R. 1249. That case was referred to a panel of Justices because it posed questions of principle concerning the recoverability of a success fee under a conditional fee agreement with after the event insurance.

PRACTICE DIRECTION 13—COSTS

Section 1

2. Entitlement to costs

Replace the second paragraph of para.2.2 with:

In making such an order, the Court may apply the provisions of CPR 3.19, **4A-159** CPR 45.43 or, as the case may be, CPR r.52.19 or CPR r.52.19A.

SECTION 4B JUDICIAL COMMITTEE OF THE PRIVY COUNCIL APPEALS

Judicial Committee (Appellate Jurisdiction) Rules 2009

In the last paragraph, replace "Re Baronetcy of Pringle of Stichill [2016] UKPC 16" with:
Re Baronetcy of Pringle of Stichill [2016] UKPC 16; [2016] 1 W.L.R. 2870 **4B-0.2**

SECTION 6   ADMINISTRATION OF FUNDS, PROPERTY AND AFFAIRS

SECTION 6A   COURT FUNDS

INVESTMENTS ON BEHALF OF CHILDREN AND PROTECTED BENEFICIARIES

Estates which have fallen to the Crown

6A-216   *Replace the second paragraph with:*
If the deceased person lived in England and Wales, write to: The Government Legal Department (Bona Vacantia), BVD, PO Box 2119, Croydon CR90 9QU, DX 325801 Croydon 51 (tel: 020 7210 4700). If the deceased person lived in Cornwall, write to: The Duchy of Cornwall, 10 Buckingham Gate, London SW1E 6LA (tel: 020 7834 7346). If the deceased person lived in Lancashire, write to: The Duchy of Lancaster, 1 Lancaster Place, Strand, London WC2E 7ED, Tel: 0207 269 1700, or, for both Duchies, write direct to the Duchy Solicitors Messrs Farrer & Co, 66 Lincoln's Inn Fields, London WC2A 3LH, Tel: 0203 375 7000. Website: *http://www.farrer.co.uk* [Accessed 11 May 2017].

SECTION 7   LEGAL REPRESENTATIVES—COSTS AND LITIGATION FUNDING

SECTION 7A1   LITIGATION FUNDING BEFORE APRIL 1, 2013

FUNDING ARRANGEMENTS

Conditional Fees

7A1-56   *Delete the fourth paragraph (beginning with "The House of Lords has held that the scheme").*

Add new paragraph 7A1-57.1:

Article 10 of the European Convention on Human Rights

7A1-57.1   In *Campbell v Mirror Group Newspapers Ltd (Costs)* [2005] UKHL 61; [2005] 4 All E.R. 793, the House of Lords held that the scheme of allowing additional liabilities to be recovered from the losing party in a defamation action was not incompatible with art.10 ECHR. MGN applied to the European Court of Human Rights, which decided that the order that MGN pay the claimant's success fees and ATE premium was an infringement of MGN's art.10 rights: *MGN Ltd v United Kingdom (39401/04)* (2011) 53 E.H.R.R. 5. In *Times Newspapers Ltd v Flood* [2017] UKSC 33, the Supreme Court declined to decide whether there was a general rule that a requirement to reimburse success fees or ATE premiums would normally be an infringement of the art.10 rights of a defendant publisher, because the United Kingdom government was not a party to the appeal. However, on the footing that there had been an infringement, there was a good reason not to deprive the claimants of the success fees and ATE premiums, namely their legitimate expectation that they would not be retrospectively deprived of their rights under the 1999 Act regime. In respect of those claimants who had been the subject of phone hacking (*Frost v MGN Ltd*) the court accepted that the defendant's art.10 rights had been engaged but concluded that, given the defendant's conduct, this was not a case where the defendant could properly invoke the rule.

Success fees

7A1-58   *Delete the first paragraph.*

SECTION 8   LIMITATION

Limitation Act 1980

Date when action "brought"

Add new paragraph at end:
In *Wells v Wood*, 9 December 2016, unrep. HHJ Godsmark QC held that a claim form issued **8-3.1** and sealed by a court after payment of an incorrect fee was effective to stop time from running for the purposes of the Limitation Act 1980.

Accrual of cause of action

Add at end:
In *Glaxo Wellcome UK Ltd (t/a Allen & Hanburys) v Sandoz Ltd* [2017] EWCA Civ 227 the Court of **8-5** Appeal held in the context of a passing off action that an accessory was liable not for his acts of assistance but for the primary actor's tortious act. Accordingly, a judge had been wrong to refuse to join two companies as additional defendants; limitation ran from the same date as for the original defendant, namely when the product was first promoted and sold.

Add new paragraph 8–10.1:

Editorial note

In *Otuo v Watchtower Bible and Tract Society of Britain* [2017] EWCA Civ 136, unrep. the Court of **8-10.1** Appeal confirmed that the correct approach to calculating the limitation period for defamation was to exclude the day on which the cause of action accrued from the computation of time for limitation: also see *Gentoo Group Ltd v Hanratty* [2008] EWHC 627 (QB), unrep.

Notes on s.32

After the ninth paragraph (beginning with "In Parkin v (1) Alba Proteins Ltd"), add new paragraph:
In *Booker v RT Financial Services UK Ltd* [2016] EWHC 3186 (Ch) the Master struck out the **8-85.1** claim, holding that the claimants had been in possession of all the primary facts within the limitation period, and the fact that the defendant might have encouraged them to believe that somebody else was the correct person to sue did not amount to deliberate concealment for the purposes of the Limitation Act 1980 s.32.

Section 33(3)(a)—delay

Delete the penultimate paragraph (beginning with "In Davidson v Aegis Defence Services"). **8-94.2**

Add new paragraph at end:
In *CD v Catholic Child Welfare Society* [2016] EWHC 3335 (QB), it was held that when considering the reasons for delay whilst it was typical for a victim of child sexual abuse to want to repress the memory and avoid disclosure of the abuse, that justification for non-disclosure was not self-proving and some assessment of the alleged victim was required.

Section 33(3)(b)—effect of delay on the evidence

After the third paragraph (beginning with "In McArdle v Marmion"), add new paragraph:
In *Davidson v Aegis Defence Services (BVI) Ltd* [2013] EWHC 590 (QB), the judge held that it was **8-94.3** appropriate to refuse a claimant's application for an extension of time to bring a personal injury action against his former employer where a delay in bringing proceedings had exacerbated existing difficulties for the court to investigate properly and determine liability.

New claim by way of set-off or counterclaim

After the first paragraph, add new paragraph:
In *Al-Rawas v Hassan Khan and Co (A Firm)* [2017] EWCA Civ 42 the Court of Appeal held that **8-108** no new claim, other than an original set-off or counterclaim, could be made after the expiry of any

applicable limitation period, except as provided by rules of court. The Limitation Act 1980 s.35(3) did not allow a counterclaim to be brought where a fresh action required to advance that claim would be out of time.

SECTION 9   JURISDICTIONAL AND PROCEDURAL LEGISLATION

SECTION 9A   MAIN STATUTES

Senior Courts Act 1981

Ouster of jurisdiction by statute

After the first paragraph, add new paragraph:

9A-71   The relevant authorities were reviewed in *R. (Privacy International) v Investigatory Powers Tribunal* [2017] EWHC 114 (Admin), 2 February 2017, DC, where a Divisional Court considered the efficacy of s.67(8) of the Regulation of Investigatory Powers Act 2000 as a statutory ouster clause. In that case it was noted (by Leggatt J at para.52), that, although it had repeatedly been said that Parliament could, in principle, exclude the possibility of judicial review by using language of sufficient clarity, it was striking that no language so far used had been held to be sufficiently clear to have that effect.

Jurisdiction where proceedings raising "academic" or "hypothetical" point of law

In the fifth paragraph (beginning with "In modern times, the appellate courts"), after "public interest for doing so.", add:

9A-77   The authorities indicate that in such a case the court has a narrow discretion to proceed, to be exercised with caution; if the only extant issue goes to costs, the court is likely to be still more cautious before deciding to hear the appeal (*Hamnett v Essex CC* [2017] EWCA Civ 6; [2017] 1 W.L.R. 1155, CA, para.37).

Costs order in favour of or against non-parties

Replace with:

9A-203   The procedure to be followed where the court is considering whether to exercise its discretion under s.51 to make a costs order in favour or against a person who is not a party to the proceedings is stated in CPR r.46.2. For information on the exercise of the discretion in this manner, see commentary following that rule (Vol.1, para.46.2.1). In *Hull and Holderness Magistrates' Court v Darroch* [2016] EWCA Civ 1220; [2017] 4 W.L.R. 6, CA, the Court of Appeal stated (obiter) that the High Court does not have power under s.51(1) to grant a third party costs order on an appeal by way of case stated or a claim for judicial review that sought to quash convictions.

SECTION 9B   OTHER STATUTES AND REGULATIONS

Civil Evidence Act 1972

Add new paragraph 9B–1063.1:

Effect of section

9B-1063.1   Section 4(2) concerns the manner in which foreign law can be proved. The sub-section provides that where a question of foreign law has been decided (as a question of fact) in one case the decision can be relied on as evidence of the same fact in other cases, subject to the conditions laid down within it. One of the purposes of s.4(2) is to enable a party in a later case to rely on the reasoned conclusions of a judge in an earlier case as to a point of foreign law without having to commission fresh expert evidence.

The procedure to be followed where a party intends to put in evidence a finding on a question of foreign law as provided by s.4(2) is stated in CPR r.33.7.

In *Joint Stock Co "Aeroflot · Russian Airlines" v Leeds, Wood and Hellard* [2017] EWHC 150 (Ch), 2 February 2017, unrep. (Warren J), the effect of s.4 was examined in detail. In this case the judge rejected the submission, made by a party opposing the admitting of evidence under s.4(2), that, although that provision clearly includes a finding or decision which was a necessary part of the reasoning leading to the ultimate decision in the earlier case, it does not include anything which did not form part of such reasoning or ultimate conclusion, anything which is simply obiter. The judge concluded that, where a judge expresses a clear conclusion about a point of foreign law which it is not necessary to decide in reaching the ultimate decision in the earlier case, it is a "finding" or "decision" on a matter "determined" within s.4(2); however, s.4(2) cannot be read in isolation and must be must be read with s.4(5) (paras 13 to 16).

Justice and Security Act 2013

Effect of this section

After the fifth paragraph (beginning with "In McGartland v Secretary of State for the Home Department"), add new paragraph:

In *Rahmatullah v Ministry of Defence* [2017] EWHC 547 (QB), 22 March 2017, unrep. (Leggatt J) **9B-1408** the judge explained (para.7) that although a s.6 declaration opens a gateway to a closed material procedure, it is only the first stage of the process and does not finally decide whether such a procedure will be used at the trial. In particular, s.7 of the 2013 Act requires the court to keep any declaration under review, to undertake a formal review once the pre-trial disclosure exercise has been completed, and to revoke the declaration if the court considers that it is no longer in the interests of the fair and effective administration of justice in the proceedings. Further, it is sufficient to justify making a s.6 declaration that the two statutory conditions are met in relation to any relevant material, and the defendants do not need to put before the court at this stage all the material which might meet the conditions (s.6(6)). Furthermore, in considering whether it is in the interests of the fair and effective administration of justice in the proceedings to make a s.6 declaration, the court should focus on whether any sensitive material on which the application is based is necessary for resolving the issues in the case before it.

SECTION 11   OVERRIDING OBJECTIVE OF CPR

C.   Giving Effect to the "Overriding Objective"—Generally (rr.1.1 and 1.2)

2.   General Application of "Overriding Objective" as Demonstrated in Decided Cases

In the sixth paragraph (beginning with "The overriding objective is not applicable"), replace "(Russell-Cooke Trust Co v Prentis [2002] EWHC 1435 (Ch); January 21, 2003, unrep. (Lindsay J.))." with:
(*Russell-Cooke Trust Co v Prentis* [2003] EWHC 1435 (Ch); 21 January 2003, unrep. (Lindsay J)).   **11-6**

SECTION 12   CPR: APPLICATION, AMENDMENTS AND INTERPRETATION

A.   Extent and Application of CPR

3.   Application of the CPR

(b)   Proceedings to which CPR do not apply (CPR r.2.1)

(i) Insolvency proceedings

Replace with:
The CPR do not apply to insolvency proceedings. This is not because such proceedings are not   **12-6**

civil proceedings, but "because they are specialised proceedings which need special rules" (*Stubbs v Gonzales (Practice Note)* [2005] 1 W.L.R. 2730, PC, at para.5). Under the Insolvency Act 1986 s.411 rules may be made in relation to England and Wales by the Lord Chancellor with the concurrence of the Secretary of State for the purposes of giving effect to Pts I to VIII of that Act (company insolvency and companies winding-up), and under s.412 for the purpose of giving effect to Pts VII to IX (insolvency of individuals, bankruptcy). Nothing in the Insolvency Act s.411 or s.412 prejudices any power to make rules of court. The Lord Chancellor is required to consult the Insolvency Rules Committee before making any rules under s.411 or s.412 of the 1986 Act. The Insolvency (England and Wales) Rules 2016 (SI 2016/1024), amongst other rules, are made under those provisions. Although CPR r.2.1 states that the CPR do not apply to insolvency proceedings, as r.12.1 of the 2016 Rules indicates the "provisions of the CPR (including any related Practice Directions) apply for the purposes of proceedings under Parts 1 to 11 of the [1986] Act with any necessary modifications, except so far as disapplied by or inconsistent with these [the 2016] Rules". Certain provisions in the 2016 Rules expressly incorporate CPR provisions; see e.g. r.12.27, which incorporates the power to seek further information and disclosure under CPR Pts 18 and 31; and r.12.58, which incorporates CPR Pt 52, subject to variation by an applicable Practice Direction.

C.   Statutory Instruments Amending CPR

4.   *Amendments and Transitional Arrangements in Amending Statutory Instruments*

(b)   2014 to date

Add new paragraph at the beginning:

12-34   Subject to transitional provisions and specified exceptions, the Civil Procedure (Amendment) Rules 2017 (SI 2017/95) came into force on 6 April 2017. The amendments it effected to CPR rr.45.41 to 45.55, Pt 52 and Pt 61 came into force on 28 February 2017, while those it effected to CPR rr.3.7A1(1) to 3.7AA, Pt 25 and Pt 44 came into force on 6 March 2017. It effected significant changes to rr.3.15 and 3.18, in order to correct the problem that arose as a result of the Court of Appeal's decision in *Sarpd Oil International Ltd v Addax Energy SA* [2016] EWCA Civ 120; amend CPR rr.45.29B to 45.29E to reflect the Court of Appeal's decision in *Qadar v Esure Services Ltd* [2016] EWCA Civ 1109; and to introduce provisions governing costs protection in environmental claims in CPR Pt 45, Section III and CPR Pt 52.

In the first paragraph, after "2016 (SI 2016/788)", replace "comes" with:
    came

SECTION 13   RIGHTS OF AUDIENCE

G.   Right of Audience Granted by the Court in Relation to the Proceedings (Sch.3, para.1(2))

4.   *Exercise of the Discretion*

(a)   Generally

To the end of the third paragraph (beginning with "It is submitted that where an application is made"), add:

13-17   A solicitor who has been struck off or suspended from practice is unlikely to be granted a right of audience as that would undermine the sanction imposed by the Solicitors' Disciplinary Tribunal (*Azumi Ltd v Zuma's Choice Pet Products Ltd* [2017] EWHC 45 (IPEC)).

(b)   Unqualified advocates providing advocacy services

Add new paragraph at end:

13-18   In the case of a solicitor who has been struck off or suspended from practice see *Azumi Ltd v Zuma's Choice Pet Products Ltd* [2017] EWHC 45 (IPEC).

(c)   McKenzie friend

After the second paragraph (beginning with "In July 2010, the Master of the Rolls"), add new paragraph:

13-19   References to the practice (descending to various levels of detail) are found in the Court Guides. See: Chancery Guide para.4.21 (Vol.2 para.1A-42); Queen's Bench Guide para.2.6.1 (Vol.2 para.1B-

14); Administrative Court Judicial Review Guide para.3.6 (Vol.2 para.1BA-20); Senior Courts Costs Office Guide paras 1.2(h) and 22.1(b) (Vol.2 paras 1C-9 and 1C-137); Mercantile Court Guide para.16.5 (Vol.2 para.2B-33).

SECTION 14 ALTERNATIVE DISPUTE RESOLUTION

A.   Introduction

1.   Negotiation, Mediation and Other Dispute Resolution Procedures

Replace the last paragraph with:

With reference to the Government's proposals on legal aid in 2011 Lord Neuberger, Master of **14-2** the Rolls, as he then was, expressed concern about what some see as the prospect of replacing legal aid-funded cases with alternative dispute resolution. Lord Neuberger warned: "If we expand mediation beyond its proper limits as a complement to justice we run the risk of depriving particular persons or classes of person of their right to equal and impartial justice under the law." (See *http://kedah.kehakiman.gov.my/?q=system/files/document/Mediation.pdf* [Accessed 21 May 2017].)

2.   Appellate Judges' Statements and Speeches on ADR—The Jackson Report/The Briggs Report—Proposals for Reform

At the end of the first paragraph, replace "[26]) and (x) Briggs L.J. in PGF II SA v OMFS Co [2013] EWCA Civ 1288." with:

[26]); (x) Briggs LJ in *PGF II SA v OMFS Co* [2013] EWCA Civ 1288; (xi) Jackson LJ in *Thakkar* **14-3** *v Patel* [2017] EWCA Civ 117 (para.31) and (xii) Vos LJ in in *NJ Rickard Ltd v Holloway* [2015] EWCA Civ 1631 (para.34).

Replace the second paragraph with:

Between 2007 and 2009, Lightman J, Lord Phillips CJ and Sir Anthony Clarke M.R. (as they then were) each delivered speeches, out of court, all of which were predicated on the greater use of ADR. They will be referred to collectively below as the "Judicial Speeches" and the speech on 8 May 2008 will be referred to as Sir Anthony Clarke's Birmingham Speech. The speeches are available at *http://www.cedr.com/articles/?item=Mediation-an-approximation-to-justice-a-speech-by-The-Honourable-Mr-Justice-Lightman* [Accessed 21 May 2017] (Lightman J); *http://webarchive.nationalarchives.gov.uk/20131202164909/http://judiciary.gov.uk/Resources/JCO/Documents/Speeches/lcj_adr_india_290308.pdf* [Accessed 21 May 2017] (Lord Phillips CJ); *http://www.civilmediation.org/downloads-get?id=119* [Accessed 21 May 2017] (Sir Anthony Clarke M.R., Brighton); *http://www.civilmediation.org/downloads-get?id=128*;   *http://webarchive.nationalarchives.gov.uk/20131202164909/http://judiciary.gov.uk/media/speeches/2008/speech-clarke-lj-mor-11042008* [Accessed 21 May 2017] (Sir Anthony Clarke M.R., Birmingham); *http://webarchive.nationalarchives.gov.uk/20131202164909/http://judiciary.gov.uk/media/speeches/2008/speech-clarke-lj-mor-08052008* [Accessed 21 May 2017] (Lord Clarke of Stone-Cum-Ebony M.R.). In 2011 Lord Dyson responded to some of the issues arising in the Judicial Speeches in a speech subsequently published under title of "A word on Halsey v Milton Keynes" (Arbitration 2011, 77(3), 337-341).

B.   ADR in the Context of the CPR

1.   Case Management

(d)   Active case management in relation to ADR after the introduction of the CPR

At the end of the second paragraph, replace "N J Rickard Ltd v Holloway, 3 November 2015, unrep., Court of Appeal (Civil Division)," with:

NJ Rickard Ltd v Holloway [2015] EWCA Civ 1631.   **14-7**

Replace the penultimate paragraph (beginning with "Proportionality and the mantra that litigation") with:

Proportionality and the mantra that litigation should be the last resort were two of the key issues in *Briggs v First Choice Holidays and Flights Ltd*, 23 September 2016, unrep., Senior Courts Costs Office. A large number of tourists had stayed at an all-inclusive holiday resort which they had booked through the defendant tour operator. Some developed gastrointestinal illnesses and others endured sub-standard accommodation and service, and had their holidays spoiled. The court decided that the claimants who had not become ill should have pursued their claims via mediation under an Association of British Travel Agents scheme. On appeal, however, Singh J held that "The costs judge's conclusion that it was inherently unreasonable for the appellants to enter into a CFA rather than a voluntary mediation scheme went too far. The costs judge had erred." *Briggs v First Choice Holidays and Flights Ltd*, 8 February 2017, unrep., Queen's Bench Division.

(f)   Judicial speeches—ADR case management post Halsey—power to direct ADR

In the fifth paragraph (beginning with "As the 10th anniversary of Halsey approached"), replace the quoted section with:

14-9   "I thought then, and I still think now, that it struck the right balance. It was careful to protect the interests of defendants who had a genuine and entirely proper desire to resist claims that they reasonably believed to be without merit. It was equally careful to support the promotion of settlement. In doing so, it sent out a clear message that neither litigation nor mediated settlement are devices which could or should be used as a means to secure unjustified windfalls for individuals who are trying it on." (See *http://webarchive.nationalarchives.gov.uk/20131202164909/http://judiciary.gov.uk/media/speeches/2013/mr-speech-compensation-culture-fact-or-fantasy* [Accessed 21 May 2017].)

(h)   Case management and cost sanctions

After the eighth paragraph (beginning with "In Laporte v The Commissioner of Police of the Metropolis"), add new paragraph:

14-11   In *OMV Petrom SA v Glencore International AG* [2017] EWCA Civ 195 the costs sanction took the form of enhanced interest: "As long as the award (of interest) was proportionate to the facts of the case, it could include a non-compensatory element to encourage parties to engage in reasonable settlement negotiations and to mark the court's disapproval of unreasonable conduct."

3.   Costs where ADR Declined

After the eighth paragraph (beginning with "For an application, and discussion, of the concept"), add new paragraph:

14-17   In *Primeview Developments Ltd v Ahmed* [2017] UKUT 57 (LC) the Upper Tribunal (Lands Chamber) decided, by reference to *Halsey v Milton Keynes General NHS Trust* [2004] EWCA Civ 576, that a party's refusal to mediate was not unreasonable. The critical issues were that the prospects of success were slight and the costs of mediation were likely to be disproportionately high.

At the end of the eleventh paragraph (beginning with "This was in fact the approach taken by the Court of Appeal"), replace "Flanagan v Liontrust Investment Partners LLP [2016] EWHC 446 (Ch) and Kupeli v Sirketi (t/a Cyprus Turkish Airlines) [2016] EWHC 1478 (QB)." with:

Flanagan v Liontrust Investment Partners LLP [2016] EWHC 446 (Ch); *Kupeli v Sirketi (t/a Cyprus Turkish Airlines)* [2016] EWHC 1478 (QB); *NJ Rickard v Holloway* [2015] EWCA Civ 1631; *Car Giant Ltd v Hammersmith LBC* [2017] EWHC 464 (TCC); *Inchbald v Inchbald* [2017] EWHC 616 (Ch) and *MacInnes v Gross* [2017] EWHC 127 (QB).

After the sixteenth paragraph (beginning with "This decision was subsequently upheld by the Court of Appeal"), add new paragraph:

In *Thakkar v Patel* [2017] EWCA Civ 117 the Court of Appeal developed PGF. Here the defendants did not ignore or refuse an offer to mediate, "but they dragged their feet and delayed until eventually the claimants lost confidence in the whole ADR process". Jackson LJ stated: "The message which the court sends out in this case is that in a case where bilateral negotiations fail but mediation is obviously appropriate, it behoves both parties to get on with it. If one party frustrates the process by delaying and dragging its feet for no good reason, that will merit a costs sanction." The court enumerated the factors that suggested there were good prospects of a successful mediation in this case.

After the last paragraph, add new paragraph:

In *OMV Petrom SA v Glencore International AG* [2017] EWCA Civ 195 Vos LJ said, at para.41, that a "blank refusal to engage in any negotiating or mediation process, ... to seek to frustrate a claimant's attempts to reach a compromise solution should be marked by the use of the court's powers to discourage such conduct."

4.   Confidentiality, without Prejudice and "Mediation Privilege" in Relation to Mediation

(d)   Without prejudice

To the end of the fourth paragraph (beginning with "See also Youlton v Charles Russell"), add:

14-18.3   In *Savings Advice Ltd v EDF Energy Customers Plc*, 17 January 2017, unrep., WL 00219540, during costs proceedings subsequent to the main action, Master Howarth allowed a party to refer to costs information provided during a mediation of the main action. This was on the basis that the duty of confidence and without prejudice privilege existed to protect the disclosure of admissions or concessions made in negotiations, not costs information in the form of purely factual statements which had been disclosed "without prejudice save as to costs".

(e) Mediation privilege

In the last paragraph, after "in this area", replace "is" with:
was

14-18.4

6. Miscellaneous Matters

Add new paragraph at end:
An interesting practice point arose in *Savings Advice Ltd v EDF Energy Customers Plc*, 17 January **14-20** 2017, unrep., WL 00219540. Master Howarth stated: "29. In my judgment it is imperative that when parties enter into a formal mediation or informal negotiations for settlement of a claim that they do so in the full knowledge of their opponent's costs. The amount of the costs of litigation condition any subsequent negotiations or mediation that may follow."

D. ADR in Particular Courts

3. Court of Appeal Mediation Scheme (CAMS)

Replace the first paragraph with:
Information about mediation in cases pending or proceeding in the Court of Appeal (Civil Divi- **14-25** sion) is found on the Court of Appeal website (*http://hmctsformfinder.justice.gov.uk/HMCTS/GetForm. do?court_forms_id=996* and *http://hmctsformfinder.justice.gov.uk/HMCTS/GetForm.do?court_forms_id=997* [Accessed 21 May 2017]).

SECTION 15   INTERIM REMEDIES

A.   Interim Injunctions

2. Principles and Guidelines to be Applied (American Cyanamid Co. Case)

(a) Principles—a serious question to be tried

After the fifth paragraph (beginning with "In the American Cyanamid case"), add new paragraph:
A claimant seeking a "quia timet" injunction must show that there is a serious issue to be tried as **15-8** to there being a real risk that the defendant intends, unless restrained, to undertake the activities sought to be enjoined. The court will not grant an injunction on the principle that if the defendant does not intend to violate the claimant's rights, the injunction would do no harm (*Rafael Advanced Defense Systems Ltd v Mectron Engenharia Industrie E Comercio SA* [2017] EWHC 597 (Comm), 27 March 2017, unrep. (Teare J)).

9. Undertaking as to Damages

(g) Fortifying undertaking

To the end of the first paragraph, add:
The difficulties in using an insurance policy as a means of providing fortification of a cross- **15-32** undertaking in damages were considered in *Holyoake v Candy* [2017] EWCA Civ 92, 28 February 2017, CA, unrep.

B.   Freezing Injunctions

4.   Third Parties

(a)   Duties of third party

In the second paragraph (beginning with "The receipt by a bank"), after "commercial judgment, provided", replace "always that is does nothing inconsistent with the underlying purpose of the injunction (Gangway Ltd v Caledonian Park Investments (Jersey) Ltd [2001] 2 Lloyd's Rep. 715, (Colman J.)." with:

15-61   that it is not colluding with or aiding and abetting a breach by the defendant of the freezing order (*Gangway Ltd v Caledonian Park Investments (Jersey) Ltd* [2001] 2 Lloyd's Rep. 715, (Colman J), as explained in *Taylor v Van Dutch Marine Holding Ltd* [2017] EWHC 636 (Ch), 27 March 2017, unrep. (Mann J), at paras 10, 12 and 17).

(c)   Restraint on third parties: the Chabra jurisdiction

Replace the first paragraph with:

15-63   In *TSB Private Bank International SA v Chabra* [1992] 1 W.L.R. 231 (Mummery J), it was held that, where the defendant is restrained from disposing of the assets of a company, the court has jurisdiction of its own motion to join the company (in effect, a third party) as a second defendant and to grant a freezing injunction against it to support the claimant's claim against the defendant, even though there is no cause of action against the company. The principles for the exercise of the Chabra jurisdiction (as it is called) were summarised by Popplewell J in *PJSC Vseukrainskyi Aktsionernyi Bank v Maksimov* [2013] EWHC 422 (Comm), 7 March 2013, unrep. Those principles were approved by the Court of Appeal in *Lakatamia Shipping Co Ltd v Su* [2014] EWCA Civ 636; [2015] 1 W.L.R. 291, CA, and stated to be as follows (at [32]): (1) the jurisdiction is exercisable where there is good reason to suppose that assets held in the name of a defendant against whom the claimant asserts no cause of action (the NCAD) would be amenable to some process, ultimately enforceable by the courts, by which the assets would be available to satisfy a judgment against a defendant against whom the claimant asserts a cause of action (the CAD); (2) the test of "reason to suppose" is equated with a "good arguable case" i.e. more than barely arguable but not necessarily one the judge believes has better than a 50% chance of success; (3) it is just and convenient to exercise the jurisdiction, which is exceptional and to be exercised with caution; (4) a common example of assets falling within the Chabra jurisdiction is where there is good reason to suppose that assets in the name of the NCAD are in truth assets of the CAD; (5) establishing substantial control by the CAD over NCAD assets may be relevant, but will not necessarily justify freezing NCAD assets; the ultimate test is that there is good reason to suppose that the assets would be amenable to execution of a judgment obtained against the CAD. Where the court exercises the Chabra jurisdiction and restrains a third party, in effect the court is granting ancillary relief in aid of, and as part of, the freezing relief granted against the defendant.

In the second paragraph, replace "(Linsen International Ltd v Humpuss Sea Transport Pte Ltd (op. cit.))." with:

(*Linsen International Ltd v Humpuss Sea Transport Pte Ltd* [2011] EWHC 2339 (Comm); [2011] 2 Lloyd's Rep. 663 (Flaux J)).

5.   "Domestic" Freezing Injunctions

(c)   Ancillary orders—asset disclosure

(ii)   Asset disclosure post-judgment

Replace the fourth paragraph with:

15-76   In *Vitol SA v Capri Marine Ltd* [2010] EWHC 458 (Comm), 9 March 9 2010, unrep. (Tomlinson J) the judge explained (at para.37) that disclosure orders made after judgment may have the dual purposes of (1) assisting in the identification or ascertainment of the location of assets which were subject or potentially subject to a freezing order, and (2) assisting the judgment creditor to locate assets against which enforcement could be sought. The judge held that the disclosure given post judgment by a judgment debtor could be used for the purposes of enforcement, not only against the judgment debtor, but also (on the basis of the alter ego theory of liability) in proceedings abroad against a third party. The enforcement of the judgment was not a purpose collateral to that for which disclosure was made.

E. Interim Payments

3. *Conditions to be Satisfied and Matters to be Taken into Account (CPR r.25.7)*

(a) Generally

(iii) Judgment predicted

After the first paragraph, add new paragraph:

Where the court is satisfied that there would be judgment for a substantial sum of money **15-104** without being satisfied what precisely that sum would be, the court has to decide "the likely amount of the final judgment" (r.25.7(4)) and cannot order an interim payment of more than a reasonable proportion of that likely amount (*Makdessi v Cavendish Square Holding BV* [2017] EWHC 650 (Comm), 30 March 2017, unrep. (Teare J) at para.6).

4. *Amount of Interim Payment (CPR r.25.7(4))*

Interim payments and periodical payments of quantum judgment

After the first paragraph, add new paragraph:

In *C v Nottingham University Hospitals NHS Trust*, 20 September 2016, unrep. (Dove J), on 11 **15-116** November 2015, judgment on liability on a clinical negligence claim (for a serious brain injury) was entered in favour of the claimant (C), and on C's application the claim was stayed for a period of five years for injury stabilisation reasons. On 28 July 2016, C applied under CPR r.25.6 for an order for an interim payment of £1m from D for specialised accommodation. The judge refused the application, principally for the reason that, as no directions had been given as to the obtaining of evidence in relation to quantum, the assessment called for by *Eeles v Cobham Hire Services Ltd* [2009] EWCA Civ 204; [2010] 1 W.L.R. 409, CA, could not properly and reliably be made, and D had not had the opportunity or indeed the need to undertake any investigation of the quantum of C's case.

APPENDIX 1 COURTS DIRECTORY

County Court Directory

County Court Directory

Schedule: County Court Directory

Replace table with: **AP-9**

Key	Proceedings and co-located courts	Relevant provisions
I	Insolvency	The Insolvency (Commencement of Proceedings) and Insolvency Rules 1986 (Amendment) Rules 2014, S.I. 2014/817
C/LLP	Company and Limited Liability Partnerships	Practice Direction 2C, paragraph 3
CDR	Chancery District Registry	The Civil Courts Order 2014, S.I. 2014/819
CEA	Certification of Enforcement Agents	Practice Direction 84—Enforcement by Taking Control of Goods
CTC	Civil Trial Centre	Practice Direction 26—Case Management - Preliminary Stage: Allocation and Reallocation
DR	District Registry	The Civil Courts Order 2014, S.I. 2014/819

GVI	Application on notice for an injunction under the Policing and Crime Act 2009		Practice Direction 65—Proceedings Relating to Anti-social Behaviour and Harassment	
MC	Mercantile Court		Practice Direction 59—Mercantile Courts	
RR	Race Relations		The Civil Courts Order 1981, S.I. 1983/713	
TCC	Technology and Construction Court		Practice Direction 63—Technology and Construction Courts	

Column 1	Column 2	Column 3	Column 4	Column 5
County Court Hearing Centre	District Registry, Chancery District Registry, Mercantile Court Or Civil Trial Centre	Civil Trial Centre to Which Cases Allocated to the Multi-Track Will Be Transferred	Additional Proceedings	Civil Trial Centres — Feeder Courts
Aberystwyth	DR	Swansea	I C/LLP	
Aldershot & Farnham		Winchester		
Banbury		Oxford	I C/LLP	
Barnet		Central London	Part of the London Insolvency District (High Court for Parts 1 to 7, County Court at Central London for Parts 7A to 11) (C/LLP should be started in the High Court)	
Barnsley	DR	Sheffield	I C/LLP	
Barnstaple	DR	Exeter	I C/LLP	
Barrow-in-Furness	DR	Carlisle	I C/LLP	
Basildon		Southend		
Basingstoke	DR	Winchester		
Bath	DR	Bristol	I C/LLP	
Bedford	DR	Luton	I C/LLP	
Birkenhead	DR	Liverpool	I C/LLP CEA	
Birmingham	DR CDR MC CTC		I C/LLP CEA GVI RR TCC	Dudley
Blackburn	DR	Preston	I C/LLP	
Blackpool	DR		I C/LLP	
Blackwood	DR	Cardiff	I C/LLP	
Bodmin		Truro		
		Manchester	I C/LLP	
Boston	DR	Lincoln	I C/LLP	

Bournemouth & Poole	DR CTC		I C/LLP	Weymouth
Bradford	DR CTC		I C/LLP GVI	Skipton
Brentford		Central London	Part of the London Insolvency District (High Court for Parts 1 to 7, County Court at Central London for Parts 7A to 11) (C/LLP should be started in the High Court)	
Brighton	DR CTC		I C/LLP CEA	Chichester, Eastbourne, Hastings, Horsham, Lewes, Worthing
Bristol	DR CDR MC CTC		I C/LLP CEA GVI RR TCC	Bath, Weston-super-Mare
Bromley		Central London		
Burnley	DR CTC		I C/LLP CEA	
		Manchester	I C/LLP	
Bury St Edmunds	DR	Cambridge	I C/LLP	
Caernarfon	DR CDR CTC		I C/LLP CEA	Llangefni
Cambridge	DR CTC		I C/LLP RR	Bury St Edmunds, Chelmsford, Peterborough
Canterbury	DR CTC		I C/LLP RR	Maidstone, Medway, Thanet
Cardiff	DR CDR MC CTC		I C/LLP CEA GVI TCC RR	Blackwood, Newport (Gwent)
Carlisle	DR CTC		I C/LLP RR	Barrow-in-Furness, Kendal, West Cumbria
Carmarthen (hearings only)	DR	Swansea	I C/LLP	
Central London	CTC		Part of the London insolvency district (High Court for Parts 1 to 7, County Court at Central London for Parts 7A to 11) (C/LLP should be started in the High Court) CEA RR	Barnet, Bow, Brentford, Bromley, Clerkenwell & Shoreditch, Croydon, Edmonton, Kingston-upon-Thames, Lambeth, Mayor's & City of London,

				Romford, Wandsworth, Willesden, Woolwich, Uxbridge
Chelmsford	DR	Southend	I C/LLP CEA	
Chester	DR MC CTC		I C/LLP TCC	Crewe
Chesterfield	DR	Derby	I C/LLP	
Chichester	DR	Brighton		
Chippenham and Trowbridge		Winchester		
Clerkenwell and Shoreditch		Central London	Part of the London Insolvency District (High Court for Parts 1 to 7, County Court at Central London for Parts 7A to 11) (C/LLP should be started in the High Court)	
Colchester	DR CTC	Southend	I C/LLP	
Conwy & Colwyn (the building has closed — hearings are listed in Llandudno Magistrates Court; all administration is undertaken at Prestatyn)		Contact the Prestatyn hearing centre for information regarding the CTC		
Coventry	DR CTC		I C/LLP	Nuneaton, Warwick
Crewe	DR	Chester	I C/LLP	
Croydon	DR CTC	Central London	I C/LLP GVI	
Darlington	DR	Middlesbrough	I C/LLP	
Dartford	CTC	Central London	CEA	
Derby	DR CTC		I C/LLP	Chesterfield
Doncaster	DR	Sheffield	I C/LLP	
Dudley (hearings take place at Dudley Magistrates' Court)	DR	Birmingham	I C/LLP	
Durham	DR	Newcastle-upon-Tyne	I C/LLP	
Eastbourne	DR	Brighton	I C/LLP	

Edmonton		Central London	Part of the London Insolvency District (High Court for Parts 1 to 7, County Court at Central London for Parts 7A to 11) (C/LLP should be started in the High Court)	
Exeter	DR CTC		I C/LLP RR TCC	Barnstaple, Torquay & Newton Abbott
Gateshead		Newcastle-upon-Tyne	CEA	
Gloucester and Cheltenham	DR CTC		I C/LLP	Cheltenham
Great Grimsby	DR CTC		I C/LLP	
Guildford	DR		I C/LLP	Staines
Harrogate	DR	York	I C/LLP	
Hastings	DR	Brighton	I C/LLP	
Haverfordwest	DR	Swansea	I C/LLP	
Hereford	DR	Worcester	I C/LLP	
Hertford		Luton	I C/LLP CEA	
High Wycombe		Reading		
Horsham		Brighton		
Huddersfield	DR CTC		I C/LLP	
Ipswich	DR	Norwich or Southend	I C/LLP	
		Carlisle	I C/LLP	
Kettering		Northampton		
Kingston-upon-Hull	DR CTC		I C/LLP CEA	Grimsby
Kingston-upon-Thames		Central London	I C/LLP	
Lambeth		Central London	Part of the London Insolvency District (High Court for Parts 1 to 7, County Court at Central London for Parts 7A to 11) (C/LLP should be started in the High Court)	
Lancaster	DR CTC		I C/LLP	None

Leeds	DR CDR MC CTC		I C/LLP TCC RR	Wakefield
Leicester	DR CTC		I C/LLP GVI	
Lewes		Brighton		
Lincoln	DR CTC		I C/LLP	Boston
Liverpool	DR CDR MC CTC		I C/LLP GVI TCC	Birkenhead, St Helens, Wigan
Llanelli		Swansea		
		Caernarfon	I C/LLP	
Luton	DR CTC		I C/LLP	Bedford, Hertford, Watford
Maidstone	DR	Canterbury	I C/LLP	
Manchester	DR CDR MC CTC		I C/LLP GVI RR TCC	Bolton, Bury, Oldham, Stockport
Mansfield	DR	Nottingham		
Mayor's & City of London	CTC	Central London	Part of the London Insolvency District (High Court for Parts 1 to 7, County Court at Central London for Parts 7A to 11) (C/LLP should be started in the High Court)	
Medway	DR	Canterbury		
Merthyr Tydfil	DR	Swansea	I C/LLP	
Middlesbrough	DR CTC		I C/LLP CEA	Darlington
Milton Keynes	DR	Oxford	I C/LLP	
Mold (hearings only – all administration is undertaken at Wrexham)	DR CDR MC	Wrexham		
Newcastle-upon-Tyne	DR CDR MC CTC		I C/LLP GVI RR TCC	Durham, Gateshead, North Shields, South Shields, Sunderland
Newport (Gwent)	DR	Cardiff	I C/LLP	
Newport (Isle of Wight)	DR	Portsmouth	I C/LLP	
Northampton	DR CTC		I C/LLP CEA	Kettering, Peterborough
North Shields		Newcastle-upon-Tyne		

Norwich	DR CTC		I C/LLP CEA	Ipswich
Nottingham	DR CTC		I C/LLP CEA Mansfield GVI RR TCC	
Nuneaton		Coventry		
Oldham	DR	Manchester	I C/LLP CEA	
Oxford	DR CTC		I C/LLP CEA RR	Banbury, Milton Keynes
Peterborough	DR	Cambridge	I C/LLP GVI	
Plymouth	DR CTC		I C/LLP CEA RR	None
Pontypridd	DR	Swansea	I C/LLP	
Portsmouth	DR CTC		I C/LLP GVI	Newport (Isle of Wight)
Port Talbot	DR	Swansea		
Prestatyn	DR	Contact the Prestatyn hearing centre for information regarding the CTC	I C/LLP	
Preston	DR CDR CTC		I C/LLP GVI	Blackburn
Reading	DR CTC		I C/LLP	High Wycombe, Slough
Romford	DR	Central London	I C/LLP	
Salisbury	DR	Swindon	I C/LLP	
Scarborough	DR	York	I C/LLP	
Sheffield	DR CTC		I C/LLP GVI	Barnsley, Doncaster
Skipton	DR	Bradford		
Slough		Reading	I C/LLP	
Southampton	DR CTC		I C/LLP CEA RR	None
Southend	DR CTC		I C/LLP	Basildon, Chelmsford, Colchester, Ipswich
South Shields	DR	Newcastle-upon-Tyne		
St Helens	DR	Liverpool		
Stafford	DR	Stoke-on-Trent	I C/LLP	
Staines		Guildford		
Stockport	DR	Manchester	I C/LLP	
Stoke-on-Trent	DR CTC		I C/LLP	Stafford, Walsall
Sunderland	DR	Newcastle-upon-Tyne	I C/LLP	

Swansea	DR CTC		I C/LLP CEA	Aberystwyth, Carmarthen, Haverfordwest, Llanelli, Merthyr Tydfil, Pontypridd
Swindon	DR CTC		I C/LLP	Trowbridge, Salisbury
Taunton	DR CTC		I C/LLP	Yeovil
Telford	DR CTC		I C/LLP	Wolverhampton
Thanet	DR	Canterbury		
Torquay & Newton Abbot	DR	Exeter	I C/LLP	
Truro	DR CTC		I C/LLP	Bodmin
Uxbridge		Central London		
Wakefield	DR	Leeds	I C/LLP	
Walsall	DR	Stoke-on-Trent	I C/LLP	
Wandsworth		Central London	Part of the London Insolvency District (High Court for Parts 1 to 7, County Court at Central London for Parts 7A to 11) (C/LLP should be started in the High Court)	
Warwick		Coventry	I C/LLP	
Watford		Luton		
Welshpool & Newtown (hearings only— all administration is undertaken at Wrexham)	DR	Wrexham	I C/LLP	
West Cumbria	DR (to be called Workington District Registry)	Carlisle	I C/LLP	
Weston-super-Mare		Bristol		
Weymouth	DR	Bournemouth	I C/LLP	
Wigan	DR	Liverpool	I C/LLP	

Willesden		Central London	Part of the London Insolvency District (High Court for Parts 1 to 7, County Court at Central London for Parts 7A to 11) (C/LLP should be started in the High Court)	
Winchester	DR CTC		I C/LLP	Aldershot & Farnham, Basingstoke
Wolverhampton	DR	Telford	I C/LLP	
Woolwich		Central London		
Worcester	DR CTC		I C/LLP CEA	Hereford
Worthing	DR	Brighton		
Wrexham	DR CTC	Wrexham	I C/LLP RR CEA	Mold, Welshpool and Newton
Yeovil	DR	Taunton	I C/LLP	
York	DR CTC		I C/LLP CEA	Harrogate, Scarborough

INDEX

LEGAL TAXONOMY
FROM SWEET & MAXWELL

This index has been prepared using Sweet and Maxwell's Legal Taxonomy. Main index entries conform to keywords provided by the Legal Taxonomy except where references to specific documents or non-standard terms (denoted by quotation marks) have been included. These keywords provide a means of identifying similar concepts in other Sweet & Maxwell publications and online services to which keywords from the Legal Taxonomy have been applied. Readers may find some minor differences between terms used in the text and those which appear in the index. Suggestions to *sweetandmaxwell.taxonomy@tr.com.*

(All references are to paragraph numbers)

Abuse of process
attempts to re-litigate decided issues, 3.4.3.2
collateral attacks upon earlier decisions, 3.4.3.3
Accelerated possession claims
claim forms, 55.13.1
Accountant General of the Supreme Court
investment, [6A-216]
Accrual
cause of action
generally, [8-5]
Addition of parties
after judgment, 19.2.6
expiry of limitation period, after
mistake, 19.5.6
generally, 19.2.1
judgment, after, 19.2.6
Additional claims
pending actions, [8-108]
time limits
statutory basis, [8-108]
Administration claims
variation of trusts
introduction, 64.2.7
Admiralty and Commercial Court Guide
general provisions, [2A-40]
Admiralty claims
applications
fax, by, [2A-135]
case management
Guide, [2A-136]
commencement
collision claims, [2A-133]
Court Guide
case management, [2A-136]
fax issue, [2A-135]
fax applications
Court Guide, [2A-135]
Admissions
form, 14.1.8
formal admissions
form, 14.1.8
liability, of
form, 14.1.8
Admissions (facts)
form
amend an admission, 14.1.8
withdraw an admission, 14.1.8
Admissions (liability)
form

Admissions (liability)—*cont.*
form—*cont.*
amend an admission, 14.1.8
withdraw an admission, 14.1.8
Affidavits
defects
generally, 32.16.2
form
defects, 32.16.2
All proceedings orders
generally, 3.11.1
Allocation of business
costs
fast track, 46.11.2
small claims track, 46.11.2
County Court
anti-social behaviour orders, 2BPD.8
committal, 2BPD.8
freezing injunctions, 2BPD.8
human rights, 2BPD.14
injunctions, 2BPD.8
freezing injunctions
County Court, 2BPD.8
human rights
County Court, 2BPD.14
injunctions
County Court, 2BPD.8
interim remedies
County Court, 2BPD.8
Practice Direction
County Court, 2BPD.8
stay of proceedings
generally, 26.4.1
Alternative dispute resolution
appellate judges' statements and speeches, [14-3]
Briggs Report (July 2016), [14-3]
case management
generally, [14-7]—[14-11]
confidentiality
privilege, [14-18.4]
threats, [14-18.4]
without prejudice, [14-18.3]—[14-18.4]
costs where declined, [14-17]
Court of Appeal, [14-25]
debt claims, C16-006
introduction, [14-2]
mediation
Court of Appeal scheme, [14-25]

Paragraph numbers marked "+" denote online/CD content; those within [...] refer to Volume 2

Barristers
misconduct
small claims, 27.14.4
Blood tests
parentage
introduction, 23BPD.3
Case management
Admiralty claims
Guide, [2A-136]
alternative dispute resolution
generally, [14-7]—[14-11]
Chancery Guide
conference, [1A-117]
clerical errors, 3.10.3
conditional orders, 3.1.4
correction of errors, 3.10.3
costs budgets
detailed assessment, and, 3.18.3
failure to file, 3.14.1
costs management
assessment of costs on standard basis, 3.18.3
effect of provisions, 3.12.1
failure to file budgets, 3.14.1
Practice Direction, 3.12.1
Court of Protection
conditional orders, 3.1.4
correction of errors, 3.10.3
liberty to apply orders, 3.1.13
security for costs, 3.1.5
stay of proceedings, 3.1.7
deposit orders
effect, [3O-12.1]
employment tribunals
deposit order, [3O-12.1]
fees (non-payment by claimants)
consequences, 3.7.2
non-payment of fees by claimants
consequences, 3.7.2
preliminary issues
stay for settlement, 26.4.1
procedural errors, 3.10.3
relief from sanctions
Mitchell v News Group Newspapers Ltd, 3.9.3
post-Mitchell decisions, 3.9.6.9—3.9.6.11
procedure, 3.8.1
revocation of order
liberty to apply orders, 3.1.13
security for costs, 3.1.5
stay of proceedings
generally, 26.4.1
introduction, 3.1.7
variation of order
liberty to apply orders, 3.1.13
Case management conferences
Chancery Guide, [1A-117]
Case management information sheets
debt claims, C16-009
Case management orders
employment tribunals
deposit order, [3O-12.1]
CE-file
Chancery Guide, [1A-45]
Chambers (hearings)
anonymity of party or witness, 39.2.14
children, 39.2.5
criteria
national security, 39.2.3.1

Chambers (hearings)—*cont.*
interest of justice, 39.2.7
national security, 39.2.3.1
patients, 39.2.5
personal financial matters, 39.2.4
publicity defeat object of hearings, 39.2.3
unjust to respondent, 39.2.6
Chancery Division
procedure Guide
generally, [1A-0]—[1A-281]
Chancery Guide
Bankruptcy Court
cross-border insolvency, [1A-226.1]
case management
conference, [1A-117]
case management conference, [1A-117]
CE-file, [1A-45]
Companies Court
cross-border insolvency, [1A-226.1]
contact details, [1A-3]—[1A-21]
costs management conference, [1A-117]
court details, [1A-3]—[1A-21]
court file
CE-file, [1A-45]
electronic filing, [1A-46]
email communications, [1A-48]
introduction, [1A-44]
online public search, [1A-47]
cross-border insolvency, [1A-226.1]
editorial introduction, [1A-0]
electronic filing, [1A-46]
email communications, [1A-48]
insolvency
cross-border cases, [1A-226.1]
introduction, [1A-2]
judges
changes in jurisdiction, [1A-80]
introduction, [1A-80]
Masters
changes in jurisdiction, [1A-80]
introduction, [1A-80]
online public search, [1A-47]
public search, [1A-47]
urgent court business
pager numbers, [1A-281]
Users' Committees
Financial List, [1A-26]
outside London, [1A-31], [1A-281]
Chancery Masters
applications, and
changes in jurisdiction, [1A-80]
introduction, [1A-80]
Change of parties
after judgment, 19.2.6
expiry of limitation period, after
mistake, 19.5.6
generally, 19.2.1
joinder
after judgment, 19.2.6
judgment, after, 19.2.6
Charging orders
interim orders
judgment payable by instalments, 73.4.4
Children
compromise
anonymity orders, 21.10.2
control of money, 21.11.3

Paragraph numbers marked "+" denote online/CD content; those within [...] refer to Volume 2

Paragraph numbers marked "+" denote online/CD content; those within [...] refer to Volume 2

Paragraph numbers marked "+" denote online/CD content; those within [...] refer to Volume 2

Paragraph numbers marked "+" denote online/CD content; those within [...] refer to Volume 2

Paragraph numbers marked "+" denote online/CD content; those within [...] refer to Volume 2

Paragraph numbers marked "+" denote online/CD content; those within [...] refer to Volume 2

Security for costs—*cont.*
claimants, against
co-claimants resident abroad and in England,
25.13.10
discretion, 25.13.1
generally, 25.13—25.13.6
impecuniosity, 25.13.13—25.13.14
insolvent claimants, 25.13.13—25.13.14
introduction, 3.1.4
nominal claimants, 25.13.17
poverty, 25.13.13—25.13.14
court powers
discretion, 25.13.1
introduction, 3.1.5
International Conventions
other, 25.13.6
introduction, 3.1.5
person other than claimant, against
assignment to avoid liability, 25.14.2
disclosure in aid, 25.14.6
Senior Courts Act 1981
costs
generally, [9A-203]
Service
address not given for service, where
defendant out of jurisdiction at time of service,
6.9.7
alternative permitted method (claim forms), by
retrospective approval, 6.15.5
deemed date (claim forms)
'relevant step', 6.14.3
directors disqualification proceedings
claim forms, [3J-19]
documents other than claim forms, of
methods, 6.20.2
'first class post', by, 6.3.3
methods
documents other than claim forms, 6.20.2
post, 6.3.3
no address given at which defendant be served
defendant out of jurisdiction at time of service,
6.9.7
place of service
last known residence, at, 6.9.7
post, by
'first class post', 6.3.3
principal office of business, at, 6.9.7
witness summonses
court, by, 34.6—34.6.1
Service by alternative permitted method
claim forms
retrospective approval, 6.15.5
Service (claim forms)
alternative method, by
retrospective approval, 6.15.5
deemed date
'relevant step', 6.14.3
'first class post', by, 6.3.3
methods
post, 6.3.3
no address given at which defendant be served
defendant out of jurisdiction at time of service,
6.9.7
post, by
'first class post', 6.3.3
principal office of business, at, 6.9.7

Service out of jurisdiction
Admiralty claims, and, 6.37.11, 6HJ.36
amendment of claim form
after service, 6.37.9
before service, 6.37.8
applications for permission
Admiralty actions, 6.37.11
amendment of claim form, 6.37.8—6.37.9
appeals, 6.37.13
claim in para 3.1(3) of PD6B, 6.37.3
claim under r.6.36, 6.37.4
content, 6.37.2
'court will not give permission unless satisfied',
6.37.5
directions, and, 6.37.7
generally, 6.37.1
'not for service out of the jurisdiction', 6.37.10
serve in Scotland or Northern Ireland, to, 6.37.6
setting aside order, 6.37.12
time limits, 6.37.1
arbitration claims
generally, [2E-13]
choice of court agreement, 6JR.35
contracts, and
employment contracts, 6JR.28
delict, 6JR.16
directions where court gives permission, 6.37.7
directors disqualification proceedings, [3J-19]
employment contracts, and
Notes, 6JR.28
exclusive jurisdiction, and
Notes, 6JR.33
injunctions, 6HJ.4
jurisdiction by agreement
Notes, 6JR.35
Notes on Rules of Jurisdiction in Judgments
Regulation
choice of court agreement, 6JR.35
contracts, 6JR.28
delict, 6JR.16
employment contracts, 6JR.28
exclusive jurisdiction, 6JR.33
jurisdiction by agreement, 6JR.35
patents, 6JR.32
quasi-delict, 6JR.16
related proceedings, 6JR.46
special jurisdiction, 6JR.28
tort, 6JR.16
patents, 6JR.32
permission required
Admiralty claims, and, 6.37.11; 6HJ.36
appeals, 6.37.13
applications, 6.37—6.37.13
directions where court gives permission, 6.37.7
generally, 6.36.1
injunctions, 6HJ.4
principles for grant, 6.37.15.1
serve in Scotland or Northern Ireland, to, 6.37.6
setting aside order, 6.37.12
time limits, 6.37.1
quasi-delict, 6JR.16
related proceedings, 6JR.46
Scotland, in
permission not required, 6.37.6
Service Regulation 1348/2000, under
generally, 6.41.2

Paragraph numbers marked "+" denote online/CD content; those within [...] refer to Volume 2

NOTES

NOTES

NOTES